Maximising the Benefits of Psychotherapy

Maximising the Benefits of Psychotherapy

A Practice-Based Evidence Approach

David Green

Consultant Clinical Psychologist, Department of Clinical & Health Psychology,
St James's University Hospital, Leeds, and Honorary Senior Lecturer, Leeds
Institute of Health Sciences, University of Leeds.

Gary Latchford

Research Director, Clinical Psychology Training Programme, Leeds Institute
of Health Sciences, University of Leeds, and Head of Adult Medical
Psychology, Department of Clinical & Health Psychology, St James's
University Hospital, Leeds.

WILEY-BLACKWELL

A John Wiley & Sons, Ltd., Publication

This edition first published 2012
© 2012 John Wiley & Sons, Ltd

Wiley-Blackwell is an imprint of John Wiley & Sons, formed by the merger of Wiley's global Scientific, Technical and Medical business with Blackwell Publishing.

Registered Office
John Wiley & Sons Ltd, The Atrium, Southern Gate, Chichester, West Sussex, PO19 8SQ, UK

Editorial Offices
350 Main Street, Malden, MA 02148-5020, USA
9600 Garsington Road, Oxford, OX4 2DQ, UK
The Atrium, Southern Gate, Chichester, West Sussex, PO19 8SQ, UK

For details of our global editorial offices, for customer services, and for information about how to apply for permission to reuse the copyright material in this book please see our website at www.wiley.com/wiley-blackwell.

The right of David Green and Gary Latchford to be identified as the authors of this work has been asserted in accordance with the UK Copyright, Designs and Patents Act 1988.

Wiley also publishes its books in a variety of electronic formats. Some content that appears in print may not be available in electronic books.

Designations used by companies to distinguish their products are often claimed as trademarks. All brand names and product names used in this book are trade names, service marks, trademarks or registered trademarks of their respective owners. The publisher is not associated with any product or vendor mentioned in this book. This publication is designed to provide accurate and authoritative information in regard to the subject matter covered. It is sold on the understanding that the publisher is not engaged in rendering professional services. If professional advice or other expert assistance is required, the services of a competent professional should be sought.

Library of Congress Cataloging-in-Publication Data

Green, David, 1950–
    Maximising the benefits of psychotherapy : a practice-based evidence approach / David Green and Gary Latchford.
       p.; cm.
    Includes index.
    ISBN 978-0-470-68315-6 (hbk) – ISBN 978-0-470-68314-9 (pbk.)
    I. Latchford, Gary.   II. Title.
    [DNLM: 1. Psychotherapy–methods.   2. Evidence-Based Practice.   3. Mental Disorders–therapy.   4. Treatment Outcome. WM 420]

    616.89'14 – dc23

2011035203

A catalogue record for this book is available from the British Library.

Wiley also publishes its books in a variety of electronic formats. Some content that appears in print may not be available in electronic books.

Set in 11.5/14 pt Minion by Toppan Best-set Premedia Limited
Printed in Malaysia by Ho Printing (M) Sdn Bhd

1   2012

Contents

List of Figures   vii

About the Authors   ix

Acknowledgements   xi

1   The Equivalence of Psychotherapies   1

2   Research Into Psychotherapy: What Works and How?   23

3   The Conventional Wisdom   45

4   The Real Experimenter   67

5   Practice-based Evidence   87

6   Using Client Feedback in Psychotherapy – The Research   109

7   Using Client Feedback in Psychotherapy – In Practice   129

8   Ideas in Action   151

9   Transforming Training and Supervision   171

10   Conclusions and Some Recommendations   195

Subject Index   211

List of Figures

Figure 5.1:   The three criteria for clinically
              significant change   92

Figure 5.2:   Possible assessment framework   102

Figure 8.1:   Norma – SRS and ORS scores   155

Figure 8.2:   Joanne – SRS and ORS scores   157

Figure 8.3:   Ruth – SRS and ORS scores   160

Figure 8.4:   Gordon – SRS and ORS scores   163

Figure 8.5:   Trevor – ORS overall and social subscale scores   166

About the Authors

Dr David Green

DG qualified as a clinical psychologist over 30 years ago. He has worked therapeutically with young people and their families in a variety of settings ever since. He has been involved in the training of clinical psychologists for over 25 years as supervisor, clinical tutor and finally as Clinical Director of the Doctor of Clinical Psychology training programme at Leeds (a post he left in 2010). He currently works as a freelance trainer and legal specialist but also provides sessional clinical input to the psychology service at St James's University Hospital in Leeds, and holds an honorary Senior Lectureship at the University of Leeds.

DG has published widely on the topic of clinical supervision and is co-author along with Richard Butler of *The Child Within: Taking the Young Person's Perspective by Applying Personal Construct Psychology*, published by John Wiley and Sons in 2007.

Dr Gary Latchford

GL is a clinical psychologist. He studied for a PhD in Edinburgh with Colwyn Trevarthen in 1989, after which he completed clinical training in Leeds in 1991. Since that time he has worked with adults with physical illness, combining research and clinical interests in chronic illness – particularly cystic fibrosis – and psychological therapies. His clinical practice is at St James's University Hospital in Leeds, and since 1996 he has also been research director on the Doctor of Clinical Psychology training programme at Leeds University.

Acknowledgements

We would like to thank all those who have so generously helped us in writing this book.

Thanks go to all our friends and colleagues on the University of Leeds Doctoral Programme in Clinical Psychology, staff and students alike, for indulging us, and for allowing us to share our emerging ideas with them, or, as they might more accurately put it, 'bang on about psychotherapy all the time'. Thanks especially to Professor Stephen Morley for his support and feedback on several early drafts of chapters, and Nigel Wainwright, who allowed us to include his new measure of the supervisory alliance.

There are many psychologists, psychotherapists and counsellors whose ideas have enriched our thinking and, at times, set us off in entirely new directions. We would like to single out Scott Miller and Barry Duncan, who set many of these ideas in motion with their excellent 'Training the Trainers' workshops. David Winter of the University of Hertfordshire added to our appreciation of the importance of client preferences. Chuck Rashleigh, Ladislav Timulak and their colleagues at Trinity College Dublin generously shared their experiences with using feedback in counselling practice.

We would especially like to thank our wives Catherine and Jennifer, and our families, for putting up with our occasional absences to write and research this book.

Finally, we greatly appreciate the help of all the clients who have taken up our invitation to provide us with regular feedback, attempted to 'put us right' in so many ways and, in so doing, played a major role in generating the ideas presented in this book. While we worry that it may sound tokenistic to thank our patients, we both feel that it is truly a privilege to be allowed into people's lives as their therapist, and this feeling, together with a fascination (and respect) for the way therapy brings about change, has only ever increased with time.

D.G. and G.L.

1

The Equivalence
of Psychotherapies

'Why,' said the Dodo, 'the best way to explain it is to do it.' (Lewis
Carroll [1896] *Alice's Adventures in Wonderland*)

Introduction

In October 2009, *Newsweek* magazine in the United States published
an article by Sharon Begley called 'ignoring the evidence'. In it, psychotherapy researchers are quoted berating psychotherapists for
taking no notice of science and instead treating patients with whatever intervention they are familiar. There is a 'widening gulf between
researcher and clinician'. One researcher, Timothy Baker, argues that
clinicians 'give more weight to their personal experiences than to
science'. The tone of the article is that this is clearly a bad thing. The
implication is that science has progressed since the early days of
therapy, and that we now know more about what therapies work and
why. Clinicians should, therefore, keep up to date in their knowledge
and change their practice accordingly.

If this is all true, it is pretty damning. The truth, though, is a bit
more complicated.

Maximising the Benefits of Psychotherapy: A Practice-Based Evidence Approach,
First Edition. David Green and Gary Latchford.
© 2012 John Wiley & Sons, Ltd. Published 2012 by John Wiley & Sons, Ltd.

Psychotherapists naturally want to be good at their job, and their clients equally naturally want to see someone who has the best chance of helping them. What is the most important factor in success? It's a reasonable assumption that this is the particular form of psychotherapy or counselling being provided. If so, can science tell us which therapies have been shown to be best? Is the *Newsweek* article right? Should therapists be directed to follow the science and train in whatever therapy has the best evidence? Are newer therapies more effective than older ones?

It's very tempting to assume that anything newer must be better. The belief in progress is perhaps strongest in medicine. Although this can sometimes lead to unrealistically optimistic expectations of the power of modern medicine to cure, there have undoubtedly been some striking and high-profile successes such as transplant surgery. In medicine a great deal of effort has gone into finding ways to evaluate and improve treatments, and then to disseminate scientific findings to clinicians in the form of guidelines.

Psychotherapy and counselling are now well established as effective frontline treatments for mental health problems. In many countries they are seen as being a part of the framework of mental health services and often offered as an alternative to drug treatments. We usually think of psychotherapy, then, as being a kind of medical intervention often (but not always) delivered alongside other forms of treatment in health settings. It's not surprising, then, that questions about effectiveness and cost benefits asked of medical treatments should also be asked of psychotherapy. It is also understandable that the same methods used to evaluate medical treatments should be used to evaluate psychotherapies. Such an approach leads directly to the views expressed in the *Newsweek* article. Therapists who do not change their practice in line with science, this argument goes, are like medical doctors prescribing out-of-date medication. At best they are less effective than they should be, at worst they are dangerous.

So what is a therapist to do? It all hinges, of course, on what the evidence actually says, and whether the evidence is reliable. The next chapter will look at whether the research methods we use to evaluate therapy are fit for purpose, and will explore some of the controversies in the area. This chapter will go straight to the heart of the matter: what is the evidence that some therapies are better than others?

Guidelines and Evidence-Based Practice

If I have diabetes and of the two drugs available one has been shown in scientific research to be better for the condition and with fewer side effects, that's the one I'd want my doctor to be aware of and to prescribe for me. How can we make sure that doctors are kept informed about best practice, and don't rely solely on their own experience (which might be out of date)? This issue has been the focus of the evidence-based practice movement. It has had two aims: to improve the quality of research and to develop methods of combining findings so that dissemination is more efficient. Perhaps the group most associated with this movement is the Cochrane Collaboration, founded in 1993. This is a not-for-profit international group of specialists who conduct systematic reviews – 'critical summaries' – of different areas of healthcare to establish current evidence for treatment and prevention. It is named after Scottish epidemiologist Archie Cochrane who is recognised as giving the initial impetus for the movement in his book *Effectiveness and Efficiency* in 1972.

The most notable impact of the evidence-based practice movement for clinicians has been the emergence of guidelines that review the current research evidence and direct them on which treatments to use. This is massively influential in medicine, providing an up-to-date overview of research that was previously beyond the scope of any individual doctor.

The success of the approach has inevitably led to it being applied to other areas of practice, including psychotherapy. In the United Kingdom, this has most prominently been in the form of guidelines from the National Institute for Health and Clinical Excellence (NICE) on the treatment of various mental illnesses. The depression guideline revised in 2009, for example, recommends cognitive behavioural therapy (CBT), interpersonal therapy (IPT), behavioural activation and couples therapy. No other therapies are supported, though the guidelines admit that counselling and short-term psychodynamic psychotherapy are 'limited options' for those people who refuse one of the recommended treatments, and go on to make it clear that the therapist needs to discuss the lack of evidence for these approaches with the patient before starting therapy. Whether therapists really tell their clients they are about to offer a treatment that NICE thinks won't work is not known.

Meanwhile in the United States, in 1994, Division 12 (Clinical Psychology) of the American Psychological Association published a list of empirically supported Treatments (ESTs) – psychotherapies for which there was thought to be supporting evidence (Chambless *et al.*, 1998). Significantly, they used the same criteria for evaluating psychotherapies as the US Food and Drug Administration (FDA) uses for drug trials – for example, at least two trials showing that the therapy is better than no treatment or produces equivalent results to any established treatment. There are now around 300 officially sanctioned ESTs, and the Division lists which therapies are recommended for particular conditions such as depression.

The key question, of course, is whether the evidence informing these guidelines – and the *Newsweek* article – is convincing. Is there clear evidence for the superiority of any one psychotherapy over another? Curiously, although this has been the focus of a growing debate since the 1970s, the question was first asked of psychotherapy in 1936, and the answer given then remains as relevant today as it was when it was written.

Saul Rosenzweig, Dodos and Common Factors

Saul Rosenzweig got his doctorate from Harvard in 1932 and remained active in psychological research until shortly before his death 72 years later. His most influential paper – 'Some implicit common factors in diverse methods of psychotherapy' was published in 1936. Just to give some context, one of Rosenzweig's classmates at Harvard was B.F. Skinner, one of the founders of behaviourism. Rosenzweig's paper was a response to the claims of proponents of the various psychotherapies popular at the time that their particular therapy was more effective than all the others, and that the reason for this was that the theory of change on which their therapy was based was right (and the others wrong).

In contrast, Rosenzweig was the first to propose that the mechanisms of change in psychotherapy might not be specific to the form of therapy, but instead be agents of change common to all therapies, which he termed 'the common factors'. It is tempting to think that one of the reasons this paper is still regularly cited in contemporary research is the quotation with which it begins: 'At last the Dodo said, "Everybody has won, and *all* must have prizes."'

The allusion was to the caucus race in Lewis Carroll's 1865 book *Alice in Wonderland*, in which the Dodo instigates a confused race with no rules in order for the participants to shake themselves dry. Rosenzweig argued that competition between different schools of therapy was similarly misguided, because all were equally effective. This became known as 'the dodo bird hypothesis', a poetic touch that we suspect has captured the imagination of many subsequent researchers.

Rosenzweig's paper was a reflective one – it contained no data to support his assertions. Reading it now, in some ways it also seems very dated – the psychotherapies mentioned include psychoanalysis and Christian Science rather than CBT and IPT, for example. In other ways, however, it has not dated at all. Rosenzweig's opening argument is that all proponents of psychotherapies can produce successful cases to support assertions that they work. Unfortunately, he argues, they tend then to imply that this evidence also demonstrates that their own brand of therapy is better than the others. As someone surveying this from a more detached position, he argues that the logical conclusion to reach is that, if so many different therapies based on conflicting theoretical approaches can produce successful outcomes, then the reasons for success are unlikely to lie within any one theory.

His basic logical point was that the success of any therapy cannot be used as evidence that the therapy has brought about change in the way it claims to – it provides evidence that the therapy works, but not why it works. Rosenzweig's belief was that therapies that appeared to be very different actually had more in common than the proponents realised – that the effectiveness of therapies was a result of unrecognised factors common to them all.

What did he think these factors might be? Rosenzweig makes a few suggestions. He argues that the relationship with the therapist may allow for some social reconditioning to occur, and also suggests that catharsis may be a common consequence of different therapeutic approaches. He also focuses on the effect of the therapist's personality. Though hard to quantify, he argues that there is a shared understanding of the qualities needed in a good therapist, and that good therapists are distributed across different schools of therapy.

Interestingly, his next possible factor is the coherent structure for understanding that all therapies offer. Rosenzweig describes this in terms of personality – that therapies offer a consistent and persuasive schema for the client to achieve greater personality organisation. In 1936 personality was a key concept in psychotherapy – Rosenzweig's definition of an established psychotherapy was one based on a general theory of personality, and he refers to mental disorder as a conflict of disintegrated personality constituents. Although the terminology of therapy has changed over the years, the notion that therapies may be providing a coherent and believable structure by which clients can begin to understand and solve their problems remains a persuasive idea.

Rosenzweig's next argument comes even now as a refreshing acknowledgement of the complexity of psychological problems and the limits of our understanding. Put bluntly, he argues that psychological events are so complex that many different, equally justified formulations are possible, and that each may contain a certain amount that is accurate. Thus no one therapy or interpretation has a monopoly on truth. In addition, personality is so complex that it is likely that there are very many ways to effect a change in organisation. Again, to put it bluntly, different therapies may target different aspects but have a similar overall impact. The implication is that therapists' formulations do not have to be completely accurate to have a therapeutic effect, and that different foci in therapy can bring about similar therapeutic change.

Rosenzweig's paper is still immensely provocative. Though not based on research itself, it anticipates much of the psychotherapy research to take place over the subsequent 70 years – from studies comparing different therapies, examining the therapeutic alliance or the accuracy of a formulation, to dismantling studies aiming to identify the active ingredients in therapy. It also anticipates many of the concepts which have become associated with the processes of therapy, most obviously the common or non-specific factors that may underlie effectiveness. He also stressed the importance of the confidence that therapist and client have in the therapy-that it needs to appear credible to the client and evoke allegiance in the therapist. Both of these factors are reflected in the consistency of the therapist in adhering to the treatment approach.

Three other things are worth noting from this paper. First, Rosenzweig recognised that equivalence of therapies was only true when they were appropriately used. He limits his conclusions to accepted therapies, competently applied. Second, he did not rule out the possibility that some forms of treatment may be better suited to particular kinds of cases. He also considers the potential importance of matching patient and therapist in terms of personality. Finally, there is another possible solution to the logical conundrum of many therapies claiming differential effectiveness but all producing successful outcomes: rather than the explanation being that success is due to non-specific factors common to them all, perhaps each type of therapy utilises specific and distinct factors, but these are equally effective. In Rosenzweig's terms, these factors may have an impact in different ways but produce similar overall changes. We'll return to this point later.

After Rosenzweig: Does Therapy Actually Work?

Although he had particular views about differences between therapies, Rosenzweig never doubted that psychotherapy was effective.

This has not always been accepted, however, and 20 years after his paper the majority opinion seemed to reject it. In two papers, Hans Eysenck (1952, 1965), perhaps the most famous psychologist of his generation, argued that 75% of patients get better regardless of whether they receive psychotherapy (though he was more hopeful for treatments based on 'modern learning theory'). Although his conclusions were founded on reviews of a small number of studies, they were extremely influential at the time, leading many to conclude that traditional psychotherapy was ineffective. By the end of the 1960s, however, the weight of evidence was turning decisively against this view, as exemplified by Bergin's (1971) review of a much larger number of well-conducted studies. By this time the methods used to study psychotherapy outcome had grown increasingly sophisticated, taking their lead from medical trials. Even so, reviews that listed the outcome of different studies tended to add to the debate about the effectiveness of psychotherapy rather than end it. The decisive blow finally came in the 1970s and was made not by a psychotherapy researcher, but by an educational psychologist called Gene Glass, whose innovation in the way information can be summarised from different studies would change not just psychotherapy, but the way the whole of medicine is practised. Before we come to this, we need to understand the methods for conducting research that had by then become increasingly popular, and that provided the raw data for Gene Glass's innovation.

A Well-conducted Study: The Randomised Controlled Trial

What is a well-conducted study? How can a reader determine that an investigator's conclusions are justified, that the research has been conducted without bias and presents a fair and truthful account? As psychotherapies became more popular, and increasingly formed an accepted part of mental health services, it was natural for investigators to draw on the research methods used to evaluate other interventions in health. In fact, medicine had addressed the problems of trustworthiness some time before with the randomised controlled trial (RCT), and this became the method of choice for psychotherapy investigators looking at outcome.

The first RCT in medicine is usually thought to date from 1946 and examined whether streptomycin was an effective treatment for pulmonary tuberculosis. Since then countless RCTs have been conducted, and have undoubtedly made a huge contribution to the development of medical practice. Put simply, RCTs enable a fair and unbiased comparison of treatments for particular conditions so that policy makers and clinicians have evidence rather than opinion on which to base treatment decisions.

To illustrate, suppose that a new drug is invented to treat the common cold. In an RCT the experimenter attempts to control for all the things that can bias a fair comparison so that a treatment can be properly evaluated. First, the new treatment is compared with something else – usually an existing treatment, but sometimes no treatment. Second, the appropriate group is targeted – in this case, people with a cold. The treatment is designed for the common cold so it would be unhelpful and unfair to include patients with the 'flu. Third, everyone agreeing to take part is randomised – that is, they are randomly allocated to either the new treatment or the old one with everyone having an equal chance of being in either group. They are randomised so that the two groups are likely to be comparable, and no one group is stacked with body builders with a fierce resistance to the common cold, for example. This randomisation is double blind – neither the patient nor the experimenter knows which treatment they are getting. This is to prevent the knowledge influencing either the patient ('I'm on the new wonder drug so I must be feeling better') or the experimenter ('I've spent years researching this great new drug and they must be feeling better'). The trial is then carried out, with each group receiving one or other of the treatments. At the end of the trial, an appropriate assessment is taken – in this case, whether they still have a cold. At this point the experimenter is able to crack the code on who was receiving which treatment, and compares the two groups to see if one has better outcomes than the other. In RCTs, then, the aim is to eliminate potential confounds so that a pure comparison between two treatments can be carried out.

When reading an RCT, then, although the methodological rigour with which they are carried out can vary considerably, you may have a certain degree of confidence in the conclusions. It therefore seems absolutely appropriate to utilise these methods in evaluating psychotherapy. Unfortunately, techniques that are relatively unproblematic when comparing two drug treatments become much more complicated when comparing psychotherapies – but more on this later.

How have these methods been used in psychotherapy research? Generally, to show that a particular psychotherapy is effective (i.e., comparing it with a no-treatment control) or to compare two or more psychotherapies to see if one is differentially more effective. The latter, of course, also provides evidence about the effectiveness of psychotherapies in general

The problem with individual RCTs, however, is that even the best of them remains just a single study, and when the sample size is small the results are often inconclusive – traditional inferential statistics usually require quite large numbers of participants if there is to be a good chance of detecting a significant difference between groups. Worse, when several similar studies are carried out, it is not uncommon for the results to vary, making an objective interpretation difficult.

An obvious solution is to write reviews gathering together the results of many RCTs in order to summarise their results. The first reviews of existing research are now known as narrative reviews. In them, the authors (usually experts in the field) offer an overview and interpretation of the existing literature. Though such reviews can be valuable and interesting, the opinions are just opinions – there is no attempt to present a mathematical summary of the findings of previous studies. This means, of course, that two reviews may potentially feature very different opinions and reach opposite conclusions about what current research is saying.

In essence, this was the situation described earlier regarding the effectiveness of psychotherapy, with Eysenck reviewing research and finding no evidence for effectiveness, and others arguing the opposite.

An important way to improve reviews would be to find some way of representing the data from individual studies. Luborsky, Singer and Luborsky (1975) reviewed 40 psychotherapy outcome studies using a 'voting system' whereby each study that produced a statistically significant result in favour of a particular therapy was added to a tally. When they looked at the votes for different therapies, they found little evidence for any difference in effectiveness between therapies and resurrected Rosenzweig's use of the dodo bird metaphor in what became a highly influential paper.

Although this method did acknowledge the importance of the data in individual studies, reducing the data to a tick in favour of a treatment clearly meant that a lot of potentially important information was lost. A way of retaining this information and producing a more comprehensive way of summarising the data was the logical next step and appeared soon after. It was devised by Gene Glass, who called his method 'meta-analysis'.

Gene Glass and Meta-analysis

Psychotherapy research was the very first area in which the new method of meta-analysis was tested. As the inventor, Gene Glass, was an educational researcher, this seems quite puzzling. In fact, Glass was someone who felt that he had personally benefited from psychotherapy early in his career and was quite irritated by Eysenck's (1965) criticisms. He also argued that Eysenck's conclusions were based on poor methodology – arbitrary decisions about what studies to include (just 11 studies), and very crude interpretation of available data. In response, Glass chose to apply the ideas he was developing on synthesising data from multiple studies to the issue of the effectiveness of psychotherapy.

A key innovation in Glass's approach was to use effect sizes in his calculations. Studies tend to report whether there were any statistically significant differences between groups but, as said earlier, this is influenced by the number of people in the study and can be misleading. It also leads to a focus on whether the results were significant or not, with any non-significant results tending to be ignored. Within a research article, however, there is usually enough information to calculate an effect size, an incredibly useful statistic reflecting the magnitude of the effect of the therapy. Effect sizes are based on standardised mean differences between groups – Glass defined this as the mean difference between the treatment and control group divided by the standard deviation (a measure of variability) of the control group. Using an effect size as the unit of outcome for each study gives meta-analysis a number of advantages: effect sizes are not influenced by sample size; effect sizes tell you *how large* the difference was between groups and not just whether it was significant or not (to give you an idea about how to interpret effect sizes, if you compared the heights of 15 and 16 year olds you would get a small effect size, if you compared the difference between the heights of 13 and 18 year olds you would get a large effect size); effect sizes enable you to compare the results of different studies even when they have used different outcome measures. Most important of all, effect sizes from different studies can be combined to produce an overall effect size, thus mathematically representing a summary of them. A common way of representing an effect size is Cohen's (1992) *d*, which reflects the size of the difference between groups.

Glass's meta-analysis was published in a paper with Mary Smith in the *American Psychologist* in 1977, and expanded in book form three years later (Smith, Glass and Miller, 1980). It presented a meta-analysis of nearly 375 controlled studies of psychotherapy and counselling representing nearly 50,000 participants. The authors found very clear evidence of the effectiveness of psychotherapy – they cite that on average the typical therapy client is better off than 75% of people receiving no treatment. Glass pointed out that this figure is by coincidence exactly the same figure that Eysenck had cited as the number of people who recover without therapy. Eysenck's attempt at a rebuttal, calling the new technique 'mega-silliness', now seems quaint in an era in which meta-analysis is pivotal in evidence-based medicine.

Subsequent researchers have confirmed Glass's work. Grissom (1996), for example, analysed data from 46 meta-analyses and calculated that the probability that any random client was better off receiving psychotherapy was $.7 \pm .2$, which he referred to as 'the magical number'. This figure sounds impressive, and it is. Rosenthal

(1990) compared the effect size obtained by Glass for psychotherapy with the effect size obtained in one of the key studies on azidothymidine (AZT) for AIDS – generally regarded as one of the most significant medical breakthroughs of the last 20 years. He found that the effect size for psychotherapy was significantly greater than that for AZT.

So Psychotherapy Works – Are Therapies Equivalent?

Glass's meta-analysis went further than examining the effectiveness of psychotherapy. He gave his new method a challenge – to determine whether some therapies are more effective than others. This is actually much trickier than determining whether psychotherapy works, which involves simply pooling data from all studies comparing a psychotherapy with a control group. Summarising different comparisons of therapies would be meaningless – for example, one study might find a behavioural therapy is more effective than a psychodynamic; another might find the opposite, so pooling the effect size is nonsense. In fact, there are many different studies comparing therapies, and often huge differences in study quality, duration, severity of problem and a host of other factors. Glass's solution was to group similar psychotherapies together into small categories (based on expert opinion) and compare these. He reports on four in the book, two (behavioural versus non-behavioural) in the paper. He found little evidence for any difference between therapy types when this was done, though the method for categorising different therapies is inevitably open to differing opinion. More convincing is a subset of his analysis, which looks at the studies that have both a behavioural and a non-behavioural arm (around 50) and finds similar effect sizes for both.

Glass's study was followed by a number of similar papers replicating and refining his approach, as well as, initially, arguments from behaviourally oriented researchers that many key behavioural papers had been ignored. A key response to this and other criticisms was the work of husband and wife team David and Diana Shapiro, based in Sheffield in the United Kingdom (Shapiro and Shapiro, 1982). They refined Glass's method – for example, they included only studies that directly compared two or more treatments and had a control group – and made a particular effort to include the behavioural studies alluded to by critics of Glass's paper. They identified 143 outcome trials, a selection dominated by behavioural interventions (featured in 134 studies) and group therapy approaches (52% of studies). Most studies were of treatment of phobias and anxiety-related disorders, with only ten looking at depression, for example. Their meta-analysis confirmed the effectiveness of therapy compared with a placebo, and found that in comparison differences between therapies were modest, accounting for less variance than the target problem.

One of the most thoughtful uses of Glass's method has been by Bruce Wampold and colleagues (Wampold *et al.*, 1997) who tried a different solution to the problem of using meta-analysis to compare different therapies: they looked at the pattern of differences rather than the size. They only included studies (114) that directly compared two or more established therapies, and randomly assigned a positive or negative to the effect sizes from each comparison. The overall effect size for all the studies will therefore be zero, but they reasoned that, if there really is no difference between therapies, the distribution of scores will be small. This is, indeed, what they found.

A final example is one of the most comprehensive – Luborsky *et al.*'s (2002) attempt to revisit the equivalence question. They conducted a meta-analysis of meta-analyses, examining data from 17 meta-analyses of studies where active treatments were compared with each other. These covered common problems such as depression and anxiety, and common therapies, such as cognitive and psychodynamic. They found that the difference between them was small. Chambless (2002) has argued that the differences between therapies might be larger for particular problems and raises the possibility of matching treatment to problem. The idea that some therapies work much better for particular problems is a seductive notion, though others have argued that this is misguided – that the way the therapy is delivered is much more important (Messer and Wampold,

2002). A comprehensive examination of this issue would require a huge amount of effort – analysing good quality data on every combination of condition and competing therapy – and we don't have this kind of data. Luborsky *et al.* titled their 2002 paper 'The dodo bird verdict is alive and well – mostly', and this seems to us an apt summary. So far, the balance of evidence from these large meta-analyses suggests that the dodo still reigns.

Curiously, these large-scale meta-analyses do not find their way into treatment guidelines. Instead, guidelines rely on meta-analyses of treatments for particular conditions such as depression, and on individual studies.

Meta-analysis for Particular Conditions

There are now many meta-analyses summarising research into effective treatments for particular conditions. Some find no difference between the treatments studied – Rosa-Alcázar *et al.* (2008), for example, looked at 19 studies of the treatment of obsessive compulsive disorder, finding similar effect sizes for exposure with response prevention alone, cognitive restructuring alone and a combination (although all the treatments studied were different aspects of behavioural interventions). Other reviews find an advantage for a particular approach – Wolitzky-Taylor *et al.* (2008), for example, conducted a meta-analysis of 33 RCTs of treatments for phobia and found exposure-based treatments to be more effective than relaxation and cognitive-based approaches, but all were better than placebo or no treatment. Such reviews depend, of course, on the original research available. Wolitzky-Taylor *et al.* found no psychodynamic studies to include in their review, for example.

In other areas, such as depression, the findings of such meta-analyses are particularly interesting. Ekers, Richards and Gilbody (2008) conducted a meta-analysis of 17 RCTs, finding that behaviour therapy was as effective as CBT, and better than supportive counselling and brief psychotherapy. Cuijpers *et al.* (2008), looking at a larger pool of studies (53 RCTs) and comparing seven different treatments (CBT, non-directive supportive treatment, behavioural activation, psychodynamic, problem-solving, interpersonal psychotherapy and social skills training) found no large differences between them, though the dropout rate was higher in CBT.

Perhaps most provocative of these meta-analyses, however, has been Benish, Imel and Wampold (2008), who conducted a meta-analysis of 15 trials of the treatment of post-traumatic stress disorder (PTSD). For some time it has been widely assumed that exposure is a necessary ingredient of a successful intervention in PTSD. Their review, surprisingly, found no difference between the therapies and no specific, crucial ingredient necessary for a successful outcome, including exposure. A long rebuttal followed (Ehlers *et al.*, 2010), arguing that the meta-analysis was flawed in that the selection criteria was biased and that the results did not show that treatments were effective compared with natural recovery. The implication is that the researchers were also biased – they knew what they wanted to find and made the evidence fit. An even longer reply followed this (Wampold *et al.*, 2010), pointing out in great detail that the meta-analysis was notably transparent and coherent in all criteria applied and avoided the conceptual fudging that, they argued, undermined the existing guidelines on what therapies work for PTSD (the authors of which contributed to the earlier rebuttal). This is a topic that clearly raises temperatures, and in many ways it reflects the ongoing debate in psychotherapy more generally. We urge you to read all three papers and make up your mind about this. Is exposure necessary for the treatment of PTSD? Having read these papers, we would argue that at the very least this remains not proven.

The Big Psychotherapy Trials

We end, however, with attempts to study the effectiveness of different approaches within a single RCT. This has a number of advantages – it means that the conditions for the comparison can be carefully controlled, and the type of patients seen by therapists using the different therapies will be similar in terms of severity. In order to get meaningful data, however, the studies need to be large. Such studies span several different sites – with teams of therapists working on the same project in different cities, in a series of 'mini-RCTs'. When all these data are pooled together, the study has the power to detect differences between treatments. Few such studies have been conducted because of expense, but those that have been completed have proved to be very influential.

We'll begin with the largest of them: Project MATCH (1997), a US study of three treatments for alcohol abuse, had 1726 participants. It involved multiple sites and compared 12-step facilitation (based on Alcoholics Anonymous), CBT coping skills, and motivational enhancement therapy (MET, based on motivational interviewing), all offered as either outpatient or follow-up to inpatient treatment. It also included an attempt to match patient characteristics with the treatment offered. The results showed no differences between treatments – all were effective in terms of abstinence at one year follow-up – and very little evidence for matching.

The UK Alcohol Treatment Trial (UKATT, 2005) was a British version of Project MATCH, conducted at five centres offering either MET or a new intervention called social network behavioural therapy. The researchers found no differences in outcome between the treatments, though interestingly there were differences at individual sites (Davidson, 2008) so if these individual RCTs at the different sites had been published separately the results would have been misleading.

The most well known of these trials, however, is the US National Institute for Mental Health (NIMH) Treatment of Depression Collaborative Research Project (Elkin *et al.*, 1989; Shea *et al.*, 1992). It is generally considered a landmark study – well planned and well executed. It involved 250 patients with unipolar depression randomly allocated to therapists (psychologists and psychiatrists) at different sites administering cognitive therapy, interpersonal therapy, medication (imipramine) with clinical management, or a placebo with clinical management. The therapists were experienced, followed treatment manuals, had expert supervision and were subject to fidelity tests to ensure they were providing what they were supposed to be providing. The results showed no significant differences between treatments. Interestingly, there were again some differences between treatments at some sites.

Other Sources of Evidence?

We've now looked at the main sources of research evidence for examining differences in effectiveness of psychotherapies. We're going to finish with something slightly different. A common criticism of research trials is that they do not reflect the everyday experience of therapists – patients tend to have single problems, therapists are highly trained in one approach, etc. If routine clinical practice involves routine outcome assessment, however, it has the potential to be another source of research evidence. This was the approach taken by a group in West Yorkshire in the United Kingdom. In two studies (Stiles *et al.*, 2006; 2008), outcomes were compared for the six approaches offered in this service (CBT, person-centred or psychodynamic therapy alone or any one of these plus one additional approach: integrative, supportive or art therapy). These studies involved a very large number of clients: 1309 in the first, 5613 in the second. In both papers they reported no difference between the treatments – they were all effective.

The usefulness of this naturalistic approach to gathering evidence on effectiveness has been cited by Jacques Barber in his inaugural address as president of the American Psychological Association in 2009 (Barber, 2009) as a bridge to the better controlled RCTs. Of course it is not an RCT – as Clark, Fairburn and Wessely (2008) have pointed out, we don't actually know what the therapists were doing. The point is, however, that they were doing what the vast majority of therapists do in real life, and their choice of therapy made no difference to outcome. The point is also, of course, that the properly controlled RCTs and meta-analyses discussed earlier have obtained the same result.

Conclusions

What are we to make of all this? Research on the effectiveness and equivalence of the psychotherapies has a long history. Psychotherapy is proven to be very effective, but is there now any scientific evidence for the superiority of one therapy over another? At the moment, we think that it is difficult to read this literature and argue convincingly that there is. The message to therapists then is to hold fast, and not switch therapies to a newer 'improved' version.

Why might research show all therapies to be equivalent? This result is, on the face of it, bizarre – that all therapies, new, old, those based on nineteenth-century ideas of the unconscious, those based on modern research into cognitive psychology, all therapies work just about as well as any other. How? This is an interesting question, and one no one knows the answer to. There are many possibilities, including the four we outline as follows:

1. All therapies really are equivalent and the reason for this is they all share the same active ingredients (i.e., common factors), mostly concerning the relationship between therapist and client.
2. All therapies really are equivalent and the reason for this is they all work in very different ways (i.e., uncommon factors), but each of these ways is equally effective.
3. Therapies are not equivalent at all and the reason we haven't spotted this yet is that our research methods are not yet good enough.
4. All therapies are roughly equivalent, but there might be some conditions where some types of therapy tend to be more effective or quicker at achieving a result; however, these differences are small and tricky to spot.

Of course the reality might be a messy combination of several of these possibilities.

At the moment the evidence we have leaves us with a default position of assuming no important differences in therapy effectiveness. This leaves us with two questions. The first is why does this large amount of evidence not find its way into evidence-based guidelines in psychotherapy? The second is, if it is not the form of therapy that makes a difference to outcome, what does?

We'll ponder these two questions in the next chapter, when we'll look more closely at the research methodologies underlying psychotherapy research, and see how much research can help us in understanding not just whether a psychotherapy works but how.

References

Barber, J.P. (2009) Toward a working through of some core conflicts in psychotherapy research. *Psychotherapy Research*, 19, 1–12.

Begley, S. (2009) Ignoring the evidence. Why do psychologists reject science? *Newsweek* (Oct 2), http://www.newsweek.com/id/216506 (accessed 11 September, 2011).

Benish, S., Imel, Z.E. and Wampold, B.E. (2008) The relative efficacy of bona fide psychotherapies of post-traumatic stress disorder: a meta-analysis of direct comparisons. *Clinical Psychology Review*, 28, 746–758.

Bergin, A.E. (1971) The evaluation of therapeutic outcomes, in *Handbook of Psychotherapy and Behaviour Change* (eds A.E. Bergin and S.L. Garfield), John Wiley & Sons, Inc, New York.

Chambless, D.L., Baker, M.J., Baucom, D.H., *et al.* (1998) Update on empirically validated therapies, II. *The Clinical Psychologist*, 51 (1), 3–16.

Chambless, D.L. (2002) Beware the dodo bird: the dangers of overgeneralization. *Clinical Psychology: Science and Practice*, 9, 13–16.

Clark, D., Fairburn, C. and Wessely, S. (2008) Psychological treatment outcomes in routine NHS services; a commentary on Stiles *et al.* (2007). *Psychological Medicine*, 38, 629–634.

Cochrane, A.L. (1972) *Effectiveness and Efficiency. Random Reflections on Health Services*, Nuffield Provincial Hospitals Trust, London.

Cohen, J. (1992) A power primer. *Psychological Bulletin*, 112, 155–159.

Cuijpers, P., van Straten, A., Andersson, G. and van Oppen, P. (2008) Psychotherapy for depression in adults: a meta-analysis of comparative treatments. *Journal of Consulting and Clinical Psychology*, 76, 909–922.

Davidson, R. (2008) Accredited, brand named psychotherapies and the standard of evidence. *Clinical Psychology Forum*, 191, 48–52.

Ehlers, A., Bisson, J., Clark, D.M., *et al.* (2010) Do all psychological treatments really work the same in posttraumatic stress disorder. *Clinical Psychology Review*, 30, 269–276.

Ekers, D., Richards, D. and Gilbody, S. (2008) A meta analysis of randomized trials of behavioural treatment of depression. *Psychological Medicine*, 38, 611–623.

Elkin, I., Shea, M.T., Watkins, J.T., *et al.* (1989) National Institute of Mental Health treatment of depression collaborative research program. General effectiveness of treatments. *Archives of General Psychiatry*, 46, 971–982.

Eysenck, H.J. (1952).The effects of psychotherapy: an evaluation. *Journal of Consulting Psychology*, 16, 319–324.

Eysenck, H.J. (1965) The effects of psychotherapy. *International Journal of Psychiatry*, 1, 97–178.

Grissom, R.J. (1996) The magical number .7 +/– .2: meta-meta-analysis of the probability of superior outcome in comparisons involving therapy, placebo, and control. *Journal of Consulting and Clinical Psychology*, 64, 973–982.

Luborsky, L., Singer, B. and Luborsky, L. (1975) Comparative studies of psychotherapy. *Archives of General Psychiatry*, 32, 995–1008.

Luborsky, L., Rosenthal, R., Diguer, L., *et al.* (2002). The dodo bird verdict is alive and well – mostly. *Clinical Psychology: Science and Practice*, 9, 2–12.

Messer, S.B. and Wampold, B.E. (2002), Let's face facts: common factors are more potent than specific therapy ingredients. *Clinical Psychology: Science and Practice*, 9, 21–25.

National Institute for Health and Clinical Excellence (2009) *The Treatment and Management of Depression in Adults (update)*. Clinical Guideline 90. http://www.nice.org.uk/CG90niceguideline (accessed 11 September, 2001).

Project MATCH (1997). Matching alcoholism treatment to client heterogeneity. *Journal of Studies on Alcohol*, 58, 7–29.

Rosa-Alcázar, A., Sánchez-Meca, J., Gómez-Conesa, A. and Marín-Martínez, F. (2008) Psychological treatment of obsessive–compulsive disorder: a meta-analysis. *Clinical Psychology Review*, 28, 1310–1325.

Rosenthal, R. (1990) How are we doing in soft psychology? *American Psychologist*, 45, 775–777.

Rosenzweig, S. (1936) Some implicit common factors in diverse methods of psychotherapy. *American Journal of Orthopsychiatry*, 6, 422–425.

Shapiro, D.A. and Shapiro, D. (1982) Meta-analysis of comparative therapy outcome studies: a replication and refinement. *Psychological Bulletin*, 92, 581–604.

Shea, M.T., Elkin, I., Imber, S.D., *et al.* (1992) Course of depressive symptoms over follow up: the NIMH TDCRP. *Archives of General Psychiatry*, 49, 782–787.

Smith, M.L. and Glass, G.V. (1977) Meta-analysis of psychotherapy outcome studies. *American Psychologist*, 32, 752–760.

Smith, M.L., Glass, G.V. and Miller, T.I. (1980) *The Benefits of Psychotherapy*, Johns Hopkins University Press, Baltimore.

Stiles, W.B., Barkham, M., Mellor-Clark, J. and Connell, J. (2008) Effectiveness of cognitive–behavioural, personcentred, and psychodynamic therapies in UK primary care routine practice: replication in a larger sample. *Psychological Medicine*, 38, 677–688.

Stiles, W.B., Barkham, M., Twigg, E., *et al.* (2006) Effectiveness of cognitive-behavioural, person-centred and psychodynamic therapies as practised in UK National Health Service settings. *Psychological Medicine*, 36, 555–566.

UKATT Research Team (2005) Effectiveness of treatment for alcohol problems: findings of the randomised UK alcohol treatment trial (UKATT). *British Medical Journal*, 331, 541–546.

Wampold, B.E., Mondin, G.W., Moody, M., *et al.* (1997) A meta-analysis of outcome studies comparing bona fide psychotherapies: empirically, 'all must have prizes.' *Psychological Bulletin*, 122, 203–215.

Wampold, B.E., Imel, Z.E., Laska, K.M., *et al.* (2010) Determining what works in the treatment of PTSD. *Clinical Psychology Review*, 30, 923–933.

Wolitzky-Taylor, K., Horowitz, M., Powers, M. and Telch, M. (2008) Psychological approaches in the treatment of specific phobias: a meta-analysis. *Clinical Psychology Review*, 28, 1021–1037.

2

Research Into Psychotherapy: What Works and How?

Psychology had modelled itself after the hard sciences, with physics as the shining example. But they had taken the old Newtonian clockwork as their example. To modern physics there was no tick-tock world independent of the observer, no untouched mechanism, no way of describing a system without being involved in it. (Gregory Benford [1980] *Timescape*)

Introduction

In the last chapter we looked at the guidelines that have emerged in recent years to direct clinicians to the psychotherapies deemed to have best available supporting evidence. Though the attempt to ensure that therapies reflect the developing evidence base seems sensible, in practice that evidence base is less straightforward and considerably harder to interpret than at first appears.

This chapter begins by looking more closely at the actual research methods and considering their suitability for the job at hand of investigating psychotherapy effectiveness. Along the way, armed with some new and intriguing methods, we will revisit the question of the effectiveness of different therapies by looking at it from a different

Maximising the Benefits of Psychotherapy: A Practice-Based Evidence Approach, First Edition. David Green and Gary Latchford.
© 2012 John Wiley & Sons, Ltd. Published 2012 by John Wiley & Sons, Ltd.

direction – is the individual clinician or the choice of therapy more important to outcome? Finally, we will return to the split between researchers and clinicians hinted at in the *Newsweek* article, but this time from the perspective of clinicians asking how research into psychotherapy can be made more relevant to their everyday experience of practice.

Trials and Psychotherapy

As we saw in the previous chapter, psychotherapy researchers have looked to medical trials for the methods with which to test effectiveness. The argument is that if we are to take psychotherapy seriously as a treatment – and recognise its potential for good and harm – then we need to take the mechanisms by which we evaluate it seriously too. We believe that all reasonable psychotherapists and counsellors should have no difficulty agreeing with this in principle. The problem, however, is that the methods commonly used in medical research may not transfer so easily to research into psychotherapy.

On the surface, the trend to evaluate psychotherapy using methods such as the RCT, which are derived from medicine, seems logical. These methods are tried and tested and generally work very well in drug trials. In fact, the idea of randomisation in an experiment even predates medical research and was first used in the design of agricultural field trials. Using these research methods means that information about the effectiveness of psychotherapy can be obtained and communicated in a form familiar to commissioners and consumers of health services. It also offers the advantage of conferring credibility to both the researchers and the therapy.

Adopting these methods is more than a convenient tool, however, and has much deeper implications. Medical methods of evaluation are predicated on the illness and the treatment having certain properties – for example, that the illness is diagnosable and able to be correctly categorised (e.g. a bacterial infection), and that the treatment is able to be clearly specified (e.g. a particular amount of an antibiotic drug given a specified number of times each day). The role of physicians, meanwhile, is reduced to an 'interchangeable constant' because they don't know whether they are giving a medication or placebo (Shapiro and Shapiro, 1997). The treatment is like a black box on a flow chart with patients flowing in and outcomes measured on the other side. Beutler (2009) recalls that the then director of the NIMH when announcing the collaborative depression trial that it funded, described psychotherapy as being like aspirin. The implication is clear – that RCTs would enable the isolation and identification of the active ingredients of psychotherapy, as it does in medicine (Klerman, 1986).

Specifying diagnosis and treatment is therefore essential to this approach. In applying these methods to psychotherapy, the assumption is made that these properties are also true in psychotherapy: that the 'illness' (such as depression) can be categorised and the treatment (psychotherapy) quantified. It is not clear at all whether this is actually true, however. To quantify psychotherapy in the same way as a medical treatment risks ignoring the potentially important role of the context in the individual case – the nature of the condition and the complexity of the therapeutic relationship. If mental distress is easily quantifiable and if psychotherapy acts like a drug so that it doesn't matter who gives it to you or the context in which it is given as long as it's taken, then these issues will not be important. Unfortunately for researchers, it isn't, it doesn't, and it is.

First, mental distress is not easily quantifiable. Type of bacterial infection can be determined by growing cultures in a laboratory; classification of mental distress continues to be a topic of controversy. In fact, there is profound disagreement about whether such a classification system of mental distress is viable or even desirable – the British psychologist Dave Pilgrim (2007) has pointed out that the effort that has gone into producing and revising detailed classification systems for mental health problems based on symptom or behaviour legitimises a biomedical model of mental illness and conveys the impression that the disorders they describe, such as depression, are discrete entities analogous to medical conditions. In fact, the classifications are prone to unnerving flexibility – there are clearly cultural influences on the presentation of some conditions, and regular revisions to the classification system. Post-traumatic stress disorder wasn't recognised until 1980, for example. One of the most influential systems, the Diagnostic and Statistical Manual of Mental Disorders (DSM), will publish a fifth edition in 2013 and has already attracted criticism for plans to loosen diagnostic criteria and introduce new disorders that seem to overlap with what many would consider normal behaviour. Even for conditions that most would feel more confident could be categorised, such as depression, the process may not be so simple. Depression was seen as a form of anxiety until DSM-II in 1968 and there is still a continuing debate about whether depression and anxiety are separate entities, two aspects of the same underlying one, or form a tripartite with mixed depression/anxiety (Clark and Watson, 1991).

Second, drug trials are able to specify exact doses and constituents so that the effects of a treatment can be carefully evaluated. If the dose a patient received varied, it would make it more difficult to interpret the results. Psychotherapy is simply not like this. There are many hundreds of different psychotherapies; for the analogy with drug treatment to hold, we would need to be able to identify the active ingredients in them, and to be able to regulate the doses given. Despite the very many claims of very many types of therapy, there is as yet no convincing evidence for any causal link between a proposed active ingredient in psychotherapy and a successful outcome. Just because the theory behind a particular psychotherapy provides a rationale for a key component (such as finger movement in eye movement desensitization and reprocessing therapy [EMDR]), it doesn't follow that there is necessarily evidence to support this assertion. This hasn't stopped researchers from attempting to pin down the key ingredients in particular therapies and to ensure that these are delivered in a consistent way – in the same doses – in trials. When particular therapies are the subject of trials, this does seem to follow a logic – if it is to provide evidence for a particular form of therapy, this therapy needs to be very carefully controlled and hence avoid confusion around the type of therapy being examined. It therefore needs to be delivered in the same way by different therapists in the trial, and it needs to be recognisable as that form of therapy to other clinicians. The most common method of ensuring consistency in psychotherapy trials is to produce a manual and train therapists to use this when delivering the therapy. Though this goes some way to solving the problem of consistency, unfortunately it introduces another set of problems that risks undermining the whole enterprise.

Read the Therapy Manual

Recall that medical trials require the target condition and treatment to be clearly specified, and all attempts made to control for anything that might influence the outcome – researchers refer to this as high internal validity and it means that, if a significant finding emerges, you can be fairly sure it was because of the drug and not something else. The downside is that such studies may suffer from low external validity – they may no longer have much in common with routine clinical practice so generalisation of the results beyond the trial may be difficult. In psychotherapy trials this problem is magnified. Specifying the target population most often means that patients are included only if they have a single diagnosis, such as depression. After all, the argument goes, it would not be a fair trial of treatment for depression if some of the patients also had alcohol problems or anxiety. The problem, of course, is that in routine clinical practice patients' problems are messy, and co-morbidity is often the norm rather than the exception. Though Crits-Christoph, Wilson and Hollon (2005), among others, have argued that many trials do include participants with complex, co-morbid problems, most clinicians still do not recognise trials as reflecting routine clinical practice. Indeed, if the principles of an RCT are followed, there will always be differences.

Perhaps the most important is the necessity to regulate treatment to ensure high internal validity – if therapy were delivered in very different ways by the different therapists in a trial, the results might be hard to interpret. Using a manual to standardise the way the therapy should be delivered comes at a considerable price, however.

First, someone has to write the manual. These are often very pre-scriptive, describing the way the therapy should be undertaken in some detail. They are hopefully written by experts in the field being studied. But how do they make decisions about what to include? Clearly, the evidence base doesn't begin to provide answers to detailed questions such as the timing and duration of therapy or specific strategies such as homework tasks. In practice, those writing the manual must use their own experience to describe what they con-sider best practice. The resulting manual may often be very useful, but the details should nevertheless not been seen as being directly based on empirical evidence. Most importantly, as Westen, Novotny and Thompson-Brenner (2004) have pointed out, the trial then becomes a test of the manual rather than the therapy. As a conse-quence, any evidence for effectiveness that emerges from the trial is for that particular manual and the author's interpretation of the therapy rather than the therapy itself. Given the time and expense involved in large trials, another consequence is that the manual may be around for a long time, and may inadvertently inhibit further developments in practice. In fact, manuals have proliferated not just as research tools but as guides to practice, being used for teaching and disseminated.

Are manuals a good or bad thing? As we will see in the next chapter, perhaps surprisingly there is no convincing evidence that they actually improve practice (Duncan and Miller, 2006). They clearly do take control away from the therapist and patient, who have considerably less choice as a result. It has been argued that this may ensure therapists stick to the script of what are known to be effective therapies. Wilson (1998), for example, cites good evidence that clini-cal judgement is often unreliable – 'actuarial prediction is usually superior to clinical judgment' (p. 205). His preferred solution is to direct clinicians to a manual rather than consider ways of improving their judgement. Weisz, Weersing and Henggeler (2005) argue that many therapy manuals actually allow flexibility and creativity by the clinicians using them. The substantial concern about the way trials and manuals are used to evaluate ESTs remains, however – allowing flexibility in the way manuals are used does not necessarily mean that this results in something akin to normal clinical practice. Instead, it raises questions about those manuals that allow less flexibility, especially in the light of the finding by Kendall *et al.* (2008) that creativity when using a manual seems to be essential in engaging the patient in treatment.

More fundamental is the implicit message being conveyed: that a manual can capture the essential ingredients of an effective psychotherapy. It is part of an increasing trend to simplify therapies (particularly CBT); to fillet a treatment and train less experienced practitioners to deliver it. The danger is that this reductionist and mechanistic view underestimates the power of the therapy. When delivered by an unsupported therapist who lacks the experience to match their intervention to the needs of a client as they change throughout the course of therapy, there is a real danger of the client deteriorating: 'Generally effective interventions can have a detrimental impact when used with inappropriate timing and tact' (Boswell, Castonguay and Wasserman, 2010, p. 722).

RCTs and the Little Black Box

In a trial, then, the manualised therapy stands in for the actual therapy. The way it is delivered is standardised and the scope for individual variation limited. Anything outside the scope of the manual is considered noise, and a threat to internal validity – it is important that every patient gets the same treatment. But how is this really possible in practice? The problem is that psychotherapy is quite unlike a drug. Even the most comprehensive manual cannot accurately encompass the varieties of contexts of psychotherapy and the variety of ways in which it plays out. Worse, by focusing on techniques, therapy manuals make assumptions about the active ingredients of therapy that go far beyond the evidence. Other aspects of therapy, such as the therapeutic relationship between the therapist and client and the other common factors first described by Rosenszweig, are usually dismissed as 'non-specifics': factors that can't be controlled but which are peripheral to the question at hand, on the effectiveness of therapeutic technique. It is far from clear, however, that such factors really are peripheral, and it remains at least a reasonable hypothesis that such factors have a greater impact on outcome than the techniques that are the focus of the trial. So by trying to minimise 'contamination' by these factors, trials might be excluding the most powerful ingredients of the therapy. Such dilemmas rarely bother drug trials.

Does this mean that RCTs are worthless? Not at all. Though not the precise and unbiased tools they are sometimes thought to be, they are an important method for investigating psychotherapy. They are the best way of evaluating whether a treatment is actually effective. Put simply, they can answer questions that other research methods cannot. It is worth recalling the early enthusiasm for debriefing interventions after a trauma. This approach involved a structured intervention for groups of people who had recently experienced a trauma – such as bank staff after an armed raid – and involved guiding people in talking about their experiences. It was thought to help people process their memories and thereby avoid developing post-traumatic stress symptoms, which seemed very plausible. Early investigations reported that patients gave positive feedback on their experience of debriefing, and for several years many organisations set up debriefing teams ready to provide this intervention when needed. It took properly conducted RCTs of debriefing and subsequent systematic reviews before the truth became clear: that patients may feel positive about debriefing at the time, but at follow-up this group was on average no better off and a significant number of people were worse (Rose *et al.*, 2002). It is hard to imagine how such an important finding could have emerged without the discipline provided by an RCT.

Notwithstanding the concerns raised earlier, using an RCT to determine whether a therapy is effective seems a useful and relatively unproblematic use of the method. When it is used to compare treatments, however, some of the problems in the approach become more apparent. One well-known finding is an association between the allegiance of the researchers – what therapists they themselves believe to be effective – and the outcome of the trial. Luborsky *et al.* (1999)

found that the allegiance of the researchers accounted for 69% of the variance in outcome of the trial, though this is not necessarily evidence of a conscious bias on the part of the researcher (Leykin and DeRubeis, 2009).

So RCTs have a role, but it is as one of a number of methods for investigating psychotherapy. Buhringer and Pfeiffer-Gershel (2008), reflecting on the failure of all the major hypotheses in the Project MATCH trial to match patients with combinations of treatments, summarise the current situation for psychotherapy researchers succinctly. We know therapies such as CBT work but we don't know how. The change process, they argue, is likely to be extremely complex. Future researchers need to do more to understand it, but 'the classic black box randomized controlled trial will not help us' (Buhringer and Pfeiffer-Gershel, 2008, p. 706).

Therapist Versus Therapy

RCTs may be a black box in terms of revealing mechanisms of change, but with the right methods they may still reveal more about what is important to a successful outcome. The large multi-site trials described in the previous chapter represent an important resource of information about therapy provided by different clinicians with hundreds of clients. As new methods of statistical analysis are developed, it is becoming possible to ask much more complex questions than previously, though we need to be prepared for the answers, too, to be more complicated.

A key question asked of these data, and one that continues the discussion from the previous chapter, is this: what has the greatest effect on outcome, the therapy or the therapist delivering it? In other words, is it the technique (as proponents of manualised therapy would argue) or is it the person (as those who argue for the importance of the therapeutic relationship would argue)?

Unsurprisingly, we know that there are differences in outcomes obtained by different therapists in routine practice. We also know that effective therapists consistently get better outcomes with their clients (Brown *et al.*, 2005). Are such differences also present in well-controlled trials, and if so are differences between therapists more important than differences between the therapies being delivered?

Several researchers have re-examined data from large multi-centre trials with this question in mind. They tend to find a great deal of variation in the outcomes obtained by different therapists. Huppert *et al.* (2001), for example, looked at the performance of the 14 CBT therapists who took part in the Multicenter Collaborative Study for Treatment of Panic Disorder. Although they were all highly trained and using a manualised therapy, there were large differences in the overall effect sizes they achieved with their patients, which ranged from 0% to 18%. The researchers also found no relationship between the outcomes the therapists achieved and how experienced they were with CBT, or their adherence to the manual – so the variation does not appear to be because some therapists were less competent in CBT or less faithful to the manual, though there was a relationship with overall experience as a psychotherapist.

Project MATCH (1998), the multi-site alcohol intervention study, was unusually large, providing a wealth of information on the outcomes of the 80 therapists involved. Again, differences between therapists have been found for a number of outcomes such as abstinence and patient satisfaction. Most of the differences are accounted for by exceptionally poor outcomes in a minority of patients, though close examination shows that different therapists are associated with the different types of poor outcome. The therapist effects were most prominent at follow-up. Curiously, experience of therapist was not associated with outcome in two of the trial arms (CBT and MET), but was negatively associated with outcome in the third (12-step, a variation of Alcoholics Anonymous).

Crits-Christoph and Gallop (2006) agree that therapist effects are worthy of study but warn that research finding differences tends to draw attention, and that the many trials that find no therapist differences in their results tend to address this issue very briefly and are seldom cited. Nevertheless, any study that finds variation in the outcomes obtained by therapists, even when using manualised therapies designed to minimise variation in delivery, raises interesting questions.

Perhaps the richest and most unusual contribution to this debate is a series of papers analysing data from the NIMH Treatment of Depression Collaborative Research Project. McKay, Imel and Wampold (2006) looked at whether there were consistent differences in outcome obtained by the psychiatrists in the project when prescribing either an anti-depressant (Imiprimine) or a placebo. Though the Imiprimine was found to be better than placebo, who the patient saw rather than what they were prescribed had by far the biggest impact: 7% to 9% of the variability in outcome was due to the psychiatrist and only 3.4% to the Imiprimine. Looking closely at the data reveals a further rather startling fact – the top third performing psychiatrists in the study achieved better outcomes using the placebo than the bottom third did using Imiprimine. It seems clear then, that there is something going on in these clinical sessions way beyond the psychoactive effects of a medication.

Data from the NIMH study have also been used in an innovative way to tackle head on the question of whether the therapist or the therapy is most important to outcome. In order to tackle such a complex question a suitably complex method is needed and this has been applied to the NIMH data. Hierarchical linear (multilevel or mixed effect) modelling is a statistical technique that captures different levels of variation in the data. This enables, for example, analysis of RCT data not just to compare outcomes from the arms of a trial, but also to include the different therapists as another level. In this way, the different outcomes of each therapist are not lost in the final analysis and interesting questions may be asked about the contribution of different factors to outcome. In 2006, *Psychotherapy Research* published two articles that used a variant of this statistical technique to compare the relative contributions of the therapist and therapy to outcome (Hill, 2006). Though both used exactly the same data from the NIMH study, they came up with radically different conclusions. On the one hand Elkin *et al.* (2006a) found little support for the importance of individual therapists, with no significant overall effect due to the therapist (2.3%). On the other hand, Kim,

Wampold and Bolt (2006) found 8% of the variance in outcome was attributed to the therapist and 0% to the particular treatment. What are we to make of this? Clearly, there were differences in the way they applied the statistical technique, which may not be immediately obvious to most readers. In essence, at the level of the individual patient, Elkin *et al.* (2006b) used data collected throughout therapy to produce a single figure for rate of change to use as the outcome score, arguing that using more observations increases reliability. In contrast, Kim, Wampold and Bolt used a simpler pre-test post-test model with emphasis on the final outcome score rather than rate of change, arguing that functioning at the end of therapy is the key outcome of interest. Wampold and Bolt (2006) further argue that using rate of change, far from increasing reliability, actually undermines it by anchoring the rate of change profiles to the baseline measure with an assumption that these contain no measurement error.

The journal asked several respected researchers to comment on the disagreement between these papers (Crits-Christophe and Gallop, 2006; Soldz, 2006). In general they praise both and see their use of these statistical procedures as legitimate but complex, and that the results therefore demand a complex understanding. Disconcertingly, it is suggested that the studies are underpowered given the statistics employed. This is particularly troubling considering the data were from one of the larger psychotherapy trials conducted to date (with 17 therapists treating 205 clients). The differences in the ways both researchers applied the statistical model make direct comparisons of their findings difficult, but this still leaves open the question of which is the better analysis? The answer to this depends upon your understanding of how acceptable it is to anchor baseline observations in longitudinal multilevel models. As Stephen Soldz (2006) pointed out in his commentary on these papers, most clinicians know very little about the use of models in statistics, yet it is hard to see how the most interesting questions in psychotherapy – about how it actually works – can be investigated without using an appropriately complex approach. This does at least mean that researchers are finally able to respond to the criticism of therapists that their methods are unable to capture the complexities of psychotherapy. The implication of using these new, powerful and technically complex methods, however, is that there is a growing gulf between how psychotherapy is investigated and the ability of clinicians to comprehend it.

Academia Versus Practice

The *Newsweek* article described in the previous chapter featured psychotherapy researchers berating clinicians for ignoring research evidence and following their own judgements about which therapies to deliver. As we have tried to show here, the reality is much more complex. Perhaps clinicians could be forgiven, too, for themselves accusing some researchers of becoming remote from practitioners, writing journal articles more for other researchers than clinicians, and focusing on whatever therapies are fashionable rather than what practitioners are actually doing.

The introduction of therapy manuals, too, has received mixed reviews from practitioners. Although many are undoubtedly clinically useful and certainly a good training tool, there is also a danger that they convey a reductionist message about the nature of therapy – that therapy can be successfully delivered by minimally trained staff as long as they keep to the set of instructions in the manual. This neglects the important area of negative outcomes of therapy. Psychotherapy is a powerful intervention, but as in all potent therapies there is a risk that a client will be made worse.

Lilienfeld (2007) has argued that psychotherapists need to become more sophisticated in their understanding of the potential harmful effects of therapy. He cites a frequently cited estimate that 10% of clients deteriorate in psychotherapy, though he argues that this figure is actually difficult to determine: estimates tend not to distinguish those whose deterioration is unrelated to therapy and would have been even worse without it, for example; neither do they include the possibility that someone who improved with psychotherapy might have improved even more without it. The action of therapies, too, is complex: some may be associated with a heightening of symptoms in the short term but reduction long term, or have different impacts on different symptoms. Reviewing the literature, Lilienfeld identifies a small number of potentially harmful therapies that should be avoided. More than this, he also argues that research that presents averaged data on outcome may be masking wide individual variability that includes deterioration. This is a risk in all therapies, and he highlights the importance of monitoring progress for all clients so that deterioration can be spotted early. Castonguay *et al.* (2010) develop these ideas further. They argue that effective psychological therapies can nevertheless be harmful when delivered without regard for context, such as by a therapist rigidly adhering to a treatment manual and unresponsive to the current needs of the client. They emphasise the importance of supervision and (early) training in minimising harmful effects, and include a list of training recommendations. These cover general principles such as monitoring change and awareness of potential harm, and also a number of recommendations reflecting the importance of the skilful and appropriate delivery of therapy, grounded on a good therapeutic relationship and with due consideration of the expectation and choices of the client. This feels a long way from a manualised treatment, at least as such treatments are often implemented.

How can research and practice be brought closer together? There has certainly been a conscious move towards better quality and more sophisticated research. There have also been attempts to link theories and discoveries from psychological research with new developments in psychotherapy, in the belief that this scientific foundation will lead to more effective psychotherapies matched for particular psychological problems, in the manner in which biological research influences new drug treatments. This is a seductive argument, with psychological research producing findings such as memory bias in depression, which may well be relevant for therapy. In medicine, however, a great many things can undermine the early promise of a new medication. In psychotherapy, the obvious difference is that the study of memory or fear conditioning in a lab environment is very different from the real-life, messy context in which it will be applied – therapy is an extremely complex process in which success is likely to be due to multiple factors. When one factor is changed, such as a therapy procedure based upon research evidence, it would need to be extremely significant to stand out against all the other factors influencing outcome.

Whether the therapist or the therapy is more important to therapy outcome is one of the most important questions in therapy today and it's surprising that it is not more widely debated. It is reflected in the attempts by the American Psychological Association to produce guidelines for practitioners on effective practice. In 2002 a task force was set up to describe empirically supported treatments (Nathan and Gorman, 2002). This was responded to by a different task force describing the components of empirically supported therapeutic relationships (Norcross, 2002, 2011), then a later task force describing the evidence for principles of therapeutic change for clients with particular types of problem (Castonguay and Beutler, 2006). More recently, a further task force led by John Norcross and Bruce Wampold (2011) reviewed the evidence for whether adapting psychotherapy for the individual client results in improved outcomes, and found that this was demonstrably effective for a number of variables such as culture and client preferences.

The implications of whether the therapist or therapy has primacy in terms of outcome are quite profound – a good deal of the resources used in researching, training and providing therapies make the implicit assumption that type of therapy is the most important factor in successful outcomes. Unfortunately, the question is unlikely to be answered satisfactorily any time soon – as we have seen, it requires large numbers and complex analysis, and some level of agreement around use of statistical models. There is a limit, then, on what the research can tell us.

Concluding Thoughts

In a thought-provoking paper, Larry Beutler (2009) expressed a belief that studies that have used RCTs to identify evidence based psychotherapies have dominated clinicians' awareness of psycho-therapy research. He acknowledges the benefit that RCTs have brought – particularly in identifying harmful therapies – but on the whole believes that the reliance on RCTs has been unhelpful. He also believes that the findings of this research are commonly misunder-stood by practitioners. He highlights three myths commonly held about psychotherapy research. First, that psychotherapy would be more effective if everyone followed the evidence base and practised ESTs exclusively. In fact, most trials of psychotherapy have compared an EST with a no-treatment control group. This provides evidence that the EST is effective, but not that it is any better than the thera-pies currently being used in practice. There are some studies that have compared ESTs with routine clinical practice (treatment as usual) and this reveals few differences (Lipsey and Wilson, 1993; Shadish *et al.*, 2000; Wampold, 2001).

The second myth is that CBT or cognitive therapy outperforms relational or insight-oriented therapies. As we saw in the previous chapter, there is no convincing evidence for this (e.g. Wampold *et al.*, 1997). The literature at the moment reflects the arguments from either side: from time to time advocates of CBT point out evidence that appears to show an advantage for this therapy (e.g. Tolin, 2010). Meanwhile, advocates of other therapies (e.g. psychoa-nalysis) may similarly cite research that supports their views (e.g. Leichsenring and Rabung, 2008). We don't know whether some therapies will emerge in time as offering a clear advantage for par-ticular problems (e.g. behavioural therapies for phobias), but we are not there yet, and there is certainly no evidence that some therapies are uniformly superior to others.

Beutler's third myth is that the relationship between the patient and therapist is the most important factor in terms of the outcome of therapy. While there is certainly a significant correlation between the therapeutic relationship and outcome, how important is it? There is actually some good quality research on this topic (Horvath and Symonds, 1991; Martin, Garske and Davis, 2000; Stevens, Hynan and Allen, 2000), and the consensus is that the therapeutic relationship actually accounts for very little of the variance in outcome. This needs some context too, though. Looking at the many different factors that may have an impact on outcome in psychotherapy and measuring the contribution they each make is a difficult undertaking. The most well-known attempt is by Bruce Wampold (2001), who found that the contribution of the client and factors outside treatment accounted for the vast majority of the variance in outcome from psychotherapy (87%). Of the portion accounted for by the treatment (13%), Wampold found that the therapeutic alliance was by far the most important factor, much bigger than the contribution of the therapeutic model. We may develop improved methods for analysis and a better picture of this complex subject over time, but for now the clear message is that the contribution of the therapeutic alliance is important, but perhaps not as important as many believe. At the very least it still leaves a lot more to be explored and explained.

So where do we go from here? Beutler (2009) believes that RCTs are not fit for purpose if we are to find out more about the active ingredients of therapy and why therapy works: 'The real influences in psychotherapy include effects that are associated with variables that are non-randomly distributed aspects of the therapist, the relationship and the patient' (Beutler, 2009, p. 310). RCTs would therefore exclude the very things of interest. Such questions, he believes, are best answered by naturalistic and quasi-experimental studies.

This is a conclusion now being reached by many others. Donald Peterson of Rutgers University in the United States is a widely published and extremely experienced psychotherapy researcher. Although still strongly committed to the importance of a scientific basis to psychotherapy, in 2004 he acknowledged that there are times in clinical practice when scientific knowledge is limited, calling for what amounts to a mutually respectful, broader collaboration between researcher and clinician and the knowledge they bring.

We'll look at what this might mean later. Before that, we'll look more closely at what research can tell us about change process in therapy: what do we know already about why therapies work, and, if we are to reject the notion that the best way to improve is simply to adopt an empirically supported treatment, how we can make our existing practice better?

References

Benford, G. (1980) *Timescape*, Victor Gollancz, London.

Beutler, L.E. (2009) Making science matter in clinical practice: redefining psychotherapy. *Clinical Psychology: Science and Practice*, 16, 301–317.

Boswell, J.F., Castonguay, L.G. and Wasserman, R.H. (2010) Effects of psychotherapy training and intervention use on session outcome. *Journal of Consulting and Clinical Psychology*, 78, 717–723.

Brown, G.S., Lambert, M.J., Jones, E.R. and Minami, T. (2005) Identifying highly effective psychotherapists in a managed care environment. *The American Journal of Managed Care*, 11, 513–520.

Buhringer, G. and Pfeiffer-Gershel, T. (2008) Combine and match: the final blow for large-scale black box randomized controlled trials. *Addiction*, 103, 706–710.

Castonguay, L.G. and Beutler, L.E. (eds) (2006) *Principles of Therapeutic Change That Work: Integrating Relationship, Treatment, Client, and Therapist Factors*, Oxford University Press, New York.

Castonguay, L.G., Boswell, J.F., Constantino, M.J., *et al.* (2010) Training implications of harmful effects of psychological treatments. *American Psychologist*, 65, 34–49.

Clark, L.A., Watson, D. (1991) Tripartite model of anxiety and depression: psychometric evidence and taxonomic implications. *Journal of Abnormal Psychology*, 100, 316–336.

Crits-Christoph, P. and Gallop, R. (2006) Therapist effects in the National Institute of Mental Health Treatment of Depression Collaborative Research Program and other psychotherapy studies. *Psychotherapy Research*, 16, 178–181.

Crits-Christoph, P., Wilson, G.T. and Hollon, S.D. (2005) Empirically supported psychotherapies: comment on Westen, Novotny, and Thompson-Brenner. *Psychological Bulletin*, 131, 412–417.

Duncan, B.L. and Miller, S.D. (2006) Treatment manuals do not improve outcomes, in *Evidence-based Practices in Mental Health: Debate and Dialogue on the Fundamental Questions* (eds J.C. Norcross, L.E. Beutler and R.F. Levant), American Psychological Association, Washington, DC, pp. 140–149.

Elkin, I., Falconnier, L., Martinovitch, Z. and Mahoney, C. (2006a) Therapist effects in the National Institute of Mental Health Treatment of Depression Collaborative Research Program. *Psychotherapy Research*, 16, 144–160.

Elkin, I., Falconnier, L., Martinovitch, Z. and Mahoney, C. (2006b) Rejoinder to commentaries by Stephen Soldz and Paul Crits-Christoph on therapist effects. *Psychotherapy Research*, 16, 182–183.

Hill, C.E. (2006) Introduction to special section on therapist effects. *Psychotherapy Research*, 16, 143.

Horvath, A.O. and Symonds, B.D. (1991) Relation between working alliance and outcome in psychotherapy: a meta-analysis. *Journal of Counseling Psychology*, 38, 139–149.

Huppert, J.D., Bufka, L.F., Barlow, D.H., *et al.* (2001) Therapists, therapist variables, and cognitive-behavioral therapy outcome in a multicenter trial for panic disorder. *Journal of Consulting and Clinical Psychology*, 69, 747–755.

Kendall, P.C., Gosch, E., Furr, J. and Sood, E. (2008) Flexibility within fidelity. *Journal of the American Academy of Child and Adolescent Psychiatry*, 47, 987–993.

Kim, D., Wampold. B.E. and Bolt, D.M. (2006) Therapist effects in psychotherapy: a random effects modelling of the National Institute of Mental Health Treatment of Depression Collaborative Research Program data. *Psychotherapy Research*, 16, 161–172.

Klerman, G.L. (1986) Keynote address. Delivered to the annual meeting of the Society for Psychotherapy Research, Wellesley, MA.

Leichsenring, F. and Rabung, S. (2008) Effectiveness of long-term psychodynamic psychotherapy: a meta-analysis. *Journal of the American Medical Association*, 300, 1551–1565.

Leykin, Y. and DeRubeis R.J. (2009) Allegiance in psychotherapy outcome research: separating association from bias. *Clinical Psychology: Science and Practice*, 16, 54–65.

Lilienfeld, S.O. (2007) Psychological treatments that cause harm. *Perspectives on Psychological Science*, 2, 53–70.

Lipsey, M.W. and Wilson, D.B. (1993) The efficacy of psychological, educational, and behavioral treatment: confirmation from meta-analyses. *American Psychologist*, 48, 1181–1209.

Luborsky, L., Diguer, L., Seligman, D.A., *et al.* (1999) The researcher's own therapy allegiances: a 'wild card' in comparisons of treatment efficacy. *Clinical Psychology: Science and Practice*, 6, 95–106.

Martin, D.J., Garske, J.P. and Davis, M.K. (2000) Relation of the therapeutic alliance with outcome and other variables: a meta-analytic review. *Journal of Consulting and Clinical Psychology*, 68, 438–450.

McKay, K.M., Imel, Z.E. and Wampold, B.E. (2006) Psychiatrist effects in the psychopharmacological treatment of depression. *Journal of Affective Disorders*, 92, 287–290.

Nathan, P.E. and Gorman, J.M. (eds) (2002) *A Guide to Treatments That Work*, 2nd edn, Oxford University Press, New York.

Norcross, J.C. (ed.) (2002) *Psychotherapy Relationships That Work*, Oxford University Press, New York.

Norcross, J.C. (ed.) (2011) *Psychotherapy Relationships That Work: Evidence-based Responsiveness*, 2nd edn, Oxford University Press, New York.

Norcross, J.C. and Wampold, B.E. (eds.) (2011) Adapting psychotherapy to the individual patient. *Journal of Clinical Psychology*, 67 (special edition).

Peterson, D.R. (2004) Science, scientism, and professional responsibility. *Clinical Psychology: Science and Practice*, 11, 196–210.

Pilgrim, D. (2007) The survival of psychiatric diagnosis. *Social Science and Medicine*, 65, 536–44.

Project MATCH Research Group(1998) Therapist effects in three treatments for alcohol problems. *Psychotherapy Research*, 8, 4, 445–474.

Rose, S.C., Bisson, J., Churchill, R. and Wessely, S. (2002) Psychological debriefing for preventing post traumatic stress disorder (PTSD). *Cochrane Database of Systematic Reviews*, Issue 2. Art. No.: CD000560. DOI: 10.1002/14651858.CD000560.

Shadish, W.R., Matt, G.E., Navarro, A.M. and Phillips, G. (2000) The effects of psychological therapies under clinically representative conditions: a meta-analysis. *Psychological Bulletin*, 126, 512–529.

Shapiro, A.K. and Shapiro, E.S. (1997) *The Powerful Placebo: From Ancient Priest to Modern Medicine*, Johns Hopkins University Press, Baltimore, MD.

Soldz, S. (2006) Models and meanings: therapist effects and the stories we tell. *Psychotherapy Research*, 16, 173–177.

Stevens, S.E., Hynan, M.T. and Allen, M. (2000) A meta-analysis of common factor and specific treatment effects across outcome domains of the phase model of psychotherapy. *Clinical Psychology: Science and Practice*, 7, 273–290.

Tolin, D.F. (2010) Is cognitive-behavioral therapy more effective than other therapies?: A meta-analytic review. *Clinical Psychology Review*, 30, 710–720.

Wampold, B.E (2001) *The Great Psychotherapy Debate: Models, Methods and Findings*, Lawrence Erlbaum Associates, Mahwah, NJ.

Wampold, B.E. and Bolt, D.M. (2006) Therapist effects: clever ways to make them (and everything else) disappear. *Psychotherapy Research*, 16, 184–187.

Wampold, B.E., Mondin, G.W., Moody, M., *et al.* (1997) A meta-analysis of outcome studies comparing bona fide psychotherapies: empirically, 'all must have prizes'. *Psychological Bulletin*, 122, 203–215.

Weisz, J.R, Weersing, V.R. and Henggeler S.W. (2005) Jousting with straw men: comment on Westen, Novotny, and Thompson-Brenner (2004). *Psychological Bulletin*, 131, 418–426.

Westen, D., Novotny, C.M. and Thompson-Brenner, H. (2004) The empirical status of empirically supported psychotherapies: assumptions, findings, and reporting in controlled clinical trials. *Psychological Bulletin*, 13, 631–663.

Wilson, G.T. (1998) Manual-based treatment and clinical practice. *Clinical Psychology: Science and Practice*, 5, 363–375.

3

The Conventional Wisdom

Don't let us forget that the causes of human actions are usually immeasurably more complex and varied than our subsequent explanations of them. (Fyodor Dostoyevsky)

Something is happening but you don't know what it is. (Bob Dylan)

Introduction

In his book *The Affluent Society*, first published in 1958, the Canadian economist J.K. Galbraith coined the term 'the conventional wisdom' to describe the way in which certain ideas dominate intellectual debate by dint of being both repeated and widely acceptable (Galbraith, 1987) rather than necessarily being useful or convincing. In contrast to the physical sciences, Galbraith reckoned the inherent uncertainties and evidential rules of the social sciences always give commentators enough wriggle room to adopt beliefs that have widespread appeal even if their veracity is largely untested. He must have known some very principled physicists because few career scientists appear to treat their hypotheses in the disposable manner that Popper recommended (Kuhn, 1962). Not many of us are comfortable with sacrificing our hard-won wisdoms in the name of progress.

Maximising the Benefits of Psychotherapy: A Practice-Based Evidence Approach,
First Edition. David Green and Gary Latchford.
© 2012 John Wiley & Sons, Ltd. Published 2012 by John Wiley & Sons, Ltd.

In Galbraith's elegant prose: 'A vested interest in understanding is more preciously guarded than any other treasure.'

In the world of psychotherapy, evidence-based practice has the air of an idea whose time has come. There is an attractive logic to the basic argument that the everyday delivery of psychological treatments should be founded on the results of carefully conducted scientific research. Once well-defined interventions have been identified, it makes both economic and moral sense to try and ensure that the winning formula is reproduced consistently and cheaply for the greatest public benefit. These ideas have a widespread appeal, especially at a time of escalating healthcare costs. Nobody – be they client, clinician or service manager – wants to waste precious resources on practices that will prove ineffective or even potentially harmful. So evidence-based practice falls within Galbraith's definition of a conventional wisdom in that it passes the acid test of acceptability. Those who challenge its principles risk being shamed as unethical charlatans (Begley, 2009). But someone has to ask inconvenient questions, so here goes:

- Although there is a wealth of outcome evidence indicating that, by and large, psychotherapy works, do we know enough about how therapies (and therapists) achieve their results?
- Do therapists who adhere most closely to prescribed treatment protocols get better outcomes than their less obedient colleagues?
- How likely is it that healthcare professionals will comply with the strictures of treatment manuals?
- How compatible is evidence-based practice with the service-user movement in the mental health field?
- What do you do when the best supported approach doesn't appear to work?

Mechanisms of Change

There is generally a 'big idea' at the heart of each distinctive school of psychotherapy. People can be helped to resolve their difficulties by confronting their fears; or understanding their unconscious motives; or finding a different tale to tell about themselves, and so on. Therapeutic interventions are subsequently designed around these fundamental principles. When those interventions prove effective, it is very tempting to presume that we don't have to think very hard about how these benefits might have been achieved. Things have worked out just as Wolpe or Freud or White or whoever said they would. However that would be to confuse reasons with causes. The reason why Albert Ellis developed rational-emotive therapy (RET) was that he believed many individuals experienced difficulties in their lives because of the sloppy ways they thought about their experiences. It does not, however, necessarily follow that, when clients improve after being treated with RET, they have done so by adopting a more rational attitude to their circumstances. There could be another mechanism of change at play, which we have not considered because of our pre-existing theoretical assumptions.

In the field of criminology, Smith, Clarke and Pease (2002) reported research investigating a series of crime reduction initiatives such as the use of CCTV or cycle patrols, all of which were associated with falling crime levels. However, a careful analysis of the available data indicated that each of these community interventions appeared to be having its impact from the time it was publicly announced rather than when each scheme actually started to function. Quite how this anticipatory effect operated was unclear. Were criminals misreading the likelihood of detection? Were police officers paying extra attention to the crimes targeted by the forthcoming initiative? The important point is that the timing of the reported changes was inconsistent with the theory of change on which these interventions were originally designed. The authors made a comparison with the classic Hawthorne experiment at the General Electric Company in Michigan before the Second World War when a number of diverse organisational changes resulted in increased production levels. Light levels increased; light levels decreased. More comfort breaks for workers; fewer comfort breaks for workers. Every alteration to the working environment seemed to provide a stimulus to production:

It makes intuitive sense that better working conditions would improve productivity. In the same way it is clear that street lighting or closed circuit television should work by increasing surveillability. Plague reduction should work by drowning witches, and fever should be reduced by the extraction of overheated blood. We have been too ready to assume that how crime prevention *should* work is the way that crime prevention *does* work. (Smith, Clarke and Pease, 2002)

Could there be similar tales to tell from the world of psychotherapy? It turns out there are quite a few.

Bell and pad

The 'bell and pad' treatment for nocturnal enuresis can be fairly described as having withstood the test of time. The method was introduced by Mowrer and Mowrer in 1938 and reckoned by the developers to have a 100% guaranteed success rate. It turns out they were somewhat overstating the likely effectiveness of this novel treatment – but not a lot. When over 60 years later, in 2004, Butler reviewed the available evidence on the treatment of nocturnal enuresis in children, the bell and pad (albeit in a modernised more user-friendly form) remained the proverbial treatment of choice with an estimated initial success rate of 65–70% tempered by a post-treatment relapse of 15–30% (Butler, 2004). There seems little doubt that Mowrer and Mowrer were onto something important. They had designed their intervention following classical conditioning principles, arguing that some youngsters needed help to establish the conditioned association between experiencing sensations of a full bladder and waking up that most children acquire before the age of five. The bell and pad equipment works because the first drops of urine act as an electrical conductor that completes a circuit and sets off an alarm. Hence waking up becomes associated with the sensations of needing to urinate. In an ironic reversal of Pavlov's famous experiment with drooling dogs, the unconditioned response of waking up when a loud bell rings is replaced by the conditioned response of waking up when your bladder is full. However, while children often rapidly learn to wake up just as they begin to urinate in the night, the real treatment benefits occur when they wake up *before* this point and, better still, enjoy a complete dry night's sleep during which they have not had to get up and go to the toilet at all. Classical conditioning theory struggles to explain this pattern of learning. Other learning theorists have suggested that Skinner's operant conditioning paradigm offers an alternative theoretical rationale for the effectiveness of the bell and pad in that the shock of being rudely awakened from slumber is an aversive experience that children will learn to avoid if possible. However, in Butler's opinion this analysis is also intellectually inadequate. He prefers to acknowledge that even after more than 60 years of therapeutic success the precise mechanism by which the bell and pad operates remains 'open to conjecture'.

EMDR

EMDR has emerged in the twenty-first century as a popular treatment for post-traumatic symptoms such as disturbing intrusive thoughts and images (Shapiro, 1995). The therapy consists of inviting the traumatised individual to concentrate on their upsetting memories while simultaneously attending to some form of bilateral stimulation such as repeated side-to-side finger movements. This process is repeated until the client can tolerate recalling these troubling episodes with minimal distress, at which point the therapy shifts focus and the client is invited to develop alternative constructions of their traumatic experiences. Since Shapiro invented this approach in 1987, a series of research papers have attested to its efficacy, which appears to compare favourably with more established forms of therapy for PTSD (Bisson *et al.*, 2007; Seidler and Wagner, 2006). However, the precise mechanism by which EMDR achieves its results remains a matter of, sometimes heated, debate.

Gunter and Bodner (2008) reported a series of three experiments they had conducted to test alternative explanations for EMDR's success. The first experiment tested the prediction that eye movements induce a state of relaxation in clients that enables them to confront previously unbearable stimuli. In fact, when participants were asked to recall unpleasant memories when moving their eyes or keeping them stationary, they reported higher levels of arousal in the movement condition. The second study tested what is known as the inter-hemispheric communication hypothesis; this posits that EMDR works by promoting connections between the left and right hemispheres of the brain, thus enhancing the individual's capacity to recall troubling past experiences without becoming emotionally overwhelmed. Lateral eye movements should be more effective than vertical eye movements in establishing these connections. However, when Gunter and Bodner put this prediction to the empirical test, they found no differences in treatment outcome. Vertical eye movements worked just as well as lateral eye movements. The final experiment investigated a working memory hypothesis that proposes that EMDR procedures serve as distracters, which take up a significant amount of the client's available working memory and so dilute their capacity to pay full attention to their upsetting recollections. For this explanation to have credibility, distracting activities other than following eye movements should have comparable effects. Gunter and Bodner were able to demonstrate that when participants were asked to attend to an auditory tracking task (listening closely to a tape recording) while simultaneously recalling an unpleasant memory, their ratings of how upsetting they found their recollections reduced as anticipated. The use of a visual distracter task (copying a complex drawing) had a comparable effect.

Overall the authors concluded that that, while EMDR is an effective treatment for PTSD, it is probably no more effective than other available therapies. They suggest that the most probable mechanism of change in EMDR concerns the limited capacity of working memory to handle both detailed memory recall and a concurrent intellectual task. Hence there is probably nothing special about the eye-movement exercises – holding a series of digits in mind while remembering a traumatic experience would probably have the same effect.

Solution-focused therapy

Solution-focused therapy (SFT) was developed by De Shazer and colleagues working in the family therapy tradition (O'Connell and Palmer, 2003). It is a brief future-oriented approach that questions the assumption that we need to understand how our clients' problems have arisen before we can help them move on with their lives. Indeed it suggests that inviting folk to dwell at length on their difficulties runs the risk of making recovery even harder. So SFT therapists like to draw attention to exceptions to their clients' prevailing tales of woe. They focus instead on accounts of successful coping and aim to replace 'problem-saturated' conversation with 'solution talk.' The general thrust of the approach is to help clients articulate what they wish to achieve from therapy and then support progressive movement towards those aims. Oftentimes people do not find it easy to articulate what therapeutic success might look like beyond some amelioration of troubling symptoms (such as feeling less anxious or depressed). De Shazer devised the 'miracle question' to help his clients develop an elaborated picture of what their preferred futures might look and feel like if they were able to make the most of the opportunity offered by therapy. It is worded as follows:

Imagine when you go to sleep one night, a miracle happens and the problems we've been talking about disappear. As you were asleep, you did not know that a miracle had happened. When you wake up what will be the first signs for you that a miracle has happened?

You would expect that such a pragmatic results-oriented school of psychotherapy would be highly suited to good quality outcome research but, somewhat surprisingly, this has not been the case (Corcoran and Pillai, 2009). However, whenever such studies have been conducted, inclusion of the miracle question is considered the sine qua non of SFT inclusion criteria.

On the other hand, a qualitative study reported by Lloyd and Dallos in 2008 revealed that not all consumers of SFT hold the miracle question in such high regard. This exploratory paper sought feedback from a small group of mothers all of whom had consulted a psychologist for help regarding their learning disabled child. Therapy was delivered following SFT principles and the mothers were asked to identify what aspects of the consultation they had found particularly helpful or unhelpful. In several ways this client feedback was consistent with expectations (e.g. the emphasis on the future rather than the past, and a focus on family strengths were appreciated). However, the miracle question itself got a stunningly bad press. All seven of the mothers in the study found it 'irrelevant or baffling'. Of course service users have no special, you might even say miraculous, powers that allow them to detect the active ingredients of psychological therapies (Humphreys and Wilbourne, 2005). It should give pause for thought, though, when the alleged cornerstone of a treatment intervention is described in such consistently critical terms.

Challenging Mechanisms of Change

A fine example of an 'insider' being prepared to ask difficult questions about mechanisms of change was Longmore and Worrell's 2007 paper entitled 'Do we need to challenge thoughts in cognitive behaviour therapy?' The authors carefully evaluated the available evidence that identifying and directly countering clients' unhelpful beliefs were mediators of change in successful CBT. Their review of so-called component analysis studies suggested that the addition of a cognitive component to a basic behavioural approach to the treatment of anxiety and depression did not consistently enhance therapy outcome. They also examined the evidence for linking changes in clients' thinking to their symptomatic improvement. If cognitive shifts mediate therapeutic gains, changes in thinking should consistently precede reported reductions in levels of depression or anxiety. Otherwise we could argue that cognitive change is *a* consequence, rather than *the* cause, of symptomatic improvement. Although Longmore and Worrell cited a number of studies demonstrating close correlations between measures of mood and altered belief patterns, they concluded that evidence demonstrating a convincing cause *then* effect relationship was 'somewhat limited'.

Interestingly, Longmore and Worrell did not place any great weight on the consistent finding within both the CBT and wider psychotherapeutic literature indicating that many clients respond surprisingly quickly to a range of treatments and that these rapid improvements seem to augur very well for longer term outcomes. Lambert (2005) reviewed this evidence and noted that large numbers of clients appeared to get better well before their official course of treatment had finished – some almost before it had started! While nobody quite understands how these, somewhat unanticipated, gains have been achieved, Lambert concludes that their timing suggests they are unlikely to be the result of specific technical interventions.

Meta-analyses

While each of the papers cited so far may well have given pause for thought to readers who imagined they already knew how their favoured psychotherapeutic approach achieved its success, individual examples no matter how compelling cannot provide a credible overview of a research domain. For that we need some independent scholars who are prepared to undertake the painstaking study required to complete a systematic review of the relevant scientific literature. Fortunately two recent meta-analyses have summarised the current knowledge base.

Kazdin (2007, 2008) argued that understanding the mechanisms of change in psychotherapy promised major improvements for the services that can be offered to clients but have as yet received surprisingly little research attention. The crucial question is: 'Can changes that occur during the course of therapy be reliably linked with subsequent clinical improvements?' This requires collection of data at multiple points in the course of treatment and sophisticated statistical analysis of the pathways by which a given therapy might help individuals recover. This is a high standard that, in Kazdin's view, few research studies have yet met with one notable exception. A wide evidence base, both biological and psychological, supports the claim that exposure therapies for anxiety disorders work on the extinction model. No other proposed mediators in psychotherapy, be they model-specific or generic factors have yet met Kazdin's criteria for being recognised as an 'evidence-based mechanism of change'.

Two Scandinavian researchers, Johansson and Høglend, also undertook a thorough meta-analytic review of the extant research literature analysing mediators of change in psychotherapy in 2007. They identified 61 papers published between 1986 and 2006 but concluded that *not one* of these research studies had met the demanding standards needed to support claims that any mechanism responsible for therapeutic progress had been scientifically demonstrated.

Partly this conclusion stemmed from the predominant use of regression analyses to examine the influence of hypothetical mediators on therapy outcome. These basically correlational statistics are not best placed to establish cause-and-effect relationships. More recently published papers (Henderson *et al.*, 2009; Neacsiu, Rizvi and Lineham, 2010) have employed latent growth curve analysis to test predictions about model-specific mechanisms of change, and this promises to be a more valid and sensitive way of tracking the process of change in psychotherapy. Criteria of good practice in the use of this statistical technique (e.g. use of several measures of goodness of fit; application of 'growth mixture models' where multiple trajectories of change are anticipated) have been published (Jung and Wickrama, 2008), and future research of this ilk on psychotherapy mediators is likely to increase in popularity. Having said that, the sceptical consumer might also reflect that researcher allegiance is likely to influence the interpretation of data as much in psychotherapy process research as it has in outcome studies (Luborsky *et al.*, 1999) and systematic literature reviews (Littell, 2005).

Of course it's not just psychotherapists who might be tempted to make exaggerated claims about the special qualities that their favoured intervention possesses relative to the competition. There is a respected body of opinion within the field of pharmacology that argues that there is minimal evidence that different brands of psychotropic medication work better for some psychiatric conditions than for others. Rather, all drugs prescribed for mental health problems induce abnormal states of consciousness that may or may not prove helpful depending on the response, in the broadest sense, of the individual patient (Moncrieff, 2008). This is not a point of view to which major pharmaceutical companies are likely to subscribe.

So it seems reasonable to conclude that there is a lot more to discover about how psychotherapy works and we would be well advised to take any claims to the contrary with a substantial pinch of salt.

But does this gap in understanding really matter? If the soup is tasty and nourishing, do we need to become pre-occupied with how individual ingredients contribute to the overall effect? Well probably yes . . .

The Question of Adherence

If we know that a treatment package works, but we aren't clear about which components of the package are contributing to the beneficial outcome, how best might we proceed? At first glance the answer seems pretty obvious. Carry on delivering the 'Full Monty'. The whole point of carefully assessing how well therapists in treatment efficacy trials adhere to manualised guidelines is to enable others to faithfully replicate those procedures. However, closely following protocols has its price. If we don't know with any great confidence why a therapy intervention works, the likelihood is that we will incorporate a number of inert or even potentially injurious components in our treatment protocol. This may dilute the effectiveness of the intervention and it will undoubtedly increase the cost and complexity of training therapists to criterion levels of adherence (Rakovshik and McManus, 2010). However, it is arguable that, given the current limited understanding of psychotherapy mediators, this is still a sound strategy to adopt – provided that 'properly' conducted evidence-based interventions prove more helpful to clients than the treatment-as-usual regimes they aspire to replace. For example, a series of research papers investigating the efficacy of multidimensional family therapy has indicated that, when therapists drift away from prescribed protocol, the outcomes for their clients are likely to deteriorate relative to therapy that has been provided by the proverbial book (Liddle, 2010). A similar empirical case has been made for closely following CBT treatment manuals (Hogue *et al.*, 2008) but, as ever, not all the available evidence points in the same direction. Huppert and colleagues (2001) noticed with interest that, although all the therapists in their multicentre CBT outcome trial for the treatment of panic disorders satisfied their study's adherence criteria, there was considerable variability in the outcomes achieved by their clients. The effect sizes for individual therapists ranged from 0–18%, so some therapists were highly effective while others seemed to have made minimal difference, even though all were delivering the same tightly controlled treatment protocol. The researchers tested a few a priori hypotheses about variables that might sort the wheat from the therapeutic chaff but came up with nothing approaching a convincing explanation for these interesting and important differences. In particular, they found no clear relationship between how closely therapists stuck to the treatment guidelines provided and the outcomes for their clients. If anything, the trend in the data suggested that those who adhered most closely to the manual's dictats were somewhat less effective than those who appeared to have exercised some discretion in the way in which they conducted therapy sessions. It is, however, also important to remember that no one in this study was permitted to entirely 'do their own thing'.

In an extensive literature review, Perepletchikova and Kazdin (2005) reviewed research examining the relationship between treatment fidelity (i.e., how closely an intervention followed manualised therapy guidelines) and outcome for the client. They were surprised both at how little empirical evidence they could unearth and the very different tales that these studies told. Certainly a number of investigators had found the expected positive correlation between adherence and improved outcome but just as many, including the very large NIMH study into treatment of depression (Shaw *et al.*, 1999), found no such relationship. The authors' overall summary is worth quoting directly: 'Quite surprisingly, there is very little evidence that provides a strong link between how well or faithfully treatment is carried out and the extent to which clients improve.'

This summary is essentially a restatement of the conclusions drawn in an earlier review on the same topic conducted by Miller and Binder (2002) and is largely in accord with recent formal meta-analysis conducted by Webb and colleagues (2010). However, the latter paper does also raise the interesting possibility that procedural correctness may pay dividends when working with some specific clinical populations (such as depressed individuals) but not others.

Keeping Clinicians on Track

Casting aside for the moment any reservations about our understanding of change mechanisms in psychotherapy and the optimal level of fidelity to treatment manuals, we move onto the supremely pragmatic question of therapist training. What is the best way to help clinicians learn the ropes of specific therapies? How much is that process likely to cost? Do therapists easily transfer skills developed on specialist training courses into their everyday working practices? Are they likely to notice if their standards are slipping?

Offering interested clinicians a 'taster' experience of working within a novel theoretical framework is a relatively undemanding (and cheap) exercise. They might reasonably be expected to get a grasp of basic principles and, if the ideas take hold and are supplemented by further reading and supervision, even change their practice somewhat. However, the most that an educational intervention of this intensity could aspire to would be therapists whose work is 'informed by' a particular theoretical affiliation. Establishing good enough adherence levels to an explicit treatment manual requires a much, much more substantial commitment from all concerned.

From the educators' perspective, the focus of assessment should shift from traditional academic assignments, such as essay writing, to close scrutiny of a trainee's performance in ongoing therapy (most likely by continuous review of videotape recordings). This is time-consuming and therefore expensive work that can be further complicated by the challenge of establishing criteria by which to decide if adequate standards of competence have been demonstrated. Although a range of checklists and rating scales have been developed to aid in this task (e.g. The Cognitive Therapy Scale – Revised, produced by Blackburn *et al.*, 2001), the level of inter-rater agreement when it comes to judging clinical skills is consistently lower than more traditional academic assessments such as second-marking an exam answer (Keen and Freeston, 2008). When these disparate opinions are 'moderated', to use the educational jargon, the final decisions are likely to be determined as much by 'horse trading' between assessors as by referral to objective performance criteria (Tweed, Graber and Wang, 2010). There is also the thorny issue of how good is good enough? As the reader will now realise, there is no simple relationship between adherence and outcome so clients' symptomatic improvement cannot act as an indicator of technical competence. The alternative is to create a statistical decision-making tool that is pragmatic but unashamedly arbitrary (Rakovshik and McManus, 2010).

There is a further subtlety to be considered. Do we wish to produce therapists who adhere consistently to manualised instructions, or is the goal of professional training to equip practitioners to demonstrate the higher level skill of being flexibly competent in their use of a particular theoretical model? The gist of this discrimination lies in the judgement exercised by the individual clinician in deciding quite when and, to some extent, how any given intervention is to be delivered. Barber *et al.*, (2007) sum up this notion of psychotherapeutic competence as 'the judicious application of communication, knowledge, technical skills, clinical reasoning, emotions, values, and contextual understanding for the benefit of the individual and community being served'. This definition of the effective application of scientific research findings falls somewhere between the explicit clarity of evidence-based practice procedural correctness and the fuzzier realms of the tacit knowledge that is taken to underlie much of the mystery of higher level professional capability across a range of high-status trades (Eraut, 2000). While there is something attractive and plausible about this context-specific application of research findings to the peculiar circumstances of a particular client in a particular therapeutic relationship, there must come a point at which the empirical justification for working within a specific framework gets diluted to the point where it loses plausibility. As Beutler (2009) has argued, we can't have it both ways. When the scientific evidence suggests an explicitly described intervention is likely to be effective, it's pushing it somewhat to deliver your own personalised version of said intervention and still claim full membership of the evidence-based practice club (Waller, 2009). There is a case to be made for inventive treatments that are informed by theoretical models and relevant research findings (Grawe, 1997), but if you opt for that route you cannot simply rely on established evidence to support your practice. You and your client(s) had better start producing some evidence of your own as well!

Resistance to Change

While a commitment to continued professional development is probably written into the job descriptions of all psychological therapists, there has not been a universally enthusiastic response to the invitation to embrace the principles of evidence-based practice. It has been suggested that in some quarters this reluctance is linked to a limited awareness of research findings allied to a preference for experientially acquired insights over the results of formal scientific enquiry (Boisvert and Faust, 2006). However, resistance to externally imposed change is not an unusual phenomenon in the field of occupational psychology. Reason (1997) describes how organisations tend to respond to industrial accidents by becoming increasingly prescriptive (and more likely proscriptive) about what should and should not be done in their workplace. As a consequence the zone of 'allowable action' granted to employees gradually shrinks, often to the point where workers feel they have to break the rules to some degree just to get the proverbial job done. The net result can be that safety procedures are frequently circumvented in the interests of operational efficiency. The risk, of course, is that one of these moment-to-moment judgements goes awry and another accident occurs leading to further, more restricting, updating of safety procedures, which, in due course, sets off the cycle again. The examples that Reason provides in his book *Managing the Risks of Organizational Accidents* are generally from the chemical or transport industries rather than the health sector, but it is arguable that any attempts to limit the autonomous decision making of experienced healthcare professionals might be even more vigorously resisted in medical settings.

Transfer of Training

It would be most unfair to portray the various professions who practise psychotherapy as dyed-in-the-wool traditionalists determined to carry on doing what they've always done impervious to any new developments in the field. On the contrary, a commitment to personal and professional development is an established part of our working culture. We are only too happy to sign up for courses and swan off to conferences whenever we get the chance. However, our good intentions of transferring the new knowledge gained on these educational ventures into our everyday professional practice are frequently frustrated. A neat little paper published by Miller and Mount in 2001 illustrates nicely the problems that need to be overcome. The authors had provided a 'one-shot' workshop on motivational interviewing (MI) for a group of 22 counsellors working with young offenders. The two-day event was well constructed and included both didactic and experiential components. Participants were provided with both a textbook and a therapy manual, and a series of before-and-after measures were taken (self-report, video role-play, etc.) to ensure that the counsellors were able to conduct interviews according to the requirements of the MI model. On completion of the two-day workshop, this feedback told an encouraging tale. However, the workshop organisers wanted to check that their efforts would have an enduring impact on the counsellors' ways of working, and undertook a detailed follow-up study some four months later. The follow-up consisted of a self-report questionnaire and close analysis of videotaped recordings of actual consultations workshop participants had subsequently held with their clients. These two sources of information provided the researchers with very contrasting accounts of the workshop's impact. The questionnaire replies suggested that the counsellors had grasped MI principles and put them into regular practise to the evident benefit of their clients. However, when the videotapes of therapeutic interviews were analysed, the researchers could identify hardly any examples of what they considered the hallmarks of MI. There seemed little evidence either that the counsellors had changed their ways of working or that their clients were responding differently to their interventions. The major consequence of the workshop therefore seemed to be in the enhanced sense of self-efficacy as MI therapists reported by the counsellors. Unfortunately this belief did not appear related to any consistent behavioural changes. Miller and Mount wryly reflected that this experience may have ended up doubly handicapping the well-intentioned counsellors in that they were now not only no more effective as MI therapists than when they started but they no longer saw any need to attend further training courses!

This disappointing outcome is not an isolated finding. The default position is that continued professional development (CPD) activity for a range of healthcare professionals has minimal lasting impact on their subsequent practice (Davis *et al.*, 1995). This is particularly the case for brief one-off courses such as that described, but it would be foolish to assume that more intensive and enduring training experiences always result in better established shifts in therapists' behaviour. Brosan and colleagues reported a study in 2006 in which they evaluated therapy tapes of 13 United Kingdom-accredited CBT therapists of whom seven failed to meet published criteria for CBT competence. It is, however, important to note that those participants who had most recently completed their training were the ones who were most likely to be performing to expected standards. In a follow-up study (Brosan, Reynold and Moore, 2008), the same group of researchers compared the 22 CBT therapists' appraisal of their performance on a therapy tape with that provided by an expert observer. In a finding that echoed the wider social psychology literature on positive biases in self-appraisal (Dunning, Heath and Suls, 2004), the greatest divergence in opinion was between the self-ratings of the least competent therapists and the judgements of the independent assessor.

None of the foregoing arguments should be taken to imply that it is impossible to enable mental health professionals to become highly motivated and effective proponents of evidence-based practice or for all of us to benefit from feedback so that we learn to appraise our own performance more accurately across a range of contexts. However, it is fair to say that this is not likely to be a straightforward or inexpensive undertaking. Consequently evidence-based practice initiatives tend to be more successful when they operate at both an organisational and an individual level (Aarons and Sawitzky, 2006). A good example of this thoughtfully negotiated application of scientific evidence to a major mental health problem is the community partnership model espoused by Becker *et al.* (2009) in developing a preventative programme aimed at reducing the prevalence of eating disorders in the female undergraduate population of a number of US universities. Overall, however, it is probably fair to describe the task of achieving a high degree of fidelity to any treatment intervention delivered across a number of sites by a range of professionals as challenging, bordering on daunting (Zvoch, 2009).

References

Aarons, G. and Sawitzky, A. (2006) Organizational culture and climate and mental health provider attitudes toward evidence-based practice. *Psychological Services*, 3, 61–72.

Barber, J., Sharpless, B., Klosterman, S. and McCarthy, K. (2007) Assessing intervention competence and its relation to therapy outcome: a selected review derived from the empirical literature. *Professional Psychology: Research and Practice*, 38, 493–500.

Becker, C., Stice, E., Shaw, H. and Woda, S. (2009) Use of empirically supported interventions for psychopathology: can the participatory approach move us beyond the research-to-practice gap? *Behaviour Research and Therapy*, 47, 265–274.

Begley, S. (2009) Ignoring the evidence. Why do psychologists reject science? *Newsweek* (Oct 2), http://www.newsweek.com/id/216506 (accessed 11 September, 2011).

Beutler, L. (2009) Making science matter in clinical practice: redefining Psychotherapy. *Clinical Psychology: Science and Practice*, 16, 301–317.

Bisson, J., Ehlers, A., Matthews, R., *et al.* (2007) Psychological treatments for chronic post-traumatic stress disorder. Systematic review and meta-analysis. *British Journal of Psychiatry*, 190, 97–104.

Blackburn, I., James, I., Milne, D., *et al.* (2001) The Revised Cognitive Therapy Scale (CTS-R): psychometric properties. *Behavioural and Cognitive Psychotherapy*, 29, 431–446.

Boisvert, C. and Faust, D. (2006) Practicing psychologists' knowledge of general psychotherapy research findings: implications for science–practice relations. *Professional Psychology: Research and Practice*, 37, 708–716.

Brosan, L., Reynold, S. and Moore, R. (2006) Factors associated with competence in cognitive therapists. *Behavioural and Cognitive Psychotherapy*, 35, 179–190.

Brosan, L., Reynold, S. and Moore, R. (2008) Self-evaluation of cognitive therapy performance: do therapists know how competent they are? *Behavioural and Cognitive Psychotherapy*, 36, 581–587.

Butler, R. (2004) Childhood nocturnal enuresis: developing a conceptual framework. *Clinical Psychology Review*, 24, 909–931.

Corcoran, J. and Pillai, V. (2009) A review of the research on solution-focused therapy. *British Journal of Social Work*, 39, 234–242.

Davis, D., Thompson, M., Oxman, A. and Haynes, R. (1995) Changing physician performance: a systematic review of .the effect of continuing education strategies. *Journal of the American Medical Association*, 274, 700–705.

Dunning, D., Heath, C. and Suls, J. (2004) Flawed self-assessment. Implications for health, education, and the workplace. *Psychological Science in the Public Interest*, 5, 69–106.

Eraut, M. (2000) Non-formal learning and tacit knowledge in professional work. *British Journal of Educational Psychology*, 70, 113–136.

Galbraith, J. (1987) *The Affluent Society*, Penguin, London.

Grawe, K. (1997) Research-informed psychotherapy. *Psychotherapy Research*, 7, 1–19.

Gunter, R. and Bodner, G. (2008) How eye movements affect unpleasant memories: support for a working-memory account. *Behaviour Research and Therapy*, 46, 913–931.

Henderson, C., Row, C., Dakof, G., *et al.* (2009) Parenting practices as mediators of treatment effects in an early-intervention trial of multi-dimensional family therapy. *American Journal of Drug and Alcohol Abuse*, 35, 220–224.

Hogue, A., Henderson, C., Barajas, S., *et al.* (2008) Treatment adherence, competence, and outcome in individual and family therapy for adolescent behavior problems. *Journal of Consulting and Clinical Psychology*, 76, 544–555.

Humphreys, K. and Wilbourne, P. (2005) Knitting together some ripping yarns. *Addiction*, 101, 4–5.

Huppert, J., Bufka, L., Barlow, D., *et al.* (2001) Therapists, therapist variables, and cognitive-behavioral therapy outcome in a multicenter trial for panic disorder. *Journal of Consulting and Clinical Psychology*, 69, 747–755.

Johansson, P. and Høglend, P. (2007) Identifying mechanisms of change in psychotherapy: mediators of treatment outcome. *Clinical Psychology and Psychotherapy*, 14, 1–9.

Jung, T. and Wickrama, K. (2008) An introduction to latent class growth analysis and growth mixture modeling. *Social and Personality Psychology Compass*, 2, 302–317.

Kazdin, A. (2007) Mediators and mechanisms of change in psychotherapy research. *Annual Review of Clinical Psychology*, 3, 1–27.

Kazdin, A.E. (2008) Evidence-based treatment and practice: new opportunities to bridge clinical research and practice, enhance the knowledge base, and improve patient care. *American Psychologist*, 63, 3, 146–159.

Keen, A. and Freeston, M. (2008) Assessing competence in cognitive-behavioural therapy. *British Journal of Psychiatry*, 193, 60–64.

Kuhn, T. (1962) *The Structure of Scientific Revolutions*, Chicago, University of Chicago Press.

Lambert, M. (2005) Early response in psychotherapy: further evidence for the importance of common factors rather than 'placebo effects'. *Journal of Clinical Psychology*, 16, 855–869.

Liddle, H. (2010) Treating adolescent substance abuse using multidimensional family therapy. Evidence-based psychotherapies for children and adolescents, in J. Weisz and A. Kazdin (eds) *Evidence-based Psychotherapies for Children and Adolescents*, Guilford Press, New York, pp. 416–432.

Littell, J. (2005) Lessons from a systematic review of effects of multisystemic therapy. *Children and Youth Services Review*, 27, 445–463.

Lloyd, H. and Dallos, R. (2008) First session solution-focused brief therapy with families who have a child with severe intellectual difficulties: mothers' experiences and views. *Journal of Family Therapy*, 30, 5–28.

Longmore, R. and Worrell, M. (2007) Do we need to challenge thoughts in cognitive behavior therapy? *Clinical Psychology Review*, 27, 173–187.

Luborsky, L., Diguer, L., Seligman, D.A., *et al.* (1999) The researcher's own therapeutic allegiances – a 'wild card' in comparisons of treatment efficacy. *Clinical Psychology: Science and Practice*, 6, 95–132.

Miller, S. and Binder, J. (2002) The effects of manual-based training on treatment fidelity and outcome: a review of the literature on adult individual psychotherapy. *Psychotherapy: Theory, Research, Practice, Training*, 39, 184–198.

Miller, W. and Mount, K. (2001) A small study of training in motivational interviewing: does one workshop change clinician and client behaviour? *Behavioural and Cognitive Psychotherapy*, 29, 457–471.

Moncrieff, J. (2008) The creation of the concept of an antidepressant: an historical analysis. *Social Science & Medicine*, 66, 2346–2355.

Mowrer, O.H. and Mowrer, W.M. (1938) Enuresis: a method for its study and treatment. *American Journal of Orthopsychiatry*, 8, 436–459.

Neacsiu, A., Rizvi, S. and Linehan, M. (2010) Dialectical behavior therapy skills use as a mediator and outcome of treatment for borderline personality disorder. *Behaviour Research and Therapy* 48: 832–839.

O'Connell, B. and Palmer, S. (2003) *Handbook of Solution-Focused Therapy*, Sage, London.

Perepletchikova, F. and Kazdin, A. (2005) Treatment integrity and therapeutic change: issues and research recommendations. *Clinical Psychology: Science and Practice*, 12, 365–383.

Rakovshik, S. and McManus, F. (2010) Establishing evidence-based training in cognitive behavioral therapy: a review of current empirical findings and theoretical guidance. *Clinical Psychology Review*, 30, 496–516.

Reason, J. (1997) *Managing the Risks of Organizational Accidents*, Ashgate, Aldershot.

Seidler, G. and Wagner, F. (2006) Comparing the efficacy of EMDR and trauma-focused cognitive-behavioral therapy in the treatment of PTSD: a meta-analytic study. *Psychological Medicine*, 36, 1515–1522.

Shapiro, F. (1995) *Eye Movement Desensitization and Reprocessing: Basic Principles, Protocols, and Procedures*, Guildford, New York.

Shaw, B., Elkin, I., Yamaguchi, J., *et al.* (1999) Therapist competence ratings in relation to clinical outcome in cognitive therapy of depression. *Journal of Consulting and Clinical Psychology*, 67, 837–846.

Smith, M., Clarke, R. and Pease, K. (2002) Anticipatory benefits in crime prevention, in *Analysis for Crime Prevention: Crime Prevention Studies*, vol. 13 (ed. N. Tilley), Criminal Justice Press, Monsey, NY.

Tweed, A., Graber, R. and Wang, M. (2010) Assessing trainee clinical psychologists' clinical competence. *Psychology Learning and Teaching*, 9, 50–60.

Waller, G. (2009) Evidence-based treatment and therapist drift. *Behaviour Research and Therapy*, 47, 119–127.

Webb, C., De Rubeis, R. and Barber, J. (2010) Therapist adherence/competence and treatment outcome: a meta-analytic review. *Journal of Consulting and Clinical Psychology*, 78, 200–211.

Zvoch, K. (2009) Treatment fidelity in multisite evaluation. A multilevel longitudinal examination of provider adherence status and change, *American Journal of Evaluation*, 30, 44–61.

4

The Real Experimenter

All professions are conspiracies against the laity (George Bernard Shaw)

Introduction

When George Kelly, the originator of 'personal construct theory', surveyed the rise and rise of behaviour therapy in the early 1960s, he found much to admire. Here was a psychotherapy that was explicitly experimental in name and deed. Individuals who had been trapped by fearful thoughts and feelings were invited to embark on behavioural adventures to test out their theories and confront their anxieties about exactly what would happen if they took certain scary courses of action. Therapists supported their clients by helping them design experiments; anticipate potential outcomes; and review the results of their initiatives. So far, so good in Kelly's opinion. Where he fell out with the 'new kids on the block' was not so much in what they and their clients got up to together but in the way in which psychologists chose to describe their efforts in the professional journals through which the new ideas of the behaviour therapy movement were disseminated. He reckoned all sense of a joint therapeutic enterprise had got lost in the language of objective science. The

Maximising the Benefits of Psychotherapy: A Practice-Based Evidence Approach,
First Edition. David Green and Gary Latchford.
© 2012 John Wiley & Sons, Ltd. Published 2012 by John Wiley & Sons, Ltd.

therapist was labeled the experimenter (E) and the client was termed the subject (S). The clear implication was that the psychologist was the dominant partner in the relationship designing helpful tasks for the client to conduct. To put it bluntly, the client's job seemed to be to do what they were told and trust in the wisdom and sound judgement of the therapist. Kelly held a contrary view of the therapeutic relationship. If clients were prepared to put themselves into perilous positions that they had formerly avoided like the proverbial plague, while their psychologists cheered from the sidelines, Kelly had no doubt who he thought was the senior experimenter in the partnership. The client was the one taking all the risks and the client was the one who drew the most important conclusions from the venture. The therapist's role was not insignificant but it was supportive and subsidiary – a technical adviser with both scientific credibility and an ethical concern for the client's well-being. Kelly liked to compare his notion of the psychotherapeutic alliance with his, somewhat idealised, view of the manner in which a postgraduate student and their research supervisor might negotiate their respective roles. The student is the expert on the subject area, while the supervisor is the expert on the means of investigation.

Not all former research students will recognise this portrayal of their working relationship with their supervisor as a meeting of equals, but we get Kelly's point. When we write or talk about our therapeutic work, we tend to overstate the importance of our contribution to proceedings and downplay the part that our clients play in determining the outcome of our combined efforts. It is probably a fair criticism to suggest that the evidence-based practice movement has continued that ignoble tradition. This chapter attempts to correct the imbalance and so is dedicated to 'real experimenters' the world over.

Outcome Predictors

When Lambert penned his influential 1992 narrative review estimating the contributions made by a range of factors to psychotherapy outcome, the headline-grabbing finding was the low predictive power he attributed to the theoretical model and technique adopted by the therapist, which he reckoned might explain a mere 15% of the total variance. Wampold and colleagues' (1997) subsequent meta-analysis suggested that even this low figure might prove an over-estimate. Their analysis indicated that all treatment factors combined accounted for only 13% of the variance in final outcome, and that the majority of that contribution was related to the quality of the therapeutic alliance established between the client and the therapist. However, both Lambert and Wampold considered that client-related factors exercised a significantly stronger influence on the end result of therapy. Lambert estimated that 40% of final outcome could be attributed to client and extra-therapeutic factors, while Wampold reckoned these combined influences explained a mighty 87% of the total variance. In part these figures represent a timely reminder of the powerful role that random life events play in determining our day-to-day mental well-being, but they also underline the recurrent message that clients don't just respond to psychological treatments, they play a central role in shaping the course and outcome of therapy. They might, for example, decide not to bother . . .

Dropout in Psychotherapy

While substantial resources have been devoted to researching out-comes in psychotherapy, and particularly to studies seeking to deter-mine which brand of psychological treatment might be most effective in treating particular mental disorders, there is a surprising dearth of investigations into another, some might argue more fundamental, problem. How come so many people who seek psychological help fail to stay the course? The seriousness of this issue has been long recognised. A meta-analysis conducted by Wierzbicki and Pekarik (1993) concluded that the average client dropout rate from psycho-therapy services for adults was 47%, and that this figure was likely to exceed 50% for client groups such as those misusing drugs who have historically been harder to engage in treatment. Furthermore, there is little sign that retention rates have improved over the last 15 years or so since that review was undertaken. Barrett *et al.* (2008) summarised the results of their updated systematic review of dropout in psychotherapy as follows:

- Of 100 people who contact a mental health service:
    - only 50 will attend the initial assessment session
    - 33 will return for their first therapy appointment
    - only 20 will attend the third therapy session
    - 17 will still be engaged in therapy at session 10.

Even those who take faith in the evidence that much of the benefit that clients receive from therapy occurs in the early stages of treatment should find these statistics alarming. In fact, follow-up studies on individuals who drop out of therapy (when they can be contacted) suggest that their degree of psychopathology remains within the clinical range that prompted referral to mental health services in the first place (Cahill *et al.*, 2003).

Despite some familiar concerns about inconsistencies in the definition and measurement of dropout in psychotherapy, the message from over 30 years of research is unambiguous (Bados, Balaguer and Saldaña, 2007). Far too many people who turn to specialist services for help with psychological problems gain no relief from their suffering because they choose not to stay in therapy. It does not seem to matter what brand of therapy they are offered. Although one comparative study (Cuijpers *et al.*, 2008) reported that non-completion rates for CBT were significantly higher than those recorded for a group treated with problem-solving therapy, no form of psychological treatment claims to have solved this seemingly intractable problem (see Masi, Miller and Olson's [2003] review of systemic therapy, for example). When it comes to dropout, the reverse Dodo judgement probably applies: none have won and none deserve prizes!

It is interesting to reflect on the possible reasons behind the relative lack of research into the high dropout rates associated with psychological therapies. A marketing professional would no doubt recognise that advertising the fact that up to half one's customers jump ship is not a sound strategy for promoting a product. However, we expect higher ethical standards from our clinicians and scientists. For example, if a research study were to report success rates based only on those participants who completed a full course of therapy, they would present a heavily biased picture of the potency of the therapy being investigated. There is limited value in discovering an apparently highly efficacious intervention if the majority of those offered treatment is unwilling or unable to tolerate its requirements. It is therefore current good practice in outcome research to report data on what is termed an 'intention to treat' sample rather than just those who satisfied the full treatment protocol. As anticipated, the therapeutic benefits of even the best supported interventions don't tend to look quite so impressive once this important correction has been made. It makes similar sense to try and ensure that full and accurate information on patient dropout is collected when auditing the effectiveness of local mental health services (Connell, Grant and Mullin, 2006).

There has also been a timely move to investigate quite why so many individuals fail to stick with a contract into which, we presume, they have entered voluntarily. While early studies had tended to try to identify retrospectively those patient characteristics that were associated with premature termination (such as social class, gender or diagnostic category), more recent research has sought to understand the choice to withdraw from therapy from the patient's perspective. A good example of this approach is the prospective study examining families' experiences of 'barriers to treatment' reported by Kazdin and colleagues (1997). Over 200 families had been referred to an out-patient clinic providing a specialist service for young people with anti-social behaviour problems. This client group is recognised as being at high risk of premature termination of therapy. The researchers tested a number of related hypotheses concerning which families might drop out of treatment and when. As expected from past research findings, several established risk factors were associated with failure to engage with the service, such as the socio-economic status of the family and the severity of the referred child's behavioural problems, but this was far from the whole story. When families were asked by researchers independent of the service what might have got in the way of their making maximum use of the therapy on offer, they were able to identify a number of specific factors (environmental stressors that acted as obstacles to attendance; demands of treatment; perceived relevance of the treatment on offer; and relationship with the therapist), all of which were included in a Barriers to Treatment Participation Scale (BTPS). Statistical analysis of families' feedback regarding their experience of these various hindrances indicated that they were powerful predictors of dropout over and above the recognised population risk factors. Interestingly, the most powerful predictor of all was the parents' view of the relevance/irrelevance of the treatment provided for their child. Kazdin and his colleagues noted that, when these perceived barriers to participation were low, they could act in a protective way that enabled even the families most at risk of dropout to 'stick with the programme'. Conversely, when 'at risk' families met multiple obstacles, the likelihood of their completing therapy fell even further. The researchers also suggested that this form of investigation offered some insight into the mechanisms whereby families make the decision to opt out of, or stay in, therapy and hence provided a tentative basis on which intervention strategies to reduce premature termination might be designed. In similar vein, a UK study of attrition from an adult psychotherapy service in the NHS (Self *et al.*, 2005) noted that, while clients from socially deprived backgrounds were most likely to drop out of therapy, those who progressed beyond the early stages of engagement tended to stay the subsequent course of their treatment just as well as other clinic attenders. The authors suggested that the practical implication of this finding was to make strenuous efforts to stay in business with these 'at risk' clients through the early stages of the treatment pathway.

Ogrodniczuk and his colleagues (2005) have conducted a meta-analysis of strategies for reducing premature termination in psychotherapy that have been empirically investigated. The literature their search identified is limited. For example, they unearthed no controlled studies comparing the effectiveness of more than one intervention. Nonetheless, they discovered a number of promising ideas such as offering time-limited treatment contracts and providing reminders of upcoming appointments. In the absence of any compelling evidence of the superiority of any one approach, the authors recommend that therapists be prepared to mix and match the techniques to try and minimise dropout from treatment while always being 'mindful of the patient's perspective regarding the nature of the problem and his or her preferences and expectations of how it should be addressed'. This message was echoed in a narrative review of studies related to building successful therapeutic alliances during initial assessment interviews (Hilsenroth and Cromer, 2007) that also advocated paying close attention to the client's 'lay' theories about how their difficulties might have arisen.

Overall, therefore, the tendency of consumers of psychotherapy services to 'vote with their feet' can be seen as a reminder of the commercial power that they possess and their right to expect that providers will respond to their preferences. It was not always thus . . .

The Service-user Movement

Evidence-based practice is not the only currently influential policy initiative in the mental health field. Since the early twentieth century, there has been an increasing push to give a greater say to those who have been on the receiving end of psychiatric and psychological treatments – the 'service users' to employ our present-day jargon. There are two compelling reasons for taking this movement seriously. The first is moral. The history of care for mental health patients in the United Kingdom, North America, and indeed across the world is littered with examples of maltreatment and abuse that were allowed to occur because those individuals had been denied any power of protest. Treatment was given to them not negotiated with them. Not before time, the human rights of those who seek psychological help are nowadays being appropriately recognised.

The second driver behind the growth of the service user movement is more economic than ethical. The old free-market principle that 'the customer knows best' has infiltrated our hospitals and consulting rooms. Within the United Kingdom this ambition to improve healthcare standards by empowering consumers to take their custom to whomsoever they please was captured in the policy document *Creating a Patient-Led NHS* (Department of Health, 2005). The opportunity to get better value for money from the public purse while simultaneously correcting a long-running social injustice has understandably proved to be a politically inviting combination to successive governments.

However there is, at the very least, a potential tension between asserting the right of consumers to choose their preferred form of psychological treatment and prescribing what will likely prove the most effective intervention for their condition as determined by the available scientific evidence. The contrast in emphasis is perhaps best illustrated in the notion that the goal of care for individuals with major mental health problems should be 'recovery' rather than symptom alleviation (i.e., supporting individuals in rebuilding their lives rather than focusing primarily on reducing their psychopathology). Recovery is conceptualised as a highly personal, client-led process in which sufferers seek to make constructive meaning of their disturbing experiences, often helped by others who have struggled with comparable challenges (Anthony, 1993). The four core values of the recovery movement have been defined as:

- person orientation – where the individuality of each client is respected
- person involvement – in which collaborative discussion characterises all therapist/client communication
- self-determination – the fundamental right of clients to make choices about their treatment
- growth potential – a primary emphasis on the person's strengths and capacity to learn from experience (Farkas *et al.*, 2005).

It makes little sense to polarise the differences between the service user and evidence-based practice movements. As consumers we would surely want to have our decisions informed by the best available research findings and just as surely many of us will sometimes feel that we neither want to make, nor are entirely capable of making, complex medical judgements and prefer to follow the guidance of a trusted health professional (Adams and Drake, 2006). However, there is an inherent incompatibility between the two principles if the research on which evidence-based practice recommendations have been made has not been designed with service users' priorities in mind. For example, have the outcome measures employed assessed the kind of psychological and social changes that matter most to those recovering from mental health crises, like maintaining important relationships or finding employment? Have an adequate number of properly funded studies been conducted into the efficacy of novel interventions such as those advocated by proponents of the recovery model of care? Despite recent moves to include service users in the design phase of psychotherapy research studies, there remains a troublesome gap between what commissioners of research, such as major pharmaceutical companies, are prepared to fund and what those in receipt of mental health care want to discover (Rose, Fleischman and Wykes, 2008).

A final more subtle consequence of the increasing political influence of the consumer voice in healthcare is the recognition that how well patients feel they have been treated may matter as much as whether their condition has improved. The ends do not justify the means. Clients of mental health services, just like patients in general medical hospitals, appreciate the sense of control that comes from being well informed; the feeling of autonomy that flows from shared decision taking; and the basic self-regard that stems from being treated respectfully.

Client Preferences

While it is reasonably straightforward to make a principled case for respecting clients' preferences when deciding how best to treat their complaints, the empirical evidence supporting that policy has proved harder to collect. For example, King *et al.*'s (2005) meta-analysis found that whether or not clients were allocated to their preferred form of treatment had minimal to no effect on psychotherapy outcomes. However, this overall judgement masked some dramatic differences between individual studies. A subsequent meta-analysis (Swift and Callahan, 2009) has therefore examined issues of study design to try and make better sense of the conflicting evidence. This review identified three main experimental designs that have been employed to investigate the relationship between client preference and outcome in the treatment of a range of psychological disorders. The simplest design straightforwardly compares outcomes for two matched client groups, one of whom gets the therapy they want and the other of whom gets the therapy they don't want. The second design takes advantage of data from large-scale RCT research projects in which by definition all participants are randomly allocated to the various treatment and control arms of the study. Inevitably some will have found themselves with their therapy of choice while some will not, and the outcomes for these two groups can subsequently be compared. The third and final design is the partially randomised preference trial (PRPT) in which all participants who express a preference get to receive the treatment option they want while the remainder gets randomly allocated to the various arms of the study. Swift and Callahan included 26 studies conducted over a period of 40 years in their meta-analytic review and were able to compare outcomes for over 1000 clients who received their preferred form of therapy with those for a similar number of participants who did not receive their personal choice of treatment. They report three noteworthy findings. First, dropout rates for those who received their preferred therapy were about half those recorded for the comparison group. Second, despite a wide variation in the results of individual studies, there was overall a 'small but significant' effect on outcome when clients received their treatment of choice. Finally, the effect sizes reported by studies employing the PRPT design were significantly lower than those reported by researchers using the other two experimental designs, probably because no one in the PRPT studies ever gets allocated to a therapy option that they really don't fancy at all.

Shared Decision Making

In practice, if not in principle, it is hard to envisage many people supporting entirely unilateral decision making by either party in the therapeutic relationship. The circumstances in which autocratic 'doctor knows best' prescription of treatment is justifiable are few and far between. However, it is also highly unlikely that a financially squeezed public health service will happily fund whatever form of therapy takes the particular fancy of individual patients. When practitioners advocate prioritising client preference over the systematic collection of evidence about the efficacy of the treatments they provide, commentators are appropriately wary of their motives (Goldacre, 2008). The mid-position between these two extreme positions on the 'Who's in charge of therapy?' spectrum has been termed 'shared decision-making' (SDM).

Advocates of this approach assert that active client participation in decisions concerning their healthcare is associated with a range of benefits both in terms of increased consumer satisfaction and improved medical outcomes (Adams and Drake, 2006). However, little of the empirical evidence in support of the SDM position has been gathered in the field of mental health and there are a number of potential reasons why it might be unwise to assume that findings from physical health settings will generalise straightforwardly into the psychotherapy consulting room. Will some users of mental health services (such those suffering from dementia) have the necessary capacity to participate meaningfully in discussions regarding their future treatment? Is there a risk that users of psychotherapy services will lack the motivation to take up the SDM invitation either by dint of past experience; or as a result of side effects of medication; or because of the debilitating influence of their psychological condition? In our view none of these concerns justifies failing to try and engage, and even educate, our clients in sharing important decisions regarding their treatment, but we should not naively expect that things will turn out as anticipated. For example, a well-intentioned and well-designed US study reported by Calsyn and colleagues (2003) evaluated the effects of providing homeless clients diagnosed with severe mental illness with five credible alternative care packages from which to choose. While results offered some suggestion of a small increase in consumer satisfaction compared with a control group, there were no significant differences on the crucial outcome variables of number of days homeless and recurrent experiences of psychotic symptoms. In similar vein, a recent Cochrane review entitled 'Shared decision making interventions for people with mental health conditions' (Duncan, Best and Hagen, 2010) could identify only two empirical studies, both German, that met the stipulated inclusion criteria. While one of the papers cited reported some benefits in consumer satisfaction associated with the SDM intervention, neither found any improvements over 'treatment as usual' in either clinical or health service outcomes. The authors' familiar recommendation was that more good quality research is needed before a balanced judgement on the assumed benefits of SDM in mental health care can be made.

So What?

The arguments and evidence presented in this chapter are intended to make a compelling case for viewing clients as full and active partners in the psychotherapeutic enterprise. We see little sense or justice in treating patients as passive beneficiaries of the latest advances in scientific medicine. However, we certainly do not ally ourselves with those who would happily discount the research findings on which evidence-based practice is founded. It would be both wasteful and irrational to disregard the results of carefully conducted outcome studies when determining healthcare policy at both a macro- and micro-level. Information on what is likely to work for whom – and perhaps even more importantly what probably won't work for whom (Castonguay *et al.*, 2010) – cannot be ignored. The question is how the two legitimate principles of client-directed treatment and evidence-based practice can be best integrated.

In 2005 the American Psychological Association struck the following balance in their definition of evidence-based practice in psychology: 'Evidence-based practice in psychology (EBPP) is the integration of the best available research with clinical expertise in the context of patient characteristics, culture, and preferences.'

Sceptics might consider this recommendation a masterful example of diplomatic fudge. There's something for everyone in there. Empiricists can latch onto the 'best available research' comment. Frontline practitioners can draw comfort from the recognition of their 'clinical expertise'. Finally, consumers of psychological services will note how their unique circumstances will be considered when therapy decisions are being made. However, a subsequent section of the policy statement is unambiguous in its assertion that, in many ways, the customer knows best: 'Psychological services are most effective when responsive to the patient's specific problems, strengths, personality, sociocultural context, and preferences.'

That's just about where we stand too, but grand statements of principle have their limitations. It's not always easy to work out how to translate fine intentions into viable everyday practice. Exactly how might psychotherapists get to appreciate the particular characteristics of their clients' lives? Surely a commitment to service-user involvement represents an enduring process of consultation rather than a one-off 'what form of therapy do you fancy?' decision.

What Works for Whom Revisited

The traditional model of evidence-based practice seeks to match treatment to clients on the basis of diagnostic category – what they've got rather than who they are, if you like. This logical but inevitably somewhat crude strategy has been compared to the practices of the brutal innkeeper Procrustes of Greek legend. Procrustes was wont to ply his guests with strong drink and promise them a wonderful night's sleep in his special bed. The problem came if his visitors were the wrong size for the bed, whereupon Procrustes would 'adjust' his guests to fit either by stretching them on a rack or chopping their legs off. This brutal 'one size fits all' analogy is compared to the cosily flexible metaphor of a treatment package that is 'tailored' to the unique characteristics of the individual client. No misfitting, off-the-peg standard issue uniform for you, Sir, but a personally constructed garment designed to meet Sir's exact specifications! If we want to extend the tailoring metaphor even further, we might consider 'cutting on the bias' to align the weft and the pattern of the material in the most comfortable and figure-hugging way possible. However, the Savile Row tailor knows just what information is needed to satisfy his customers' expectations. What might be the equivalent of a precise inside-leg measurement for the psychotherapist aspiring to offer comparable standards of service?

Fortunately, a Task Force of the American Psychology Association's Divisions of Clinical Psychology and Psychotherapy has recently undertaken a timely overview of evidence that might allow clinicians to 'identify effective methods of adapting therapy on the basis of characteristics of the patient (other than diagnosis)' (American Psychology Association, 2011). The Task Force duly commissioned a series of meta-analytic literature reviews conducted by respected US academics, the results of which have been published in a special edition of the *Journal of Clinical Psychology* (Norcross and Wampold, 2011). The reviews cover eight variables that might provide a credible basis for customising psychological treatments to individual clients:

- reactance/resistance level
- stages of change
- preferences
- culture
- coping style
- expectations
- attachment style
- religion/spirituality.

Reviewers were asked not only to summarise the extant state of scientific knowledge on each of these topics but also to place the current evidence base in one of the following three categories:

- demonstrably effective
- probably effective
- promising but insufficient research to judge.

Expectation and attachment style fell into the 'too soon to judge' category. Stages of change and coping style were considered 'probably effective'. The evidence base for adapting psychotherapy provision on the remaining four client characteristics – culture; preference; reactance/resistance level; and religion/spirituality – met the Task Force's criteria for being defined as 'demonstrably effective'. These final four reviews are therefore worth describing in some detail.

The meta-analysis of cultural adaptations (Smith, Rodríguez and Bernal, 2011) identified 65 studies including more than 8000 participants who met their inclusion criteria. They calculated the overall effect size in these studies of treatments specially amended for 'clients of color' as *moderately* more effective than traditional interventions with these populations. Interestingly, the effect sizes reported tended to be higher when clients, as opposed to therapists, were evaluating the outcomes of therapy. The paper describes a number of ways in which services have been tailored to meet the needs of particular patient groups (such as delivering therapy in the client's preferred language; using culturally salient metaphors; and using community facilities rather than hospital-based clinics). However, there does not as yet appear to be strong evidence that any one of these initiatives produces better outcomes than others. Rather it seems that a 'the more the merrier' principle applies, maybe reflecting clients' appreciation of highly flexible services that can respond to a range of needs and preferences. It also seems that older (i.e., over 35 years old) users of psychotherapy services are more responsive to these cultural adaptations than their younger counterparts in the community.

The review of evidence for making adjustments based on clients' religious and spiritual beliefs (Worthington *et al.*, 2011) involved over 3000 participants whose data could be included in the meta-analysis. The design of the studies followed two patterns. The first was the familiar 'running race' format in which the outcomes of a spiritually sensitive intervention were compared with the results of either a no treatment control group or with the usual 'secular' version of the therapy programme. Unsurprisingly, the amended therapy proved consistently more effective than the no treatment control conditions. Less obviously, the amended form of therapy also out-performed standard psychological treatments on both psychological (i.e., symptom improvement) and religious (i.e., spiritual well-being) measures, though the effect sizes calculated for the psychological outcomes were notably smaller. The second research design used a 'dismantling' strategy to test whether including a spiritually sensitive component to an existing psychotherapeutic intervention provided any measurable added value. Again the amended format offered clear advantages for clients in terms of attaining their spiritual goals, though the benefits were less clear-cut for psychological outcomes. The authors concluded their review by noting how infrequently studies had taken heed of the level of commitment to their particular creed that individual clients held, and guessed that this might be an important and largely uninvestigated variable that warranted further research attention.

As regards preferences, the meta-analysis (Swift, Callahan and Vollmer, 2011) largely repeats and updates the findings of the previous systematic review conducted by the same authors (Swift and Callaghan, 2009) and described earlier in this chapter. The researchers identified 36 studies that met the Task Force's inclusion criteria and concluded from their analysis that, when clients had access to their preferred form of help, they were less likely to drop out of therapy prematurely and more likely to benefit from the intervention (perhaps because they had been more prepared to 'stick with it' in the first place). There does not yet appear to be solid evidence to suggest that matching according to any particular client preference (i.e., the role the client is expected to play; the personal characteristics of the therapist such as age, gender or ethnic background; or the brand of therapy provided) confers any specific advantage in terms of treatment outcome. The one possible exception to this general statement is that, when clients have indicated that they want to receive a talking therapy as opposed to a pharmacological intervention, it probably pays to respect that wish.

Finally, the systematic review of evidence testing the hypothesis that best treatment outcomes would occur when there was an inverse relationship between the degree of directiveness displayed by the therapist and the level of resistance (or reactance) shown by the client (Beutler *et al.*, 2011) restricted its focus to research conducted with members of a single diagnostic group – those suffering from both depression and a drug abuse problem. This decision to focus on a particular clinical population avoided the risk of assuming that everyone with a particular diagnostic label, such as adolescent conduct disorder, is bound to exhibit resistant tendencies in therapy. Resistance was measured by client self-report using well-established psychometric measures. The studies also carefully avoided another form of stereotyping – the assumption that all CBT therapists are pushily directive while all psychodynamic practitioners are gently non-directive! Instead, directiveness was assessed by independent observers who used structured measures and sampled tapes of actual therapy sessions. The authors managed to identify 12 studies involving over 110 participants that met these demanding inclusion criteria. Overall the matching hypothesis was strongly supported by the evidence reviewed. When clients who reported high levels of reactance/resistance were provided with a non-directive form of therapy, they did much better than when offered a more directive alternative. The effect size calculated was large – large enough to account for 15% of the variance in therapy outcomes across the combined studies. However, the authors also noted that there was a wide range in the effect sizes reported in the 12 studies included in their meta-analysis and so concluded that there is probably more going on here than simply recognising the folly of giving instructions to people who don't like being told what to do.

Conclusion

The ideas and evidence presented in this chapter make a compelling case for maximising clients' involvement and investment in their own treatment. Perhaps that is not headline-grabbing news for most readers. Who does not advocate active therapeutic partnerships nowadays? The trick lies in creating structures that enable clients to influence the shape and course of the care they receive. This will likely not prove as simple as it sounds. Many consumers of health services expect professionals to get on with making the kind of expert decisions they have been trained, and are paid, to make. There is not much point in replacing one kind of myth of uniformity (all depressives will respond to the same treatment) with another (all Asian clients will need services delivered in a given format). However, we are prepared to hitch our wagon to one particular star – collecting continuous client feedback to enable the therapist to respond to the needs of the client session by session.

References

Adams, J.R. and Drake, R.E. (2006) Shared decision-making and evidence-based practice. *Community Mental Health Journal*, 42, 87–105.

American Psychological Association (2005) Policy statement on evidence-based practice in psychology, http://www.apa.org/practice/resources/evidence/evidence-based-statement.pdf (accessed 10 October, 2011).

American Psychological Association (2011) Evidence-Based Psychotherapy Relationships: Customizing the Treatment Relationship to the Individual Patient, http://www.apa.org/education/ce/cutomize-relationship.pdf (accessed 10 October, 2011).

Anthony, W. (1993) Recovery from mental illness: the guiding vision of the mental health service system in the 1990s. *Psychosocial Rehabilitation Journal*, 16, 11–23.

Bados, A., Balaguer, G. and Saldaña, C. (2007) The efficacy of cognitive-behavior therapy and the problem of drop-out. *Journal of Clinical Psychology*, 63, 585–92.

Barrett, M., Chua, W., Crits-Christoph, P., *et al.* (2008) Early withdrawal from mental health treatment: implications for psychotherapy practice. *Psychotherapy: Theory, Research, Practice, Training*, 45, 247–267.

Beutler, L., Harwood, T., Michelson, A., *et al.* (2011) Resistance/reactance level. *Journal of Clinical Psychology*, 67, 133–142.

Cahill, J., Barkham, M., Hardy, G., *et al.* (2003) Outcomes of patients completing and not completing cognitive therapy for depression. *British Journal of Clinical Psychology*, 42, 133–143.

Calsyn, R., Morse, G., Yonker, R., *et al.* (2003) Client choice of treatment and client outcomes. *Journal of Community Psychology*, 31, 339–348.

Castonguay, L., Boswell, J.F., Constantino, M.J. *et al.* (2010) Training implications of harmful effects of psychological treatments. *American Psychologist*, 65, 1, 34–49.

Connell, J., Grant, S. and Mullin, T. (2006) Client initiated termination of therapy at NHS primary care counselling services. *Counselling and Psychotherapy Research*, 6, 1, 60–67.

Cuijpers, P., van Straten, A., Andersson G. and van Oppen, P. (2008) Psychotherapy for depression in adults: a meta-analysis of comparative outcome studies. *Journal of Consulting and Clinical Psychology*, 76, 902–922.

Department of Health (2005) *Creating a Patient-led NHS: Delivering the NHS Improvement Plan*. Department of Health. London.

Duncan, E., Best, C. and Hagen, S. (2010) Shared decision making interventions for people with mental health conditions. *Cochrane Database of Systematic Reviews*, Issue 1. Art. No.: CD007297. DOI: 10.1002/14651858. CD007297.pub2

Farkas, M., Gagne, C., Anthony, W. and Chamberlain, J. (2005) Implementing recovery oriented evidence based programs: identifying the critical dimensions. *Community Mental Health Journal*, 41, 141–158.

Goldacre, B. (2009) *Bad Science*, Harper Perennial, London.

Hilsenroth, M. and Cromer, T. (2007) Clinician interventions related to alliance during the initial interview and psychological assessment. *Psychotherapy: Theory, Research, Practice, Training*, 44, 205–218.

Kazdin, A., Holland, L. and Crowley, M. (1997) Family experience of barriers to treatment and premature termination from child therapy. *Journal of Consulting and Clinical Psychology* 65, 453–463.

King, M., Nazareth, I., Lampe, F., *et al.* (2005) Impact of participant and physician intervention preferences on randomized trials: a systematic review. *Journal of the American Medical Association*, 293, 1089–1099.

Lambert, M. (1992) Psychotherapy outcome research: implications for integrative and eclectic psychotherapists, in *Handbook of Psychotherapy Integration* (eds J. Norcross and M. Goldfield), Basic Books, New York.

Masi, M., Miller, R. and Olson, M. (2003) Differences in dropout rates among individual, couple, and family therapy clients. *Contemporary Family Therapy* 25, 63–75.

Norcross, J. and Wampold, B. (2011) What works for whom: tailoring psychotherapy to the person. *Journal of Clinical Psychology*, 67, 127–132.

Ogrodniczuk, J., Joyce, A. and Piper, W. (2005) Strategies for reducing patient-initiated premature termination of psychotherapy. *Harvard Review of Psychiatry*, 13, 57–70.

Rose, D., Fleischman, P. and Wykes, T. (2008) What are mental health service users' priorities for research in the UK? *Journal of Mental Health* 17, 520–530.

Self, R., Oates, P., Pinnock-Hamilton, T. and Leach, C. (2005) The relationship between social deprivation and unilateral termination (attrition) from psychotherapy at various stages of the health care pathway. *Psychology and Psychotherapy: Theory, Research and Practice*, 78, 95–111.

Smith, T.B., Rodríguez, M.D. and Bernal, G. (2011) Culture. *Journal of Clinical Psychology*, 67, 166–175.

Swift, J. and Callahan, J. (2009) The impact of client treatment preferences on outcome: a meta-analysis. *Journal of Clinical Psychology*, 65, 368–381.

Swift, J., Callahan, J. and Vollmer, B. (2011) Preferences. *Journal of Clinical Psychology*, 67, 155–165.

Wampold, B.E., Mondin, G.W., Moody, M., *et al.* (1997) A meta-analysis of outcome studies comparing bona fide psychotherapies: empirically, 'all must have prizes.' *Psychological Bulletin*, 122, 203–215.

Wierzbicki, M. and Pekarik, G. (1993) A meta-analysis of psychotherapy dropout. *Professional Psychology: Research and Practice*, 24, 190–195.

Worthington, E., Hook, J., Davis, D. and McDaniel, M. (2011) Religion and spirituality. *Journal of Clinical Psychology*, 67, 204–214.

5

Practice-based Evidence

A theory must be tempered with reality. (Jawaharlal Nehru)

In theory, there is no difference between theory and practice; in practice, there is. (Yogi Berra)

Introduction

At first glance the term 'practice-based evidence' seems merely a witty riposte to the dominance of 'evidence-based practice', perhaps reassuring clinicians that practice is what counts and nodding to the importance of experience. There is much more to it than this. It represents a shift in how we think about evidence, complementing rather than replacing the research that informs the evidence-based practice guidelines discussed in earlier chapters. It is also an invitation to all clinicians to think about how they might use their own clinical practice to learn more about change in psychotherapy, and to contribute to a wider understanding. This is more than reflecting on experience, which is useful but limited; it is systematically collecting information on the process of change and outcome of psychotherapy, and becoming informed participants in the great debates about why therapy works.

Maximising the Benefits of Psychotherapy: A Practice-Based Evidence Approach, First Edition. David Green and Gary Latchford.
© 2012 John Wiley & Sons, Ltd. Published 2012 by John Wiley & Sons, Ltd.

The term 'practice-based evidence' has been used to encompass any activity in which clinicians gather scientific evidence themselves as part of their routine practice. This covers a wide range of activities, from exploring change in a single case using qualitative or quantitative data, to contributing to a large database recording change at a service level. Before progressing any further, we should say that if you have more than a passing interest in this topic we recommend you read *Developing and Delivering Practice-based Evidence* edited by Michael Barkham, Gillian Hardy and John Mellor-Clark (2010), which is a nice summary of the many different methods and applications associated with this approach. The book is good at encouraging clinicians, whether by using data from single case studies to learn more about the processes of therapy, or reflecting on how they or their services can employ measurement systems to improve their practice.

Exploring Change in a Single Case

In every session with every client, therapists have privileged access to the fundamental processes of therapy. Some are readily observable and significant – a client's report on the results of a planned homework task, such as a behavioural experiment, or reaction to a therapeutic letter, for example. Some may be brief and not immediately relevant, micro-exchanges in the ebb and flow of the conversation between therapist and client, such as the reaction to a reflection or shared formulation. All this throws light on the 'black box' of therapeutic process, and all this has the potential to inform a process of discovery by the therapist, a counterbalance to the large-scale studies that gain their potency by reducing such variability in therapy to background noise.

Most therapists have, at one time or another, reflected on the processes involved in a case that has caught their attention. To properly explore a single case demands more, however, and requires that an effort is made to gather information systematically. The challenge is to capture the important elements of therapy – if and why a client improves. The payoff is that you will almost certainly be surprised at what you find – that what you think you do that makes a difference isn't always recognised as important by your client, for example. It is an excellent way to develop your understanding and your therapeutic skills.

Bill Stiles (2005, 2007) has presented a compelling case for taking notice of the content of single case studies. He argues that every session will contain many small examples of how a therapeutic model may translate into practice – that throughout sessions therapists will be testing the model they are using based on the reactions of their clients, asking themselves how well their theory fits with their observations. He sees this as something akin to hypothesis testing in large studies. The difference is that, unlike the one or two hypotheses tested in a large study, the therapist may test very many small ideas in a single session. On their own they do not seem much, but as they build up they increase confidence in the implications for the theory. What this approach lacks in the numbers available to large studies, it makes up for in depth of analysis. In this way even a single session is an opportunity to test, refine and develop a model. Further, although the uniqueness of individual cases is unwelcome noise in large trials, Stiles argues that such cases are exactly where our therapeutic models need to evolve. Stiles' 2007 paper is an excellent introduction to using this approach. His guidance avoids being prescriptive, but in general you need some qualitative information about the process of therapy – recordings or transcripts – and some measures of process or outcome (examples are discussed later in this chapter).

A more traditional approach to a clinical case study – with a similar aim – is to focus on quantitative measures and track a client's change over time. This approach also recognises the valuable material available to therapists in their clinical work and nods to the historical importance of the single case in the development of therapeutic approaches such as behaviour therapy. This single case design is summarised in the title of a paper by Borckardt *et al.* (2008) – 'Clinical practice as a natural laboratory for psychotherapy research'. This paper is a user's guide to conducting time-series case study research; that is, a method for exploring change in a single case by plotting multiple observations before and after the intervention. This is a comprehensive guide to conducting and analysing such studies, and it is convincing in its methodological rigour – necessary in persuading those reliant on large trials for evidence that single cases have something to offer. Its focus is on A-B designs where data are gathered before and after treatment, including a baseline period and possibly a follow-up. These designs allow interesting questions to be asked about outcome and (if continuous measures are used) process. We suspect, though, that many clinicians will also find the statistical analysis contained in the approach a little overwhelming at first. However, one accessible aspect of such single case designs is that the data are usually displayed graphically (Morley and Adams, 1991), which makes the results very easy to interpret – a glance is often enough to determine whether change has occurred. Those seeking a comprehensive guide to the various possible strategies in single case experimental designs are recommended two well-regarded texts (Barlow, Nock and Hersen, 2008; Kazdin, 1982), while an accessible guide to using single case designs in practice can be found in a chapter by McMillan and Morley (2010).

Reliable and clinically significant change

A focus on outcome in a single case does raise one issue to which proponents of single case methods have given a lot of thought: how can you tell if a client has improved? This sounds simple but is not. One response might be 'if a score on an outcome measure is better at the end of therapy'. But how much improvement is enough? How do you know if the change in the score is just due to chance – the score on most questionnaires varies a little each time you complete it, so could a change in a client's score reflect variability in the measure rather than something meaningful? One way of determining if a change is reliable is to use the Reliable Change Index (RCI) developed by Jacobson and Truax (1991), computed by dividing the difference between the pre- and post-treatment scores (how much change has occurred) by the standard error of the difference between the two scores (how much the measure varies due to chance between administrations, a figure that is given in most test manuals). If you do find that a difference between scores is reliable and not an artefact of the questionnaire, does that then mean that the client has improved and actually feels better? Not necessarily, but this does raise a very interesting question – how can you define improvement? Again, Jacobson and colleagues (1999) offer guidance based on outcome scores and the distribution of these scores in populations of people who are well (in the normal range) and unwell (in the clinical range). They suggest that 'clinically significant change' be defined in terms of three criteria:

- Criterion A is about moving out of the clinical range and states that the post-treatment score should be more than two standard deviations (a measure of how spread out the data are) from the mean of the clinical population, towards the mean of the normal population.
- Criterion B is about moving towards the normal range and states that the post-treatment score should be within two standard deviations of the mean of the normal population, away from the mean of the clinical population;
- Criterion C is about moving in the right direction and states that the post-treatment score should go across a point halfway between the clinical and normal means – in other words, it is closer to the average score in the normal range than the clinical range.

Figure 5.1 illustrates the three criteria by plotting the scores of an imaginary normal and clinical population and showing how they relate to the different means, and to each other.

If you search the internet, you'll find several sites where you can calculate reliable and clinically significant change for your own data, so long as you have the properties of the outcome measures you used to hand (e.g. http://www.clintools.com/victims/resources/software/reliablechange/reliable_change_generator.html).

Of course the meaning of change should also be explored with the client and this may add a further dimension to the picture generated from the measures.

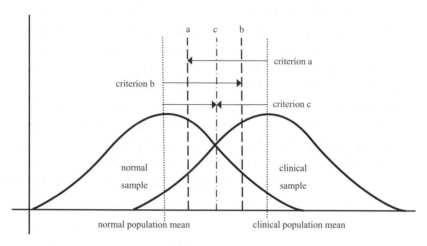

Figure 5.1:   The three criteria for clinically significant change

The hermeneutic single case efficacy design

Consideration of the many possible sources of evidence is a characteristic of what we think is probably the best introduction to using a single case to explore and link process and outcome in therapy: Robert Elliott's paper outlining what he terms the 'hermeneutic single case efficacy design' (Elliott, 2002). In this paper, he argues that single cases are actually well placed to provide evidence for the effectiveness of a therapy. In order to show that therapy is the best explanation for change, however, a convincing case needs to be developed. One part of this is that alternative explanations need to be considered and if possible accounted for, such as life events outside therapy (e.g. winning the lottery) or a measurement problem (e.g. faking good to please the therapist). The flip side of this is evidence for a causal link between process and outcome. If enough information is gathered, Elliot argues that single cases are an excellent way to do this, building on the critical eye and clinical intuition common to most therapists. Elliot suggests many possible sources of information, including quantitative (e.g. global outcome measures, weekly outcome measures) and qualitative (e.g. notes from therapy sessions). He also recommends using idiographic measures that have some of the strengths of the former but are unique to each client. Examples include 'personal questionnaires', in which the items on the questionnaire are generated for each client by their statements about the aims of therapy (Elliot, Shapiro and Mack, 1999; Morley, 2002), and repertory grids, which map clients' beliefs about themselves and the world (Fransella, Bell and Bannister, 2003). He also suggests eliciting the client's views about how and whether the intervention was helpful from either a questionnaire or an interview at the end of therapy.

Gathering this information enables change to be explored from different directions and direct evidence for effectiveness to be obtained. Elliot suggests several sources of potentially convincing evidence: the client's beliefs about the reasons for change at the end of therapy; mapping change experienced by the client with the actions of the therapist (e.g. a reduction in social anxiety at the end of therapy and a focus on social anxiety by the therapist); associations between outcome and principles consistent with the chosen therapy (such as thought diaries); change in previously stable, chronic problems; and a pairing between a significant event in therapy and a corresponding subsequent change in symptoms close in time. One case may contain many such examples, and, if they build up into a consistent pattern, the argument for therapeutic change becomes stronger.

The main message in terms of using single case data to explore therapy, then, is to choose whatever approach suits best, then plan to gather information systematically to both map the process of change and capture the effects of the intervention. It's best to measure some aspects throughout therapy. Quantitative and qualitative information are both useful, but consideration needs to be given to the reliability and validity of the measures. Thought is then needed both to define a successful outcome and provide convincing evidence that therapy is the likely cause.

The consequence of adopting this approach to single cases is not just to gather potentially useful research data; by systematically gathering information about therapy process and outcome, clinicians also benefit by becoming more aware of the session-by-session changes in their clients and, by linking change to the way they practise therapy, becoming more aware of the links between what they do and how this has an impact on the client.

Exploring Change in a Number of Cases

We are aware that up to now the emphasis in this chapter on spending time exploring and reflecting on single cases may seem at first a luxury few busy clinicians can afford. There is increasing pressure on services and individual clinicians to measure outcomes in their clients and justify their work. A practice-based evidence approach, however, sees even this as an opportunity to do more than report global outcomes to potential purchasers (though this is also pretty useful). If thought and planning are given to what data are collected, practice-based evidence can be used in a variety of ways: as a basis for scientific publication, adding evidence gathered in real-world settings to the more common publications based on RCTs and multi-site trials; as a way of monitoring the outcomes achieved by a service and comparing these with outcomes obtained in similar or higher performing services (benchmarking); and as a way of improving individual practice by drawing clinicians' attention to how their clients are doing. When enough data have been gathered on how patients with particular conditions respond to therapy, it is even possible to generate statistical models (such as growth models) that predict the rate of recovery and map how well a particular client is doing in relation to this, highlighting those appearing to fall behind and alerting the clinician (case tracking). This works particularly well when information on progress is obtained every session, as we will see later.

What has Practice-based Evidence Ever Done for Me?

As we saw in the earlier chapters looking at psychotherapy research, scientific papers based on practice-based evidence are now being recognised as a valuable source of evidence for the outcomes of routine practice in therapy. The last few years have also seen a dramatic rise in the number of services adopting a system of regular monitoring of outcomes during and at the end of therapy. There are several implications. Across the world large databases of psychotherapy outcome and process are being created. As researchers become competent in the use of new and more subtle statistical techniques such as hierarchical linear modelling which require large databases, there is the potential for interesting and novel questions to be asked across therapists, clinics, services and perhaps nations. This is quite different from the large-scale research that has preceded it: these are data drawn from real-life settings, reflecting the day-to-day practice of the clinicians most likely to be interested in the findings, and also the messiness – for example, differences in type of therapy/training of therapist/number of sessions routinely offered – associated with real-world practice.

A well-known study based on such data illustrates the benefits and perhaps anxieties associated with this new development. Jeb Brown and colleagues (2005) looked at the variability in the outcomes obtained by 281 therapists with over 10,000 clients and found that 71 therapists consistently and significantly obtained better outcomes. We don't know why they were so effective – whether it was a personal quality, something they were doing, or something unrelated to the individual – but this striking variation in the outcome of particular therapists lends some weight to those emphasising the importance of the therapist over the therapy to outcome. The ability to analyse outcome data in this way also has other implications for those delivering services, however: such data might be used as a tool to help improve practice or less helpfully as a tool to exclude therapists labelled as poorly performing. We would guess that, as monitoring of therapy outcome becomes routine, therapists might feel anxious being exposed to such scrutiny. We would argue, though, that increasing use of outcome monitoring (and perhaps process) is inevitable, and rather than being fearful therapists ought to embrace this change and become informed about what it involves and the opportunities it actually presents.

Although measuring the impact of psychological therapy is more challenging in some areas than others (for example, with patients with serious physical illness), this is more a challenge to measure the right thing than an excuse not to do it. If therapists believe they do good – and the evidence from research shows overwhelmingly that therapy is effective – then the onus is really on the individual therapist to show this. Our argument goes beyond this though. Regardless of the inevitability of increasing measurement of outcome in services being imposed by managers, we feel that therapists need to take the initiative and consider what routine measurement can do to improve their practice. We don't think that it's too far fetched to encourage therapists to embrace measurement so that they can learn more about their own outcomes and how to improve them, and feel empowered to use the data they and colleagues are collecting to ask their own questions about how therapy works. We advocate something like a workers' cooperative of clinicians and researchers!

Practice research networks

Our review of research in psychotherapy earlier implied that most clinicians are in danger of feeling excluded by current researchers. Most won't have access to the journals where researchers communicate with each other about their latest findings, and, when they do, the chances are they will be floored by new techniques such as hierarchical linear regression.

Routine measurement of process and outcome has the potential to change this. If clinicians pool their data with that obtained by other clinicians, and perhaps explore collaboration with researchers (rather than just giving them access to the data), this changes the rules: there is the opportunity for clinicians to become active producers (and we suspect more willing consumers) of psychotherapy research.

Two practice research networks in Pennsylvania in the United States (Borkovec *et al.*, 2001) and South West Yorkshire in the United Kingdom (Barkham *et al.*, 2001) provide excellent examples of networks that have both contributed to the practice of clinicians in the service and produced high quality research output.

How to set up a practice research network

Agree on whether to start one   There may already be pressure on a service to collect outcome data and we suspect most services are already doing so, but we would add that it is important for clinicians to be active participants in setting up a monitoring system. Depending on local contacts or the initial aims of the network, local researchers may be invited to contribute. Either way, an important principle is that all clinicians in a service feel that they are partners in the network and have a voice in making the important decisions in setting it up. Remember, the aim is to do more than monitor outcomes, the aim is to ensure that clinicians benefit directly from access to helpful clinical data and an opportunity to use the information to explore important aspects of therapy. The other potential partners in this enterprise are the service users. If you have good representation of clients in your service, consult them about the plans to develop a practice research network. If you don't have service user involvement where you are, see if you can help set this up!

Decide what to measure and how   Elliott and Zucconi (2006) have proposed a 'star' design as a framework for choosing measures. In this, the centre of the star represents the concepts to measure that everyone can sign up to, such as problem severity, and the arms reflect different therapeutic orientations and the factors (and measures) associated with them. Elliot also points out that there are a great number of potential things to measure – therapy is after all a complicated and subtle process – and far too much for any one network to contemplate. He suggests that in clinical practice the many years of psychotherapy research indicate that there are three main categories of things to measure: therapy outcome, therapy process and client/therapist characteristics. This seems to us a great starting point and populating these three categories with measures that are valid, reliable and easy to administer and score should be the initial aim at this stage. We would add a further important criterion: that the measures are free and easily available. We also think that it's important to measure the progress of therapy across sessions, as well as the outcome at the end of therapy. So, here are our initial recommendations, with some thoughts about where else to look.

i.   Therapy outcome (problem severity)
     There are two major players here – two well-established, highly regarded outcome measures. One is from the United States, the therapy outcome package (TOP). It is available free online (http://www.bhealthlabs.com/home.html). The other is from the United Kingdom, the Clinical Outcomes in Routine Evaluation – Outcome Measure (CORE-OM), also available free online (http://www.coreims.co.uk/index.php). Both give you the option of purchasing additional services online, including case tracking and benchmarking with outcome data. Both are extremely well validated, reliable and not bound to any theoretical model.

     These measures would suit most situations, but may be supplemented by other measures when the purpose of the intervention may include other aspects in addition to symptom reduction, such as improving adherence and coping with illness in a physical health setting. It may also be useful occasionally to add to the general battery a measure specific to the problem being treated, so that the impact of therapy can be tracked more thoroughly. For example, when treating a victim of trauma, you might add a scale assessing the different symptoms of post-traumatic stress disorder, such as the Impact of Events Scale – Revised (IES-R; Weiss and Marmar, 1997).

ii. Therapy progress
     A key part of the measurement strategy is to track change in therapy as it occurs. Recording sudden changes in symptom severity enables interesting questions to be asked about the session that preceded it. Alternatively, recording a lack of change provides useful information to the clinician (more on this later). We think that the TOPS and CORE-OM outcome measures are too long to be given every session. The CORE is available in a smaller five-item version for ongoing monitoring (CORE-5) rather than the usual 34 items. This is similarly

easily accessible and free. The other progress measure we favour is the Outcome Rating Scale (ORS; Miller *et al.*, 2003). The ORS is an ultra-brief measure with four items covering areas of life functioning. It is reliable and valid, and available free online (http://www.scottdmiller.com/?q=node/6 or http://heartandsoulofchange.com/measures). In the ORS the client completes the scale by drawing a cross on a line (a visual analogue scale), which makes it very easy to complete and score, and provides a visual cue to client and therapist on how therapy is progressing. It is designed to be a tool for therapy as much as it is an outcome measure, and the usefulness of such measures is the focus of the next chapter.

iii. Therapy process (e.g. therapeutic alliance)

For any clinician curious about what happens in therapy, process measures given regularly to the client offer a way of obtaining systematic information that can be useful for understanding the process of change in a particular client, and can build up to a resource for exploring process in therapy more generally. The most popular focus for process measures is the therapeutic alliance between clinician and client, known from research to be related to outcome. Many scales are available to measure the alliance and a comprehensive review by Cahill *et al.* (2008), commissioned by the NIMH in the United Kingdom, is available online (http://www.hta.ac.uk/project/1556.asp).

We have some suggestions, based upon quality of measure, ease of use and availability. As far as we are aware, these are all public domain and free, and available either in the original publication or from the author.

The Working Alliance Inventory (WAI; Horvath and Greenberg, 1989) is probably the most well known. It comes in three versions, full (26 item), short (12 item) and one designed for completion by couples. Each contains a form to be completed by client and therapist. You can download them free with the permission of the author (http://www.educ.sfu.ca/alliance/allianceA/), as long as they are used not-for-profit. We think the short version is the easiest to use in practice.

Alternatives include the Agnew Relationship Measure (ARM; Agnew-Davies *et al.*, 1998), a 28-item alliance measure completed by the client (a therapist version is also available). A short version has also been developed; it doesn't appear in a publication but may be available via the authors (Stiles *et al.*, 2003). The Counselor Rating Form (CRF; Barak and LaCrosse, 1975) is a 36-item measure but there is also a revised and shortened 12-item version (CRF-S; Corrigan and Schmidt, 1983), which we think is more practicable. Similarly, we prefer the shortened 12-item version of the 24-item California Psychotherapy Alliance Scales (CALPAS; Gaston, 1991; Gaston and Marmar, 1994). The revised 19-item Helping Alliance Questionnaire (HAq-II; Luborsky *et al.*, 1996) is also available.

The final suggestion is our preferred candidate. The Session Rating Scale (SRS; Duncan *et al.*, 2003) is a companion to the ORS therapy progress measure. It is a similarly brief four-item measure completed by the client and covers key dimensions of effective therapeutic relationships. Though a different take on measuring the therapeutic alliance, it is extremely brief and user friendly and, like the ORS, it uses a visual analogue scale that provides immediate feedback to therapist and client on the alliance in that session. It is also designed as a therapeutic tool, and will be discussed in the next chapter. It is available free from the same locations as the ORS (http://www.scottdmiller.com/ ?q=node/6 or http://heartandsoulofchange.com/measures/). Both measures have been found to be reliable and clinically useful (Campbell and Hemsley, 2009).

iv.   Client/therapist characteristics

Most services already record demographic client details such as employment, age and sex. We would add clinicians' therapeutic orientation, what therapy they provided and number of years' experience.

v.   Client evaluation

If the practice research network is interested, it's also possible to build in measures at the end of therapy to gain the views of the client on the therapy process. One particularly useful tool is the open-ended Helpful Aspects of Therapy form (HAT; Llewelyn, 1988). An alternative is to conduct a change interview with clients at the end of therapy, focused on their views about their experience of therapy. Guidance on how to do this, as well as a printable copy of the HAT and several other useful process tools can be accessed at the website of the Network for Research on Experiential Psychotherapies, where they are maintained by Robert Elliot (http://www.experiential-researchers.org/instruments.html)

Decide when to measure   Therapy outcome measures need to be used at least twice, before and at the end of therapy, so that meaningful outcome data can be obtained. This is a bare minimum, however, and it useful to include a baseline and to administer the outcome measure at regular intervals so that should the client drop out of therapy some data are still available. The short versions of the outcome measures described earlier are ideal for use each session.

Therapy process measures should also be used throughout therapy, either each session or every other session depending on the length of the measure and ease of use.

Figure 5.2 suggests suitable timings for the different kinds of measures.

Decide who handles the paperwork   It's essential that there is a workable system for distributing and collecting the measures in place. There are two possibilities here. Administrators may be able to do it, and to maintain a database of the results. This is often the preferred option for clinicians! While it is the easiest option for clinicians, it may not be available in all services and there is a danger that clinicians are distanced from the data. Even better, the service may pay for online support where, for example, therapists or clients type scores onto an online form, and data are collated automatically. Alternatively, clinicians may do this the old-fashioned way, but they need a supply of the measures easily to hand, a database already set up for data entry, and time to score up the measures. Although this looks like a less preferable option, it has some advantages in that

Measurement domain	Assessment	Therapy sessions								End	Follow up
Client/Therapist characteristics	■										
Therapy outcome e.g. CORE-OM	◆				◆					◆	◆
Specific outcome e.g. IES-R	○				○					○	○
Progress e.g. ORS	▲	▲	▲	▲	▲	▲	▲	▲	▲	▲	▲
Therapeutic alliance e.g. SRS	●	●	●	●	●	●	●	●	●	●	●
Client evaluation e.g. HAT										□	□

Figure 5.2: Possible assessment framework

clinicians stay very close to the data gathered from their patients. This is important if the data are to have an influence on the course of therapy for an individual.

Decide what to do with the data   If data are never used, eventually the information will *always* stop being collected. We know that gathering outcome data is now often routine, and should be an important part of the public profile of any service – data should be disseminated regularly to local service users and commissioners. Outcome data gathered from a practice research network looks pretty impressive and will serve this function exceptionally well.

Our argument here though is that such data can do much more than this: the information can make an important contribution to research evidence, and it can be used to improve individual practice. Involvement in such an endeavor is excellent reinforcement for clinicians to maintain their interest in data collection.

Using practice research network data in research

If a group of clinicians signs up to a system of data collection similar to the one outlined above, it doesn't take long before the data enable some interesting questions to be asked. This process reconnects clinicians to the evidence base, enabling curious clinicians to explore patterns in the data and investigate hunches about therapeutic practice. It presents an opportunity for the practice research network to generate and investigate questions suggested by members, perhaps in collaboration with researchers. Collaboration with other networks can also be useful, increasing the number of clients and therapists in the database. There has been some justifiable criticism of practice research networks: they are not controlled experiments and therefore involve a great deal of variability in the way therapy is delivered, the way therapists administer measures, etc. Nevertheless, they do offer an opportunity to explore matters relevant to the development of psychotherapy models in a real-world setting and offer a nice counterpoint to clinical trials. Trials establishing the efficacy of an intervention are often seen as being too far removed from routine practice to be relevant, and many see as an adequate response the effectiveness studies that follow which aim to establish the validity of treatments as they're practised in a naturalistic setting. As Barkham, Hardy and Mellor-Clark (2010) point out, however, this begs the question of what is real-world practice? In truth, there are many different real-world practices – therapy varies between individuals and settings and it is impossible to capture all this complexity in any well-controlled efficacy or effectiveness study. This is where practice research networks can make a real contribution to the evidence.

The most successful strategy is for the questions to be asked of the data gathered by the network to partially guide the choice of measures. A recent published example is a study produced by the Pennsylvania practice research network investigating what interventions were rated as most helpful by the client and the therapist (Castonguay *et al.*, 2010b). Based on data from 13 therapists who saw 121 clients, the study asked clients at the end of each session to complete a HAT (printed on a card), which the therapist then saw before the start of the next session. The results showed that clients and therapists agreed that fostering greater self-awareness in the client was particularly helpful. Few unhelpful aspects of therapy were listed, though there was emphasis on the importance of the alliance – a good fit between therapist and client.

Reflecting on the experience of the Pennsylvania practice research network, the current chair of the network, psychotherapy researcher Louis Castonguay argues that what they produced was a scientifically rigorous and clearly clinically relevant study, and that the therapists experienced their participation very positively. It is noteworthy that all the clinicians are named as co-authors on the paper and there seems to be a real sense of ownership. More than that, Castonguay argues that participation may have improved their practice.

Using practice research network data to improve practice

So far we have focused on a service or group of clinicians forming a practice research network and collaborating in collecting data to help to evaluate the service and take part in research. The other aspect to data collection is to use regularly collected data to improve individual practice. We suspect that the research cited earlier on helpful aspects of therapy has certainly made the participating clinicians even more aware of the importance of the therapeutic alliance as a potential facilitator of change. Interestingly, useful information for improving practice can come from consideration of clients who *do not* improve (Castonguay *et al.*, 2010a). Although caution is needed in ascribing causality, one of the most interesting (and provocative) studies on this topic found that an emphasis on the techniques and rationale of cognitive therapy by therapists when treating clients for depression was associated with a negative outcome (Castonguay *et al.*, 1996). Further work revealed that it was the rigid persistence of the therapists rather than the techniques themselves; worse, as client resistance to these ideas increased, so did the persistence of some therapists. The relationship disappeared when therapeutic alliance was controlled for, suggesting again that this is about the relationship rather than the particular techniques.

Such studies raise the importance of therapists listening to their clients, and a strategy for collecting regular information such as the one outlined earlier presents an opportunity to do this in a structured way so that it becomes routine. Information gathered from clients every session presents an opportunity to gather feedback on the process of therapy, which in turn offers the potential for the therapist to respond and improve the outcome for each client. It offers a way for clients to tell us what they find helpful and unhelpful, and if they feel that they are improving or not. If therapists are sensitive to the messages and prepared to adapt their work in response, it means there is the potential for certain situations, such as the unhelpful rigidity described in the research cited earlier, to be avoided.

In fact, the evidence gathered to date suggests that this potential is already being realised. Cutting across therapeutic orientation, modalities and client groups, the emerging literature on the use of client feedback in therapy promises to make a more significant impact on therapy outcomes than any other contemporary development in psychotherapy.

This will be the focus of the next chapter; the implications and how to benefit from them will be the focus for the rest of this book.

References

Agnew-Davies, R., Stiles, W.B., Hardy, G.E., *et al.* (1998) Alliance structure assessed by the Agnew Relationship Measure (ARM). *British Journal of Clinical Psychology*, 37, 155–72.

Barak, A. and LaCrosse, M.B. (1975) Multidimensional perception of counselor behavior. *Journal of Counselling Psychology*, 22, 471–476.

Barkham, M., Hardy, G.E., and Mellor-Clark, J. (eds) (2010) *Developing and Delivering Practice-based Evidence: A Guide for the Psychological Therapies*, John Wiley & Sons, Ltd, Chichester.

Barkham, M., Margison, F., Leach, C., *et al.* (2001) Service profiling and outcomes benchmarking using the CORE-OM: towards practice based evidence in the psychological therapies. *Journal of Consulting and Clinical Psychology*, 69, 184 –196.

Barlow, D.H., Nock, M.K. and Hersen, M. (2008) *Single Case Experimental Designs: Strategies for Studying Behavior Change*, 3rd edn, Allyn & Bacon, Boston.

Borckardt, J., Nash, M., Murphy, M., *et al.* (2008) Clinical practice as a natural laboratory for psychotherapy research. *American Psychologist*, 63, 77–95.

Borkovec, T.D., Echemendia, R.J., Ragusea, S.A. and Ruiz, M. (2001) The Pennsylvania Practice Research Network and future possibilities for clinically meaningful and scientifically rigorous psychotherapy effectiveness research. *Clinical Psychology: Research and Practice*, 8, 155–167.

Brown, G.S., Lambert, M.J., Jones, E.R., and Minami, T. (2005) Identifying highly effective psychotherapists in a managed care environment. *American Journal of Managed Care*, 11, 513–520.

Cahill, J., Barkham, M., Hardy, G., *et al.* (2008) A review and critical appraisal of measures of therapist–patient interactions in mental health settings. *Health Technology Assessment*, 12, 24, ix–47.

Campbell, A. and Hemsley, S. (2009) Outcome Rating Scale and Session Rating Scale in psychological practice: clinical utility of ultra-brief measures. *Clinical Psychologist*, 13, 1–9.

Castonguay, L.G., Boswell, J.F., Constantino, M.J., *et al.* (2010a) Training implications of harmful effects of psychological treatments. *American Psychologist*, 65, 34–49.

Castonguay, L.G., Boswell, J.F., Zack, S.E., *et al.* (2010b) Helpful and hindering events in psychotherapy: a practice research network study. *PsychotherapyTheory, Research, Practice, and Training*, 47, 327–344.

Castonguay, L.G., Goldfried, M.R., Wiser, S., *et al.* (1996) Predicting outcome in cognitive therapy for depression: a comparison of unique and common factors. *Journal of Consulting and Clinical Psychology*, 64, 497–504.

Corrigan, J.D. and Schmidt, L.D. (1983) Development and validation of revisions in the Counselor Rating Form. *Journal of Counseling Psychology*, 30, 64–75.

Duncan, B., Miller, S., Sparks, J., *et al.* (2003) The Session Rating Scale: preliminary psychometric properties of a 'working' alliance measure. *Journal of Brief Therapy*, 3, 3–12.

Elliott, R. (2002) Hermeneutic single case efficacy design. *Psychotherapy Research*, 12, 1–20.

Elliott, R. and Zucconi, A. (2006) Doing research on the effectiveness of psychotherapy and psychotherapy training: a person-centered/experiential perspective. *Person-Centered and Experiential Psychotherapies*, 5, 81–100.

Elliott, R., Mack, C. and Shapiro, D.A. (1999) *Simplified Personal Questionnaire Procedure*, Department of Psychology, University of Toledo, Toledo, Ohio, http://experiential-researchers.org/instruments/elliott/pqprocedure.html (accessed 6 October, 2011).

Fransella, F.R., Bell, R. and Bannister, D. (2003) *A Manual for Repertory Grid Technique*, 2nd edn, John Wiley & Sons, Ltd, Chichester.

Gaston, L. (1991) Reliability and criterion-related validity of the California Psychotherapy Alliance Scales – Patient version. *Psychological Assessment*, 3, 68–74.

Gaston, L. and Marmar C.R. (1994) The California Psychotherapy Alliance Scales, in *The Working Alliance: Theory, Research, and Practice* (eds A.O. Horvath and L.S. Greenberg), pp. 85–108, John Wiley & Sons, Inc, New York.

Horvath, A.O. and Greenberg, L.S. (1989) Development and validation of the Working Alliance Inventory. *Journal of Counseling Psychology*, 36, 223–233.

Jacobson, N.S. and Truax, P. (1991) Clinical significance: a statistical approach to defining meaningful change in psychotherapy. *Journal of Consulting and Clinical Psychology*, 59, 12–19.

Jacobson, N.S., Roberts, L.J., Berns, S.B. and McGlinchey, J.B. (1999) Methods for defining and determining the clinical significance of treatment effects: description, application, and alternatives. *Journal of Consulting and Clinical Psychology*, 67, 300–307.

Kazdin, A.E. (1982) *Single Case Research Designs: Methods for Clinical and Applied Settings*, Oxford University Press, New York.

Llewelyn, S. (1988) Psychological therapy as viewed by clients and therapists. *British Journal of Clinical Psychology*, 27, 223–238.

Luborsky, L., Barber, J.P., Siqueland, L., *et al.* (1996) The revised Helping Alliance Questionnaire (HAq-II): psychometric properties. *Journal of Psychotherapy, Practice and Research*, 5, 260–271.

McMillan, D. and Morley, S. (2010) Single Case Quantitative Methods for Practice-Based Evidence, in *Developing and Delivering Practice-Based Evidence: A Guide for the Psychological Therapies* (eds M. Barkham, G.E. Hardy and J. Mellor-Clark), John Wiley & Sons, Ltd, Chichester.

Miller, S., Duncan, B., Brown, J., *et al.* (2003) The Outcome Rating Scale: a preliminary study of reliability, validity, and feasibility of a brief visual analogue measure. *Journal of Brief Therapy*, 2, 91–100.

Morley, S. (2002) *EasyPQ – Yet another version of Shapiro's Personal Questionnaire*, University of Leeds, Leeds, http://www.leeds.ac.uk/hsphr/people/downloads/EasyPQ.zip (accessed 6 October, 2011).

Morley, S. and Adams, M. (1991) Graphical analysis of single-case time series data. *British Journal of Clinical Psychology*, 30, 97–115.

Stiles, W.B. (2005) Case studies, in *Evidence-based Practices in Mental Health: Debate and Dialogue on the Fundamental Questions* (eds J.C. Norcross, L.E. Beutler and R.F. Levant), American Psychological Association, Washington, DC.

Stiles, W.B. (2007) Theory-building case studies of counselling and psychotherapy. *Counselling and Psychotherapy Research*, 7, 122–127.

Stiles, W.B., Hardy, G.E., Cahill, J., *et al.* (2003) The short ARM (a short form of the Agnew Relationship Measure). Paper presented at the annual meeting of the North American Society for Psychotherapy Research, Newport, RI, November.

Weiss, D.S. and Marmar, C.R. (1997) The impact of Event Scale-Revised, in *Assessing Psychological Trauma and PTSD: A Practitioner's Handbook* (eds J.P. Wilson and T.M. Keane), pp. 399–411, Guilford Press, New York.

6

Using Client Feedback in Psychotherapy – The Research

The only man I know who behaves sensibly is my tailor; he takes my measurements anew each time he sees me. The rest go on with their old measurements and expect me to fit them. (George Bernard Shaw)

Introduction

So far our survey of the literature on research into psychotherapy has reflected the areas with the most publications – developing and testing models of psychotherapy with different conditions, and forays into the processes that may underlie the effectiveness of psychotherapy. The dominant paradigm, as we have seen, has been to focus on the form of therapy, and a great deal of research effort has been invested in trying to determine if one form of therapy has an advantage over another. Although much has been learnt, the payoff for this investment has not been unequivocal evidence for the superiority of any one model of therapy. For therapists trying to improve their practice, then, there is no convincing case to change therapy. Similarly, process research may just increase our anxieties by reminding us of how little evidence we have for causal relationships in

Maximising the Benefits of Psychotherapy: A Practice-Based Evidence Approach, First Edition. David Green and Gary Latchford.
© 2012 John Wiley & Sons, Ltd. Published 2012 by John Wiley & Sons, Ltd.

therapy, though a number of factors such as therapeutic alliance have been shown to be important.

So what guidance is there for a therapist hoping to improve? One of the most promising areas of research has successfully sidestepped the sometimes acrimonious debate about which therapy is better. This goes back to basics and asks, 'How does anyone get better at anything?' Well, people generally improve with practice, if they invest enough effort. Practice isn't always useful, however – we usually need some way of knowing whether we are getting better. It's difficult to imagine developing your typing skills if you can only play with the keyboard when the computer is switched off. The missing ingredient, of course, is feedback. Feedback on our performance gives us an opportunity to modify and improve, and to fine-tune.

Feedback in Therapy: Do We Need It?

Do we need feedback to fine-tune our therapy skills? You might argue that people who listen to others for a living in order to under-stand their problems and help them are already pretty good at it. So are therapists already sensitive to their clients' needs, able to pick up signs of treatment success or failure? Treatment failure might be the important issue here. As we have seen, dropout is a major problem in therapy and, if a client doesn't attend, the therapist can't help them. It's also worth recalling that a significant number of clients deteriorate in therapy (around 5–10%; Lambert and Ogles, 2004) It might be that therapists are powerless to prevent dropout or reverse treatment failure in these cases. Alternatively, they may not be aware of the problem until it is too late. In fact, there is some good evidence that the latter is true.

Hannan *et al.* (2005) ran a kind of 'head to head comparison' between man and machine in which clinicians and an algorithm were compared in the ability to successfully predict client deteriora-tion. They asked 48 therapists to predict which of 550 clients would be worse off at the end of treatment than when they started. The therapists were optimistic and predicted that only one would be worse off. In fact, 40 had a negative outcome and the therapists correctly identified only one of them. How did the algorithm fare? This used a statistical prediction based on a database gathered from many previous administrations of the measures used in the study. It was applied to 492 consecutive new clients and did pretty well, predicting all 36 of those with a negative outcome. One problem, though, was specificity – it was much less optimistic than the therapists and predicted 83 (18.2%) would get worse when in fact they did not. So, not good news for the therapists, but some consolation in that the predictive data look to be a useful tool; however, the data are a guide only and require the clinician to investigate further.

Is this a fair test of the therapists? In practice, rather than deciding early in therapy that there is a risk of deterioration, therapists may build up evidence for concern over many weeks, recording this in their case notes. In a naturalistic study, Hatfield *et al.*, (2010) examined the case notes of 70 patients who had deteriorated since the start of therapy to see if this had been picked up by their therapists using their clinical judgement. They found only 21% of the therapists had done so.

So, mixed news here: therapists are generally poor at detecting deterioration, but measures completed by clients might be a good source of evidence for risk of later deterioration and act as a kind of early warning for therapists. Would therapists use such feedback, and if so would it really make any difference to outcomes?

Feedback in Therapy: Lambert's Work

The big name in this field is Michael Lambert. In a series of six trials at the Brigham Young University student counselling centre in the United States (Harmon *et al.*, 2007; Hawkins *et al.*, 2004; Lambert *et al.*, 2001; Lambert *et al.*, 2002; Slade *et al.*, 2008; Whipple *et al.*, 2003), Lambert and his colleagues provided striking evidence that this is exactly what you find. In all, this work involved over 4000 clients. Each study employed a design in which therapists acted as their own control – for some of their clients they were randomly assigned to receive feedback on progress, and the outcomes for these clients were then compared with those for clients where no feedback was provided.

Rather than focusing on instructing therapists on what to do, the emphasis by Lambert's team has been on developing an intuitive and accessible system using a 'traffic light' as a handy rubric to inform therapists of the progress of their client. In this, each client's progress is compared with the rate of expected change and put into one of four colour-coded categories. The therapists receive a chart showing client progress that is colour coded, and with messages relevant to the category. The four conditions are: White (client is functioning in the normal range), Green (client is making reasonable progress so no change necessary), Yellow (client's progress is 'less than adequate' and there is a risk he or she will not benefit from therapy; it is recommended that the therapist reconsider the treatment plan) and Red (client is not making expected progress and there is a high risk of dropout; the therapist is recommended to review the case and choose a new course of action). Once the therapists receive this feedback, it is up to them to decide how to act upon it.

Lambert *et al.* (2001) first reported on a trial involving 31 therapists and 609 clients. The feedback intervention was particularly effective for the 66 clients whose scores predicted treatment failure (the 'at risk' group), leading to twice as many achieving significant change compared with the no-feedback condition. In fact, the effect size for this difference (0.44) was bigger than that typically found in studies comparing psychotherapies. What's more, this was at no cost to the clients who were predicted to do well – in this group feedback was associated with similar positive results but it was quicker: clients were seen for fewer sessions. These initial findings were replicated with a bigger sample (49 therapists, 1020 clients) a year later (Lambert *et al.* 2002), though rather than using random allocation this trial gave therapists access to feedback during alternate six-month periods. The study found a similar effect size for the feedback intervention for 'at risk' clients (0.40); 'on track' clients did equally well in both conditions, though the feedback condition was no quicker.

The next study (Whipple *et al.*, 2003) aimed to improve outcomes for the 'at risk' clients by adding clinical support tools (CSTs) for use by therapists after they received the feedback. The CSTs consisted of measures to be completed by the client. These focused on areas thought by the authors to be important in getting therapy back on track – the therapeutic alliance, social support and stage of change. Involving 48 therapists and 982 clients, the study found that the addition of a CST led to superior outcomes (almost double the rate of significant or reliable change) and better retention in therapy.

Hawkins *et al.* (2004) further investigated ways to increase the impact of feedback by seeing whether providing treatment progress information to the client as well as the therapist made any difference. It did – the effect was largest for this group – but this finding was not replicated in a later, larger study (Harmon *et al.* 2007), though the clients in this study were generally a less severely distressed group. This study nevertheless added to the increasing weight of evidence that feedback increases effectiveness: use of feedback improved outcome for all clients, and feedback for 'at risk' clients was especially effective when a CST was used. This resulted in double the number achieving significant or reliable change compared with the no-feedback group (42.1% vs. 21%).

Lastly, Slade *et al.* (2008) re-examined the question of whether giving feedback to the client makes a difference and also added a new question around the timing of feedback. In previous studies the practicalities involved in scoring measures meant that the feedback to the therapists was presented a week after it was taken (before the next session). If needed, the CSTs would then be given to the client so there would be an additional week before these were completed and given to the therapist. Therapists had suggested that the feedback would be better if it were collected from the client just before the session and a new system of electronic data collection enabled feedback to be transmitted to the therapist immediately, with a graph tracking weekly progress. This study included 1101 clients in the immediate feedback group where the therapist received the information electronically before the start of the session. If CSTs were needed, they were given to the client in this session and therefore available a week later (the CSTs in this study were measures of therapeutic alliance, social support, motivation for therapy and perfectionism). Clients were randomly assigned to therapist only or therapist and client feedback conditions. Results were compared with archived data from some of the previous studies, where there was a delay in receiving feedback of one week (and the CSTs of two weeks). This study once again found clear evidence that feedback to therapists worked, particularly for those at risk, and particularly when CSTs were used. There was no advantage in also giving the client access to the feedback. Interestingly, there was also no advantage in terms of outcomes in giving immediate feedback, though it was noted that these clients achieved similar change in three fewer sessions.

Putting all this together amounts to a very strong case for the use of feedback. Of particular note is that none of this research was concerned with the therapeutic orientation of the therapists – this is about providing information and not telling therapists what to do. In fact, none of these studies even examined what therapists do in response to the feedback. We only know that, whatever they do, it works.

Feedback in Therapy: PCOMS Research

The Partners for Change Outcome Monitoring System (PCOMS; Miller *et al.*, 2005) has many similarities to the feedback system developed by Lambert, and studies investigating the PCOMS approach have added to the evidence built up by Lambert's work. PCOMS utilises the Outcome Rating Scale (ORS) and the Session Rating Scale (SRS), two ultra-brief measures of client progress and therapeutic alliance designed to be administered at the start and end of each session respectively, and discussed with the therapist within the session. Interestingly, the SRS alliance measure is similar to one of the CSTs used by Lambert. The difference in the PCOMS approach, however, is that the alliance measure is used routinely in every session, regardless of whether a client is doing well or deteriorating. Where the PCOMS system is identical to Lambert's system is in the use of automated feedback on client progress based on a comparison of the change recorded for the client with clinical norms. Feedback to therapists utilises a graph of the client's progress compared with a dotted line representing the expected trajectory of change for the client given the baseline score at the start of therapy. PCOMS also uses a traffic light graphic alerting the therapist when a client's ratings on either measure falls significantly outside the established norms.

Miller *et al.* (2006) found that introducing routine feedback using the PCOMS system doubled the effect size of a telephone-based intervention. Though quite large (6424 clients, 75 therapists), this was a naturalistic study rather than a trial and a change that occurred in the service during the research (clients talking to the same therapist rather than anyone available) was a potential confound, though the effect of introducing feedback was even more pronounced for clients who had switched therapists (effect size increased from 0.02 to 0.4).

In a smaller but better controlled study in a university-based counselling service and training clinic (Reese, Norsworthy and Rowlands, 2009), 148 clients were randomly allocated to a feedback (using PCOMS) or no-feedback condition. They found significant differences in self-reported outcomes between the groups, and that change in the feedback group tended to be quicker. Focusing more on the effects on the therapists, a study by Reese *et al.* (2009) allocated therapists in training to a feedback or no-feedback group for a year to see if it made any difference to their development. Encouragingly, all the therapists improved in terms of client outcome by the end of the year, but clients of therapists receiving feedback improved more (mean gain of 8.9 points on the ORS during therapy compared with 4.01 points in the no-feedback group).

Perhaps the most striking evidence for the effectiveness of the PCOMS approach comes from a study that extended the research to couples therapy (Anker, Duncan and Sparks, 2009). In this study, 410

Norwegian couples were randomised to treatment as usual or a feedback condition. In the latter, the 10 therapists had access to the scores from the SRS and ORS every session, together with graphs plotting their clients' change so far and what the treatment response was likely to be. Couples in the feedback condition achieved nearly four times the rate of clinically significant change on the ORS than in the control condition at the end of therapy, and nearly three times the rate at six-month follow up. The effect size for the addition of feedback was 0.5, a medium to large effect.

This finding is supported by a similar study of the PCOMS approach conducted with 46 US couples (Reese *et al.*, 2010), which found that the feedback condition resulted in an effect size of 0.48 and four times as many couples reporting clinically significant change on the ORS. They also found that change was more rapid when feedback was given.

Given that once again the interventions in these studies involved no instructions to therapists to change their therapy and consisted entirely of providing additional information, these results are quite remarkable.

Feedback in Therapy: Other Research

Other research has also pointed to the usefulness of feedback, even when what is provided to the therapist is quite minimal. An RCT by Brodey *et al.* (2005) of 1374 patients in a managed behavioural healthcare setting in the United States tested the impact of providing therapists with feedback at two time points, after the assessment session and again at six weeks. Scores from items on a self-report symptom checklist were fed back to therapists in a report offering interpretations and explanations of the data, and comparative information on population norms and (at six weeks) progress over time indicating improvement or deterioration. They found that even this brief intervention produced a significant decrease in symptoms over a no-feedback condition, though they only present short-term data.

Feedback in Therapy: Other Perspectives

Other researchers, meanwhile, have approached the topic of feedback from a different theoretical perspective. Feedback is often used in motivational interviewing (MI) with clients struggling with behaviour change, such as abstention from alcohol. In such cases, presenting information on a client's alcohol consumption in a non-judgemental way is thought to increase discomfort at the gap between current and desired behaviour, and act as a lever for change. This principle is one of those underlying a study by Schmidt *et al.* (2006), which looked at the effect of providing regular feedback to the client only. In an RCT with 61 patients undertaking a cognitive behavioural self-help programme for bulimia nervosa, they examined the impact of providing personalised feedback to the client, generated and delivered in an MI (non-confrontational) style. This included letters from the therapist at the start and end of therapy, and computerised feedback on symptoms of bulimia, anxiety and depression every two weeks. The feedback intervention had no effect on dropout (contrary to the researcher's expectations), but was associated with significantly reduced symptoms of vomiting and dietary restriction.

Similarly, the concept of using feedback to increase motivation to change in the client was one of the ideas underlying an RCT by Slade *et al.* (2006) that also looked at the broader question of the use of outcome measures in community mental health teams in the United Kingdom. They asked clients and a member of staff from the team working with them to complete measures assessing needs, quality of life and therapeutic alliance every month and return them by post; both client and health professional then received feedback every three months. This group was compared with a no-feedback group. They found no advantage to the feedback group in terms of self-reported outcomes (e.g. symptoms, quality of life) but that feedback was associated with significantly fewer psychiatric in-patient days and was therefore cost effective. The population in this study (n = 160) was different from that in Lambert's studies (the majority here had a diagnosis of schizophrenia or other psychoses) and the study featured a very different timescale for feedback (only once every three months); yet it still suggests that introducing an element of feedback can have quite striking benefits.

Feedback in Therapy: Meta-analyses and Consensus

The two studies described above raise the issue of how we define feedback. As the number of studies on feedback in therapy increase, it is becoming important to obtain a consensus on its use. Four meta-analyses have now attempted to synthesise published data and the studies we have described earlier feature prominently. One (Knaup *et al.*, 2009) is undermined by inclusion criteria that are far too broad. It seems to us that it is important to distinguish studies of psychotherapy where the intention is to test the impact of regular feedback to the therapist (and possibly client) from those studies testing the impact of infrequent feedback, or the effect of feedback on the client alone (i.e., as part of a strategy to increase motivation). Of the 12 included studies in the Knaup *et al.* meta-analysis, only seven feature weekly therapist feedback; three of the included studies feature feedback given only once. They also include the Schmidt study on feedback to patients using the self-help programme described earlier. We don't think this makes sense. Although the result of this meta-analysis was positive – they still found a significant effect on mental health for clients in feedback conditions – the diverse nature of the included studies make this finding difficult to generalise. Notably, they found that frequency of feedback was a moderator.

More helpful are the meta-analyses focusing on regular feedback in psychotherapy. An early review by Lambert *et al.* (2003) of their first three studies found an effect size for feedback of 0.39. A later meta-analysis and mega-analysis involved re-analysing raw data from their six studies (Shimokawa, Lambert and Smart, 2010). This found an effect size of 0.12 for all clients, but this rose to 0.28–0.44

for clients at risk of treatment failure, and when only those clients who received at least the minimum intervention were included (four to six sessions) this rose to 0.53–0.70. Lambert's most recent review (Lambert and Shimokawa, 2011) is of nine studies, adding three studies using the PCOMS system. They found that use of feedback was associated with around a 50% drop in rates of patient deterioration, and a significant increase in rates of positive responding. Again feedback was particularly helpful for those clients at risk of treatment failure.

Overview

As can be seen by looking at the dates of the published studies described earlier, this is a very new area of research. Yet the results that are emerging are largely consistent and impressive and the overall finding that feedback has a significant impact on outcome makes a lot of sense. We know feedback is often useful in other settings and for other activities, so why should it not be useful for psychotherapy? Because it is a new area, however, many aspects of this phenomenon still seem unclear.

Unknowns: feedback to the client

For us, feedback to the client is one issue that requires further work. As seen earlier, Lambert's team have concluded that including clients in those receiving feedback makes no difference. We wonder, though, whether this reflects the way feedback is used in their approach. Lambert's team have seen feedback as information that is presented to the therapist on the progress of the client and whether the client is on track for a successful outcome. This information is presented outside the therapy room and there is no requirement (or expectation) that it will necessarily be discussed with the client. The assumption in giving the feedback to therapists is that if things are not going well they will change what they do. This might mean trying harder, or trying something different. This emphasis on the therapist as receiver of information gains some support from Lambert's finding that adding extra resources when a client is not on track (questionnaires targeting areas thought to be important to outcome such as therapeutic alliance) does make a difference. This extra information appears to guide therapists to make better choices when changing something about their therapy.

How does giving feedback to the client fit into this model? Is there a similar assumption that clients will change what they do? Giving feedback to clients on how they are doing feels to us a very different mechanism from giving feedback to therapists and we don't think we can assume that the ways this might make a difference to outcome are similar. It seems to us that a likely consequence of giving therapists feedback is that they will more successfully shape their intervention to the needs of their client. We imagine that this will often involve talking with clients either directly or indirectly about the feedback and how they are doing. In this case, simply giving clients feedback on their progress outside the context of the therapy room would perhaps make them better informed (though of course as the source of the information they may well have a better understanding of how well they are doing than the therapist) but would not guarantee that discussions take place with the therapist, and this might be the most important factor. Interestingly, in the PCOMS approach the brief measures of progress and alliance are taken and scored in the therapy session itself and there is an explicit expectation that both will be discussed with the client. Thus feedback is shared with therapist and client and discussed as part of therapy. This gives a real sense of active collaboration, of the therapist being directed by feedback from the client on how therapy is working for the client generally and in that particular session. Does the discussion make a difference? Unfortunately we don't yet have any research on this.

Unknowns: what measures to use in feedback

Among the other potentially important factors in feedback that may influence effectiveness, choice of measures also seems important to us. The work of Lambert's team shows unsurprisingly that feedback needs to be relatively timely in order to be useful. The focus in their approach to feedback is on progress in terms of symptom change. They have developed a well-regarded tool to track change in every session: the Outcome Questionnaire (OQ-45; Lambert *et al.*, 1996). Most other approaches to measurement during therapy also focus on symptoms, such as the shorter versions of the CORE outcome measure designed for sessional use (see Chapter 7). The assumption by most researchers investigating feedback has been that the important component is symptom change, though other information is included in the support tools used by Lambert. The PCOMS approach features a brief measure of symptom change but also includes an alliance measure to be used in every session. Anecdotally, therapists often find the discussion with the client about the alliance measure the most informative, but we don't know from research the relative importance of a discussion about feedback on symptom change and alliance.

A further issue is the choice of measure of symptom change. The measures used in feedback studies are nomothetic – that is, they are derived from global constructs such as anxiety and depression. They are constructed in such a way that they accurately measure the symptoms thought to be associated with the constructs (validity), and do this consistently (reliability). They are designed to be used with a population of people, so everyone gets the same measure. Interpretation of scores is by comparison with norms produced for different populations – for example, depressed or well. In this way it's possible to track someone's progress over time and then compare this with data taken from the wider population. This means you can see whether someone is off track compared with the typical scores of clients on track for change. The feedback systems described earlier all do this, and are creative in how the information is presented (using graphs, traffic lights, etc.). This approach may well be very attractive for organisations, offering the prospect of monitoring outcomes over time across the service.

In essence, however, two comparisons are being made when using feedback – the client's scores with the wider population, and the client's scores with his or her own previous scores. The assumption is that it's the former that is important, and it certainly allows for recognition of those at risk of poor outcome. The potential role of the latter is relatively unexplored though the PCOMS approach does encourage a discussion between therapist and client on the change in the client's scores over time. There may also be potential in considering idiographic measures – that is, measures designed for the individual rather than derived from global constructs. Typically, these measures would cover issues important to the individual client. The personal questionnaire described in the previous chapter on practice-based evidence is a good example. What such measures lack in terms of reliability and validity they make up for in relevance to the individual client. Change tracked over time on such measures is clearly personally meaningful, and feedback based on such change may be useful. We can see how such information could lead to therapeutically important discussions between client and therapist, and perhaps act as an early indicator of good or poor outcome as effectively as the techniques based on nomothetic measures. At the moment this issue remains unexplored.

Unknowns: the big picture

The bottom line is that there is a great deal we don't know about why feedback in psychotherapy works. This has been both a strength and a weakness. In many ways one of the reasons the feedback studies have such an impact is that the benefits of feedback have nothing to do with the form of therapy being delivered; the researchers are careful not to be directive about how therapists use the information and in principle the use of feedback may benefit therapists from all therapeutic orientations. This means that the feedback literature has largely avoided being pulled into a debate about what therapy is best, and trainers and therapists from all camps are starting to talk about incorporating sessional measures and feedback into their methods. This does mean, however, that we don't know what therapists are actually doing with the feedback. We know feedback works, but we don't yet know how or why, or ways of increasing the effect, though very many therapists are exploring this in their own practice.

There is clearly a need for more research, and a wider literature on the impact of feedback on performance in different contexts that may guide it. Claiborn and Goodyear (2005) argue for the importance of considering theory when thinking about feedback in psychotherapy. They highlight the importance of seeing the person receiving the feedback as active rather than passive, and point out that the literature suggests that how a person receives feedback is influenced by a number of variables such as self-esteem: people with high self-esteem see positive feedback as more accurate (perhaps because it accords with their self-image) but they also value negative feedback over positive (perhaps because they are less easily threatened). It seems important therefore that feedback is not seen as a threat to the autonomy of the therapist, but rather as a tool for therapists to fine-tune their practice.

Though not all the wider theoretical literature on feedback will be relevant for psychotherapy, it has highlighted a number of variables found to be associated with the effectiveness of feedback that do seem to be potentially useful. These include the accuracy and usefulness of the feedback, the attention paid by the person receiving it, and the competency of the receiver to act – in other words, the ability to change behaviour in response to the information. A key notion from this literature, however, is that simply providing feedback does not guarantee better performance. A meta-analysis and historical review of the impact of feedback on performance (Kluger and DeNisi, 1996) produced an encouraging overall effect size of 0.4, though it also showed that more than a third of interventions using feedback actually decreased performance. What makes the difference is not clear, but Kluger and DeNisi suggest that the nature of the task is important, and that feedback that directs the receiver to the task is more helpful. This finding may offer a direction for research seeking to explain the additional benefits of using CSTs, though Kluger and DeNisi were looking at a very different context for feedback (mostly memory and performance tasks).

It seems important, then, to recognise that the wider literature shows that feedback is a complex process and does not automatically guarantee increased performance. An early attempt to produce a clinical model for the use of feedback in therapy using this literature (Sapyta, Riemer and Bickman, 2005) considers some of the aspects of the feedback itself that may be important – for example, whether it is timely, the source credible, the content useful, and whether it is positive or negative. This model also includes goal commitment of the therapist as an important factor. This refers to the motivation of the therapist to use feedback to achieve a goal, and recognises the importance of supervision in maintaining the therapist's belief in being able to help the client. Again, the message here is that feedback shouldn't be seen in isolation from the beliefs and competence of the therapist. Feedback can be very useful, but only when the context allows it to be used: therapists need to be motivated to consider feedback, confident that they can respond appropriately, and empowered to act on it.

Conclusions

Using feedback in therapy sounds such a good idea that it's a surprise to find that it is a topic of only recent interest in research. Of course individual therapists may well have been using feedback more or less informally in their practice for many years, but the feedback research has shown that if this is formalised it has the potential to significantly improve practice. This benefit comes with very little cost – though access to the software enabling cases to be tracked costs money, the basic tools are free and therapists don't have to retrain, or change their preferred form of therapy at all.

We feel obliged to sound a note of caution here. The vast majority of the research we have looked at in this chapter derives from the work of a small number of researchers, all of whom think feedback is a good idea. We know that the allegiance effect can exert a powerful bias in outcome studies comparing psychotherapies, so might it also apply here? Quite possibly. We need more research by more researchers.

Though we can't rule out allegiance effects in the researchers, curiously there are some data that suggest that there was no allegiance effect in the therapists taking part in these studies. Clinicians asked to include feedback in their practice tend to be pretty sceptical. In our experience of introducing these ideas, the response of many colleagues is that feedback is unnecessary because they are already 'tuned in' to their clients. Might this also be true of some of the clinicians taking part in these studies, therefore counterbalancing any allegiance effects on the part of the researchers? In fact, Anker, Duncan and Sparks (2009) looked at exactly this as part of their study. All their therapists had said that they routinely sought informal feedback from their clients anyway and none believed that adding structured feedback would improve their outcomes. In fact, even when asked after the study whether they felt feedback had helped, only five of the 10 reported that it had. One felt that the clients in the no-feedback group had done better.

In summary, though there is much we don't know about the processes involved, there is compelling evidence that introducing feedback to therapy can have a significant beneficial effect on outcome no matter what your preferred form of therapy.

Our next chapter considers what this research might mean in real clinical practice for therapists hoping to improve their performance.

References

Anker, M., Duncan, B. and Sparks, J. (2009) Using client feedback to improve couple therapy outcomes: a randomized clinical trial in a naturalistic setting. *Journal of Consulting and Clinical Psychology*, 77, 693–704.

Brodey, B., Cuffel, B., McCulloch, J., *et al.* (2005) The acceptability and effectiveness of patient-reported assessments and feedback in a managed behavioral healthcare setting. *American Journal of Managed Care*, 11, 774–80.

Claiborn, C.D. and Goodyear, R.K. (2005) Feedback in psychotherapy. *Journal of Clinical Psychology*, 61, 2, 209–217.

Hannan, C., Lambert, M.J., Harmon, S.C., *et al.* (2005) A lab test and algorithms for identifying clients at risk for treatment failure. *Journal of Clinical Psychology*, 61, 155–63.

Harmon, S., Lambert, M., Smart, D. and Hawkins, E. (2007) Enhancing outcome for potential treatment failures: therapist-client feedback and clinical support tools. *Psychotherapy Research*, 17, 379–392.

Hatfield, D., McCullough, L., Frantz, S. and Krieger, K. (2010) Do we know when our clients get worse? An investigation of therapists' ability to detect negative client change. *Clinical Psychology & Psychotherapy*, 17, 25–32.

Hawkins, E.J., Lambert, M.J.,Vermeersch, D.A., *et al.* (2004) The therapeutic effects of providing patient progress information to therapists and patients *Psychotherapy Research*, 14, 3, 308–327.

Kluger, A.N. and DeNisi, A. (1996) Effects of feedback intervention on performance: a historical review, a meta-analysis, and a preliminary feedback intervention theory. *Psychological Bulletin*, 119, 254–284.

Knaup, C., Koesters, M., Schoefer, D., *et al.* (2009) Effect of feedback of treatment outome in specialist mental healthcare: meta-analysis. *British Journal of Psychiatry*, 195, 15–22.

Lambert, M.J., and Ogles, B.M. (2004) The efficacy and effectiveness of psychotherapy, in *Bergin and Garfield's Handbook of Psychotherapy and Behavior Change*, 5th edn (ed. M.J. Lambert), John Wiley & Sons, Inc, Hoboken, pp. 139–193.

Lambert, M.J. and Shimokawa, K. (2011) Collecting client feedback, in *Psychotherapy Relationships That Work*, 2nd edn (ed. J.C. Norcross), Oxford University Press, New York.

Lambert, M. J., Burlingame, G.M., Umphress, V., *et al.* (1996) The reliability and validity of the Outcome Questionnaire. *Clinical Psychology and Psychotherapy*, 3, 249–258.

Lambert, M., Whipple, J., Hawkins, E., *et al.* (2003) Is it time for clinicians to routinely track patient outcome? A meta-analysis. *Clinical Psychology: Science and Practice*, 10, 288–301.

Lambert, M., Whipple, J., Smart, D., *et al.* (2001) The effects of providing therapists with feedback on patient progress during psychotherapy. Are outcomes enhanced? *Psychotherapy Research*, 11, 49–68.

Lambert, M., Whipple, J., Smart, D., *et al.* (2002) Enhancing psychotherapy outcomes via providing feedback on client progress. *Clinical Psychology and Psychotherapy*, 9, 91–103.

Miller, S.D., Duncan, B.L., Sorrell, R. and Brown, G.S. (2005) The partners for change outcome management system. *Journal of Clinical Psychology*, 61, 199–208.

Miller, S.D., Duncan, B.L., Sorrell, R., *et al.* (2006) Using outcome to inform therapy practice. *Journal of Brief Therapy*, 5, 5–22.

Reese, R., Norsworthy, L. and Rowlands, S. (2009) Does a continuous feedback model improve psychotherapy outcome? *Psychotherapy: Theory, Research, and Practice*, 46, 418–431.

Reese, J., Toland, M., Slone, N. and Norsworthy, L. (2010) Effect of client feedback on couple psychotherapy outcomes. *Psychotherapy*, 47, 616–630.

Reese, R.J., Usher, E.L., Bowman, D., *et al.* (2009) Using client feedback in psychotherapy training: an analysis of its influence on supervision and counselor self-efficacy. *Training and Education in Professional Psychology*, 3, 157–168.

Sapyta, J., Riemer, M. and Bickman, L. (2005) Feedback to clinicians: theory, research, and practice. *Journal of Clinical Psychology*, 61, 145–53.

Schmidt, U., Landau, S., Pombo-Carril, M., *et al.* (2006) Does personalized feedback improve the outcome of cognitive-behavioural guided self-care in bulimia nervosa? A preliminary randomized controlled trial. *British Journal of Clinical Psychology*, 45, 111–21.

Shimokawa, K., Lambert, M.J. and Smart, D. (2010) Enhancing treatment outcome of patients at risk of treatment failure: meta-analytic and mega-analytic review of a psychotherapy quality assurance system. *Journal of Consulting and Clinical Psychology*, 78, 298–311.

Slade, K., Lambert, M.J., Harmon, S.C., *et al.* (2008) Improving psychotherapy outcome: the use of immediate electronic feedback and revised clinical support tools. *Clinical Psychology & Psychotherapy*, 15, 287–303.

Slade, M., McCrone, P., Kuipers, E., *et al.* (2006) Use of standardised outcome measures in adult mental health services: randomised controlled trial. *British Journal of Psychiatry*, 189, 330–336.

Whipple, J., Lambert, M., Vermeersch, D., *et al.* (2003) Improving the effects of psychotherapy. The use of early identification of treatment and problem-solving strategies in routine practice. *Journal of Counseling Psychology*, 50, 59–68.

7

Using Client Feedback in Psychotherapy – In Practice

What's going on,
Ya, what's going on,
tell me what's going on.

(Marvin Gaye)

Introduction

It would be understandable if some established psychotherapists did not take kindly to being advised that they should pay close attention to how their clients are responding to treatment. A case of 'teaching grannies to suck eggs' they might think. The capacity to tune into patients' experience and to convey that you have understood what they mean to say is fundamental to establishing what is widely known as 'therapeutic rapport'. It's precisely what a good psychotherapist is good at. It's what characterises expert performance in the consulting room. Putting the client at ease; listening attentively; picking up threads of conversation; validating and sometimes even anticipating the client's account of his or her life; and making it all look so easy!

There is indeed some decent evidence to be cited in defence of this 'if it ain't broke don't fix it' position. In 1995 the US magazine

Maximising the Benefits of Psychotherapy: A Practice-Based Evidence Approach,
First Edition. David Green and Gary Latchford.
© 2012 John Wiley & Sons, Ltd. Published 2012 by John Wiley & Sons, Ltd.

Consumer Reports conducted a large-scale survey of its readers asking about the experiences of those who had sought help for emotional and stress-related problems in the previous three years (Seligman, 1995). Replies were received from about 3000 individuals who had been in therapy with a mental health professional during that period. Their responses to a structured questionnaire indicated consistently high levels of satisfaction with the treatment provided. Seligman concluded bluntly that judging from their own self-report 'most respondents got a lot better'. He also noted two important differences between the way this real-life help was provided and the therapy packages evaluated in controlled trials of psychotherapy efficacy and effectiveness. First, the practitioners in the *Consumer Reports* survey were mostly free to continue providing treatment for 'as long as it takes'. Therapy trials by contrast tend to deliver a fixed pre-determined dose. Second, the course of the therapeutic conversations that were held between these 'normal' therapists and their clients were self-correcting. If one approach wasn't working the parties felt able to take another tack. This is most unlike the situation in which therapists in a manualised treatment trial find themselves where their room for manoeuvre is much more constrained.

Overall the *Consumer Reports* survey offers support both for the argument that 'treatment as usual' is a largely effective and appreciated way of delivering mental health care and that part of that effectiveness can be attributed to the responsiveness and flexibility of those providing the therapy.

Radio Luxembourg

One of us (DG) is old enough to remember the first time The Beatles hit the airwaves. In the early 1960s there were no mainstream UK radio channels that broadcast pop music. Initiatives such as pirate radio stations followed some years later. The only option open to a young British fan determined to keep up with the latest offerings in a wonderfully changing music scene was to tune into Radio Luxembourg – a commercial continental station quite prepared to give the BBC a run for its money. The musical menu on offer was absolutely spot on but access was frustratingly inconsistent. No matter how often you twisted and turned the dial on your 'tranny' to improve reception, the signal from Radio Luxembourg drifted in and out infuriatingly. Sod's Law of course guaranteed that the best reception came just when you didn't need it. Readers of a certain age may recall the regular advertisements placed by a Mr Horace Batchelor of Keynsham, near Bristol, extolling the alleged virtues of his Infra-Draw method for playing the football pools!

The reason that I have chosen to reminisce in such detail is that listening to Radio Luxembourg has frequently struck me as the perfect metaphor for describing my continued sense of being 'nearly there' in my work as a clinical psychologist. Sometimes I think my clients are coming through loud and clear and then, in an instant, I have lost them and struggle to tune in again properly. I have found myself enviously disbelieving the accounts of others who write and speak as if they constantly have their finger on their client's psychological pulse. Instead I find comfort in the old adage that 'any psychotherapist who always knows exactly what he's doing should be thoroughly ashamed of himself'. A series of empirical studies suggests I am not alone in my confusion.

Self-appraisal Bias

The first line of evidence originates in social psychology and concerns the widespread human tendency to over-estimate our own abilities. The story that over 90% of British motorists consider themselves better-than-average drivers is probably not apocryphal (Alicke *et al.*, 1995). We are nearly all prone to this positive self-appraisal bias and 'taking it easy' on ourselves in this way may well have some beneficial mental health consequences – for us, if not for our clients. Two established findings in the field of self-assessment should give us further pause for thought. The first is a pretty obvious statistical point. If everybody in an organisation reckons they are doing a better than average job, then, assuming that competence is in fact normally distributed across the workforce, it follows that the greatest mismatch between actual and self-assessed performance will be found among the least able workers. These individuals can be seen as doubly handicapped because they are both 'unskilled and unaware of it' (Kruger and Dunning, 1999) and so unlikely to take measures to improve their capability. The second worrying finding is that the more time passes the more attached we tend to become to our established views of ourselves. These 'chronic' self-appraisals hence become increasingly resistant to change (Ehrlinger and Dunning, 2003). We may be prepared to acknowledge mistakes we may have made in our foolish youth but responding to critical feedback on our current performance goes distinctly against the psychological grain (Wilson and Ross, 2000). Research with doctors across the course of their training (Wooliscroft *et al.*, 1993) and during their subsequent careers (Tracey *et al.*, 1997) indicates that health professionals are just as prone to these self-evaluation biases as the rest of the populace. Recommended strategies for helping medical practitioners make more accurate assessments of their abilities have tended to rely heavily on incorporating regular external feedback into ongoing professional training (Gordon, 1992, Joshi, Ling and Jaeger, 2004).

Implicit Knowledge

There is a well-known learning cycle, beloved of many trainers, that purports to chart the movement from uninformed ineffective performance to slick professionalism in any complicated trade. The process starts with the stage of *unconscious incompetence* in which learners think they are doing just fine but it is evident to outside observers that they still have a lot to learn. This stage is followed by that of *conscious incompetence* when the learners have become painfully aware of their limitations and are highly motivated to improve their performance. This leads into the stage dubbed *conscious competence* during which the learner makes a deliberate and sustained attempt to 'do it right'. The final stage is termed *unconscious competence* and it is only at this point that the learners are able to employ their skills in the fluent, automatic fashion that characterises true professional expertise. By now the individuals are drawing much more on their implicit, experientially acquired knowledge of what is required to do their job well than on the explicit rules of conduct on which they previously relied (Eraut, 1994). The importance of these 'tacit understandings' of what's happening in a particular work context is probably most marked where decisions have to be taken 'on the hoof' because there is no time for considered strategic deliberation about what to do next.

Most experienced psychotherapists would reckon to be operating at this stage of unconscious competence. This probably represents the standard of professional service so appreciated by the respondents to the *Consumer Reports* survey described earlier in this chapter. However, there are two important limitations to this apparently desirable style of working that warrant further discussion. First, it is not at all obvious how you might further improve your practice once this stage has been achieved. What do really expert experts do to avoid hitting a premature plateau in their professional development (Sapyta, Reiman and Bickman, 2005)? Second, there is a serious challenge to be faced when your established ways of working just don't seem to be cutting the mustard any more. If you can't articulate how you were doing it right, how are you going to be able to put it right when things go wrong?

In contrast to the 'just let it flow' approach implied by the vocabulary of unconscious competence, it appears that genuine experts in a range of fields are likely to engage in systematic self-monitoring throughout their careers and that their seemingly effortless performance is backed up by a commitment to plenty of effortful practice (Ericsson, 2009). Furthermore, that regular practice will be most usefully informed by high-fidelity feedback (i.e., information with immediate relevance to the task being undertaken). Unfortunately a lot of the feedback systems employed in the professional training of psychological therapists (such as marks on academic essays) would be considered low quality because they offer only a 'weak proxy' for the outcomes that really matter to our clients (Bransford and Schwartz, 2009). What's more the feedback we therapists do receive from our clients is not easily compared with any independent standard of expected performance. We are left to make our own judgements about how well we, and our patients, are doing. The risks inherent in this situation should by now be obvious to the reader . . .

Just How Well do Therapist and Client Accounts Tally?

One way of checking whether or not psychotherapists and their clients are on the same wavelength is to check whether their memories of shared therapy sessions concur. Llewelyn (1988) recruited 40 therapist/client pairs into an intriguing study to ask precisely that question. She asked each of the parties (independently) to reflect on their session together and record any examples of what they personally considered to have been notably helpful or unhelpful events that had occurred. Over a cumulative total of about 400 therapy sessions, she collected more than a thousand examples of therapy episodes that had been construed as either helpful or unhelpful by one or other member of the therapy pairing. When the results were subjected to a combination of qualitative and quantitative data analysis, a number of intriguing differences between the perspectives of clients and therapists emerged. Clients appreciated times when their therapists offered direct reassurance or helped them find practical solutions to problems. However, their therapists tended to consider they had done their best work when clients seemed to have reached some degree of cognitive or affective insight into their difficulties. Overall the results indicated a myriad of statistically significant differences in what therapists and their clients identified as helpful/ unhelpful, but, perhaps unsurprisingly, the greatest mismatches were reported when the outcomes of treatment proved to be the most disappointing. It is worth noting that clinicians were not asked to guess what episodes their clients might have considered helpful and vice versa, so it is possible that the two participants understood each other well enough even if they did not share the same sense of how change occurs in therapy. Possible but improbable.

Another take on this question is to ask the straightforward empirical question, 'Do therapists notice when their clients deteriorate in therapy?' (Hatfield *et al.*, 2010). The authors of this innovative study used the knowledge that a significant proportion (estimated at between 5% and 10%) of those entering therapy don't just fail to benefit much from the experience but end up feeling notably worse. By surveying outcomes at a US university counselling centre over a five-year period, Hatfield and his colleagues calculated that somewhere in the region of 8% of the clients seen by the service had met their study's criterion for reliable negative change (defined as an increase of 14 or more points on the OQ-45 questionnaire between intake session and subsequent assessments at a later stage in therapy). From an initial pool of nearly 400 such cases the researchers selected 70 for further investigation. They examined closely the progress notes written by the therapist concerned to see if they could find any indicator that the decline in the client's functioning had been registered. This occurred in only 21% of case files analysed. Reasoning that slow cumulative change might prove more difficult for therapists to pick up than dramatic session-to-session deterioration, the researchers repeated the same analysis on progress notes where clients had recorded a dramatic increase in symptom severity (defined as an increase of 30 points or more on the OQ-45) from one therapy session to the next. Of the 41 such sets of case notes they chose to analyse, they found evidence that even this 'slap you between the eyes' reduction in functioning had been registered by only 32% of the therapists.

All the foregoing evidence strongly suggests that psychotherapists in general are not as well tuned into their clients' experiences, both inside and outside the consulting room, as they imagine themselves to be. Once this failing is acknowledged, it should not be beyond our wit to develop ways to improve the accuracy of our estimates.

Kelly's First Principle

There are a number of variations on George Kelly's infamous first principle within the personal construct literature but the gist of his advice is essentially the same: 'If you want to know what's wrong with a person, why not ask them? They might just tell you.' Ask the real expert you might say. However, this general stance still begs the question about what form of interrogation will prove most helpful to both client and therapist.

We guess that the script in many 'treatment as usual' consultations follows a well-worn pathway. Therapist greets patient. Patient returns the greeting. Therapist asks something along the lines of 'How have things been since we last met?' This invitation can open up detailed conversations in which clients elaborate on key episodes in their life during which they have struggled to cope or, just as valuably, when they have risen to particular challenges. Therapists can then sensitively enquire about specific aspects of these experiences: 'What thoughts crossed your mind at that moment?' 'How do you think you managed to recover from this setback?' When the discussion takes off in this way, therapists are able to tap a rich seam of information that provides a complex and vibrant insight into their clients' lives (what qualitative researchers sometimes term a 'thick description' of events). However, there are also some serious limitations to relying entirely on this informal conversational approach to reviewing patient progress. Clients vary considerably in their willingness and ability to recount key events in their lives. The very flexibility of the interviewing approach makes it difficult to replicate. The focus on specific episodes may give a false impression of a patient's general level of functioning. Indeed it might be theoretically useful to concentrate therapeutic conversations on exceptional experiences (O'Connell, 2003). It is not possible to make reliable comparisons of the progress made by different clients or of the effectiveness of individual therapists. For these reasons a number of quantitative methods for gauging patient progress have been developed that can be categorised as being either idiographic or normative in their design. We've outlined the principles behind these approaches in earlier chapters, and also introduced you to some recommended measures. Here, we'll expand the discussion to include other useful measures, and to think about how you might incorporate them into your routine clinical practice.

Idiographic Approaches

The essence of the idiographic approach is that systems are developed to track clients' progress in their own terms. What are the unique personal goals that clients want to achieve, and how will they most easily describe their experiences?

Scaling questions

The developers of SFT (de Shazer *et al.*, 1986) incorporated regular use of what they termed 'scaling questions' into their brief therapy procedures. Clients were asked to rate the current status of their problems on a scale of 0 to 10 where 0 represented the worst things have ever been for you and 10 represented when all your therapeutic goals had been achieved. As well as providing a rough and ready indicator of progress, these scaling questions also opened up interesting conversational opportunities: 'You reckon you're a three at the moment, what would need to happen for you to change your score to a four?' 'It would no doubt be wonderful to register a perfect ten, but what score would you consider a realistic return from our work together?' This simple mechanism (and solution-focused therapists like simple) enables both client and therapist to track progress in a consistent repeatable manner that has self-evident relevance and credibility in the client's eyes. On the downside though, it is psychometrically unsophisticated and does not allow for much in the way of valid comparison of performance across patients or clinicians.

Repertory grids

The same criticisms can probably be made of the repertory grid technique, which is primarily associated with personal construct psychotherapy (Bannister and Fransella, 1977). The basic principle behind Kelly's grids is that individuals make repeated judgements on important facets of their lives (termed 'elements') using their own unique descriptors (called 'constructs'). The elements might be family members, or frightening circumstances, or images of oneself over time. The constructs would be those words that are elicited from individuals when they are asked to discriminate between members of the particular set of elements concerned (e.g. family members might be seen as 'loving', 'bossy', 'unreliable', etc). Repeated administrations of these personalised grids allow therapists to chart changes in key aspects of their clients' construing over time. While a number of complex statistical procedures mainly based on principal components and cluster analysis have been developed to analyse repertory grid data, they are not particularly user-friendly for clients (and, to be honest, most therapists). Simple grids can however be represented in a basic graphical format called performance profiling (Butler and Green, 2007).

Goal attainment scaling

Kiresuk, Smith and Cardillo (1994) attempted to develop a practical system for assessing the effectiveness of interventions that was both individual and standardised. Although initially employed in mental health settings, the approach has subsequently been adapted for use across a very wide range of human services such as education and community and social work. The basic principle behind the goal attainment scaling (GAS) approach is that client and therapist negotiate a customised set of goals that capture the aspirations they share for their work together. Each of these goals is translated into a simple five-point ordinal scale thus:

+2 Much better than expected outcome
+1 Better than expected outcome
 0 Expected outcome
−1 Worse than expected outcome
−2 Much worse than expected outcome

The parties attempt to define each of the cells on this scale in enough operational detail to allow a credible subsequent evaluation of which descriptor best represents the actual outcome of their efforts. The client is also asked to weight each of the therapeutic goals according to the level of importance he or she attaches to each of the issues identified in the goal attainment discussions. The effectiveness of the intervention is subsequently evaluated against the criteria defined on each goal attainment scale, generally via self-evaluation but potentially using an independent rater (which has proved useful in services for people with learning difficulties). Unlike the scaling questions devised by solution-focused psychotherapists, the GAS system does not lend itself easily to collecting sessional feedback but it does have the advantage of being able to collect cumulative data on how successfully an organisation or individual therapist has been in meeting client expectations. Some questions have been raised about the psychometric legitimacy of pooling data from ideographic measures in this way. For example, can it be assumed that gaps between all the points on all the scales are equidistant (like rungs on a ladder)? However, an accumulated body of empirical research suggests that the statistical justification for this approach to summation of scores is 'good enough' for most practical purposes (Marson, Wei and Wasserman, 2009)

Personal Questionnaire

Another attempt to bring a structured and systematic approach to the challenge of monitoring clients' progress is the Personal Questionnaire (Shapiro, 1961), which also respects the clients' unique priorities and uses their own words in constructing the scale. Clients are invited to make a series of statements about the difficulties with which they are struggling (e.g. 'I just can't put up with this pain'). They are then asked to produce two further statements, one that represents a recovery position (e.g. 'I can generally manage the pain OK') and one that represents an improvement position (e.g. 'Sometimes I feel I can handle the pain all right'). At the beginning of all subsequent sessions the clients are asked to say which of all possible pairs of these statements more accurately represents the way they are feeling at that moment. Shapiro borrowed this method of repeated comparisons from psychophysics and it has the dual benefit of allowing the therapist to locate the client on a precise position on the continuum from illness (his term) to recovery while providing a check on the reliability of the replies because logical inconsistency will cast doubt on the accuracy of the data. Shapiro's initially rather cumbersome procedure has been simplified by several of his followers (Elliot, Shapiro and Mack, 1999; Morley, 2002) but the approach remains time-consuming for both clinician (who must collect appropriately worded statements and construct the questionnaire) and client (who must make a series of similarly phrased judgements at each administration).

Although each of the idiographic approaches described in this section have unique characteristics, they tend also to share a common set of strengths and limitations. On the plus side, a commitment to idiographic measurement allows the clinician to develop instruments that are both uniquely relevant to individual clients and are phrased in terms that make personal sense to them. Furthermore, the negotiation of agreed goals and co-construction of tools for measuring outcome establishes a climate of collaboration that probably enhances the therapeutic alliance between the parties. On the debit side, this consultative process tends to take a long time and therapists are notoriously resistant to making even relatively minor adjustments to their established practices (Brown, Dreis and Nace, 1999). There is also the significant challenge of interpreting results. At a single-case level there is little problem in using clients as their own controls. We can recognise that personally salient goals have been achieved or that criteria for reliable change on individualised indicators have been met. What we cannot do is make confident comparisons about the effectiveness of interventions across different clients treated by different clinicians. In an era of increasing economic awareness and professional accountability this is a considerable limitation.

Normative Approaches

As explained in previous chapters of this book, the evidence-based practice movement in mental health relies largely on the results of

RCTs of various forms of psychotherapy as assessed using psycho-metrically sound outcome measures of symptom improvement. These evaluations are usually conducted on three occasions – pre-treatment baseline; end of treatment assessment; and post-treatment follow-up. Generally speaking, the measures chosen by therapy outcome researchers have been selected on scientific grounds and were not primarily designed for regular clinical use. They will prob-ably take too long to complete and score to be practical as a vehicle for providing clinicians with ongoing sessional feedback on their clients' progress. However, several brief variants of established research measures of psychopathology have been developed for repeated administration and have been validated against their lengthier progenitors. They can be usefully categorised as condition specific or generic in focus.

Condition-specific Measures

Within the United Kingdom, a government-led initiative to improve access to psychological therapies (the IAPT project) has incorpo-rated the collection of client feedback into its basic modus operandi. The scheme has been designed according to evidence-based practice principles. Clients seeking help are given a provisional diagnosis and then offered one of a range of empirically supported interventions. For example, those diagnosed with depression might be encouraged to take some structured exercise or follow a programme of behav-ioural activation. The IAPT formula aims to provide an initial rapid 'low intensity' response to clients' psychological difficulties. The effectiveness of all treatment interventions is closely monitored and swift referral on to so-called 'high intensity' therapies can be made when needed. The primary political driver behind this initiative has been the promise of supporting large numbers of people who are in receipt of state benefits because of some form of mental incapacity to return to paid employment.

The initial focus of the IAPT initiative was to offer treatment to working-age adults who suffered from common mental health problems of anxiety and depression. It therefore made sense to adopt simple screening tools that clients could complete as part of every consultation they had with the service. Furthermore, because IAPT therapists have been encouraged to use a range of communication media in their work (e.g. telephone and email contacts as well as face-to-face discussions), these measures needed to be brief and easy to complete. The two assessments adopted by the IAPT scheme for universal administration were the Patient Health Questionnaire (PHQ-9) and the Generalised Anxiety Disorder Assessment (GAD-7). Both these measures are subsets of a longer questionnaire, the Prime-MD, which was developed for use in general medical practice and supported by the pharmaceutical company Pfizer. The PHQ-9 is a nine-item scale designed to assess degree of depression (Kroenke, Spitzer and Williams, 2001) while the GAD-7 is a seven-item scale used to gauge levels of anxiety (Spitzer *et al.*, 2006). Scoring and interpretation of the measures are straightforward. Both measures are psychometrically sound (Löwe, *et al.*, 2004) and reliability and validity seem unaffected when the assessment is conducted over the phone (Pinto-Meza *et al.*, 2005). The IAPT resource pack also includes other condition-specific measures (e.g. for PTSD and social phobia) to enable clinicians to make regular appraisals of client progress, but not all are as well suited to sessional administration as the PHQ-9 and GAD-7. For example, the scale for assessing obsessive-compulsive symptoms has 42 items and asks clients to reflect on their experiences over the preceding month.

A particular strength of the IAPT philosophy is the manner in which this flow of feedback from clients is used to inform the regular supervision that is provided for therapists providing both low and high intensity interventions. The implications of the practice-based evidence movement for training mental health professionals will be considered in greater detail in a subsequent chapter of this book.

Generic Measures of Mental Health

There are two approaches to developing outcome measures that are not designed to assess treatment progress for individuals with a specific psychiatric diagnosis. The first is to produce an omnibus instrument that includes items covering a wide range of psychological problems. This strategy offers a comprehensive assessment of client functioning that aims to capture the experiences of a wide range of individuals seeking psychological help. Inevitably these instruments are none too short. The second approach is to create a briefer global measure that offers a 'big picture' analysis of how the client is coping. These instruments are easy to administer and score but may overlook some of the important personal circumstances of individual clients. So both designs have their strengths and corresponding limitations.

CORE

CORE-OM stands for Clinical Outcomes in Routine Evaluation Outcome Measure. It was originally intended to provide a fee-free system for UK practitioners and managers within mental health services to assess the effectiveness of the psychological treatments they, and their organisations, were providing using a single compact measure. The original CORE-OM (Evans *et al.*, 2000) includes 34 items all scored on a five-point scale. A total score of <20 is considered healthy while a total score of >85 indicates a severe level of client distress with various intermediary stages. A reduction of five points or more is required to meet the criteria for reliable change. The initial intention was that the CORE-OM would be a pre- and post-treatment measure that would be suitable for a wide range of clients receiving an equally wide range of psychological therapies. It was intended to be neither condition nor model specific. The CORE-OM was to be a tool designed to collect everyday 'practice-based evidence' from working clinicians (Barkham *et al.*, 2006). Much of the early data was collected 'on our patch' within the NHS in Yorkshire, UK. Interestingly, it was our experience that therapists initially saw the completion of the CORE assessments as essentially a secretarial exercise conducted by administrative staff to satisfy managers' curiosity. They were suspicious of the motives underlying the project and very rarely used the data provided by their clients to inform the nature of the treatment they delivered. Over time that stance has shifted particularly with the development of briefer 10- and 5-item versions of the original CORE-OM questionnaire that can be used on a sessional basis to track client change. All these questionnaires (along with separate versions designed for use by young people and those with learning disabilities) remain fee-free and can be provided directly to clients as well as to their therapists. The CORE brand makes its money by charging organisations to use its sophisticated computer software systems to monitor the quality of services they provide to their various customers (Evans *et al.*, 2006).

The OQ-45

The bulk of the research evidence investigating the impact of ongoing client feedback on therapy outcomes that was reviewed in the preceding chapter has been conducted by Lambert and his colleagues (Lambert, 2010). Their measuring instrument of choice has been the OQ-45 – another omnibus measure constructed following similar principles to the CORE-OM but explicitly designed to monitor client well-being on a weekly basis during routine care. Lambert sees this habitual gathering of information as the psychic equivalent of having your blood pressure recorded every time you visit the doctor.

As its name suggests, the OQ-45 is a 45-item scale that is reckoned to take between five and seven minutes to complete (Lambert *et al.*, 2004). All questions are given a rating of 1–4 and inquire into aspects of the client's social role functioning as well as their experience of a range of psychopathological symptoms. The majority of the items (36 vs. 9) are phrased negatively rather than positively. The basic scoring of the questionnaire is reasonably straightforward with a clinical cut-off point of less than 64 and a reduction of 14 points from pre-treatment baseline needed to meet the statistical criterion for reliable improvement. However, Lambert and his colleagues have developed a sophisticated feedback system for therapists that provides details of how well (or badly) treatment is progressing in comparison with empirical projections of the expected course of successful interventions with particular client groups. The 'traffic light' feedback system described in the preceding chapter was designed to alert clinicians when their clients were at high risk of treatment failure or prematurely dropping out of therapy. A later development of the feedback system also provided clinicians with a number of support tools that they might employ in response to the 'red for danger' signal. For example, if therapy is not 'on track', the clinician might employ measures to gauge the quality of the thera-peutic alliance or assess how well the client's social support system is functioning (Whipple *et al.* 2003).

The sophistication of this level of data analysis requires computer rather than hand scoring of OQ-45 responses. For this reason, clients are requested to complete their questionnaires before each therapy appointment and information on their progress is therefore only available to their therapist at the subsequent session. Somewhat sur-prisingly (from our perspective), Lambert and his colleagues have not found that providing progress reports for clients, as well as their therapists, improves outcomes, so this service does not appear to be part of their usual treatment package.

The original OQ-45 has undergone a number of revisions and developments including a shorter version for general use (the OQ-30) and a version designed for use with, and by, children and adolescents (the Y-OQ). All are psychometrically sound. Lambert and his colleagues have also employed the feedback procedures described as part of an organisational service to a managed care provider (PacifiCare) in the United States to improve the monitoring of both patient outcomes and therapist performance (Brown *et al.*, 2005).

The Outcome Rating Scale

The ORS is an archetypal example of a brief global measure of psy-chological functioning. It is short (consisting of only four items). It is easy to use (clients put their mark on a 10 cm visual analogue scale). Scoring and interpretation are uncomplicated (marks are translated to a maximum total score of 40; anything below 25 falls in the clinical range; and an increase of 5 points or more represents a statistically reliable improvement). Tracking change over time is equally straightforward (usually using a cumulative graph). While probably not as psychometrically robust as, say, the OQ-45, the ORS nonetheless correlates decently with a number of other generic measures of psychological functioning (Duncan and Miller, 2008) such as the Symptom Checklist-90-Revised (SCL-90-R) (.57) and the CORE-OM (.67).

The ORS is intended to be completed at the beginning of every therapy session and to prompt immediate discussion of the evidence it provides. The ORS was designed to be used in tandem with the SRS, which is a brief measure of the therapeutic alliance that closely mirrors the format of the ORS. The SRS (Duncan *et al.*, 2004) is administered and scored at the end of each therapy session and is intended to provide the clinician with immediate feedback of the client's experience of that particular therapeutic episode. As described in the previous chapter, Miller and Duncan, like Lambert, have also developed an organisational consultancy service entitled the Part-ners for Change Outcome Management System (PCOMS) for healthcare providers who wish to use the ORS and SRS to monitor their operations (Miller *et al.*, 2005).

The use of the ORS and SRS in everyday clinical practice will be illustrated in a series of case examples in the next chapter.

Conclusion

There is one salutary lesson to be learned from the evidence reviewed in this chapter. We psychotherapists are not as good at judging the effectiveness of the treatment we provide as we think we are. Fortu-nately there are a number of ways in which we can gain a closer appreciation of our clients' experiences. All the measures described have their strengths and limitations. One of those limitations is that they rely on a single source of information – the client's self-report. However, if you are going to restrict yourself to but one way of judging somebody's psychological well-being, it's probably as well to hear it from the proverbial 'horse's mouth' . . .

References

Alicke, M., Klotz, M., Breeitenbecher, D., *et al.* (1995) Personal contact, individuation, and the better-than-average effect. *Journal of Personality and Social Psychology*, 68, 804–825.

Bannister D. and Fransella F. (1977) *A Manual for Repertory Grid Technique*, Academic Press, London.

Barkham, M., Mellor-Clark, J., Connell, J. and Cahill, J (2006) A core approach to practice-based evidence: a brief history of the origins and applications of the CORE-OM and CORE System. *Counselling and Psychotherapy Research*, 6, 3–15.

Bransford, J. and Schwartz, D. (2009) It takes expertise to make expertise, in *Development of Professional Expertise. Toward Measurement of Expert Performance and Design of Optimal Learning Environments* (ed. K. Ericsson), Cambridge University Press, Cambridge, pp. 432–448.

Brown, J., Dreis, S. and Nace, D. (1999) What really makes a difference in psychotherapy outcome? Why does managed care want to know? in *The Heart and Soul of Change* (eds M. Hubble, B. Duncan and S. Miller), APA Press, Washington, DC, pp. 389–406.

Brown, G., Jones, E., Lambert, M. and Minami, T. (2005) Evaluating the effectiveness of psychotherapists in a managed care environment. *American Journal of Managed Care*, 2, 513–520.

Butler, R. and Green, D. (2007) *The Child Within. Taking the Young Person's Perspective by Applying Personal Construct Psychology*, John Wiley & Sons, Ltd, Chichester.

de Shazer, S., Berg, I., Lipchik, E., *et al.* (1986) Brief therapy: focused solution development. *Family Process*, 25, 207–221.

Duncan, B. and Miller, S. (2008) *The Outcome and Session Rating Scales: The Revised Administration and Scoring Manual, Including the Child Outcome Rating Scale*, Institute for the Study of Therapeutic Change, Chicago, IL.

Duncan, B., Miller, S., Sparks, J., *et al.* (2004) The Session Rating Scale: preliminary psychometric properties of a 'working' alliance measure. *Journal of Brief Therapy*, 3, 3–12.

Ehrlinger, J. and Dunning, D. (2003) How chronic self-views influence (and potentially mislead) estimates of performance. *Journal of Personality and Social Psychology*, 84, 5–17.

Elliot, R., Shapiro, D.A. and Mack, C. (1999) *Simplified Personal Questionnaire Procedure Manual*. University of Toledo, Department of Psychology, Toledo, OH, http://experiential-researchers.org (accessed on 6 October, 2011).

Eraut, M. (1994) *Developing Professional Knowledge and Competence*, Routledge Falmer, London.

Ericsson, K. (2009) Enhancing the development of professional performance: implications from the study of deliberate practice, in *Development of Professional Expertise. Toward Measurement of Expert Performance and Design of Optimal Learning Environments* (ed. K. Ericsson), Cambridge University Press, Cambridge, pp. 405–431.

Evans, R., Mellor-Clark, J., Barkham, M. and Mothersole, G. (2006) Developing the resources and management support for routine evaluation in counselling and psychological therapy service provision: reflections on a decade of CORE development. *European Journal of Psychotherapy and Counselling*, 8, 141–161.

Evans, C., Mellor-Clark, J., Margison, F., *et al.* (2000) Clinical outcomes in routine evaluation: the CORE-OM. *Journal of Mental Health*, 9, 247–255.

Gordon, M. (1992) Self-assessment programs and their implications for health professions training. *Academic Medicine*, 67, 672–679.

Hatfield, D., McCullough, L., Shelby, D., *et al.* (2010) Do we know when our clients get worse? An investigation of therapists' ability to detect negative client change. *Clinical Psychology and Psychotherapy*, 17, 25–32.

Joshi, R., Ling, E. and Jaeger, J. (2004) Assessment of a 360-degree instrument to evaluate residents' competency in interpersonal and communication skills. *Academic Medicine*, 79, 458–463.

Kiresuk, T., Smith, A. and Cardillo, J. (1994) *Goal Attainment Scaling: Applications, Theory and Measurement*. Lawrence Erlbaum, Hillside, NJ.

Kroenke. K., Spitzer, R. and Williams, J. (2001) The PHQ-9: validity of a brief depression severity measure. *Journal of General Internal Medicine*, 16, 606–613.

Kruger, J. and Dunning, D. (1999) Unskilled and unaware of it: how difficulties in recognising one's own incompetence lead to inflated self-assessments. *Journal of Personality and Social Psychology*, 77, 1121–1134.

Lambert, M. (2010) *Prevention of Treatment Failure. The Use of Measuring, Monitoring and Feedback in Clinical Practice*. American Psychological Association, Washington, DC.

Lambert, M., Morton, J., Hatfield, D., *et al*. (2004) *Administration and Scoring Manual for the Outcome Questionnaire-45*, OQMeasures, Salt Lake City, UT.

Llewellyn, S. (1988) Psychological therapy as viewed by clients and therapists. *British Journal of Clinical Psychology*, 27, 223–237.

Löwe, B., Kroenke, K., Herzog, W. and Gräfe, K. (2004) Measuring depression outcome with a short self-report instrument: sensitivity to change of the Patient Health Questionnaire (PHQ-9). *Journal of Affective Disorders*, 78, 131–140.

Marson, S., Wei, G. and Wasserman, D. (2009) A reliability analysis of goal attainment scaling (GAS) weights. *American Journal of Evaluation*, 30, 203–216.

Miller, S., Duncan, B., Sorrell, R. and Brown, G. (2005) The partners for change outcome system. *Journal of Clinical Psychology*, 61, 199–208.

Morley, S. (2002) *EasyPQ – Yet Another Version of Shapiro's Personal Questionnaire*. University of Leeds, Leeds, http://www.leeds.ac.uk/hsphr/people/downloads/EasyPQ.zip (accessed 10 October, 2011).

O'Connell, B. (2003) Introduction to the solution-focused approach, in *Handbook of Solution-Focused Therapy* (eds B. O'Connell and S. Palmer) Sage Publications, London, pp. 1–11.

Pinto-Meza, A., Serrano Blanco, A., Penarrubia, M. and Haro, J. (2005) Assessing depression in primary care with the PHQ-9. *Journal of General Internal Medicine*, 20, 738–742.

Sapyta, J., Reiman, M. and Bickman, L. (2005) Feedback to clinicians: theory, research and practice. *Journal of Clinical Psychology*, 61, 145–153.

Seligman, M. (1995) The effectiveness of psychotherapy. The consumer reports study. *American Psychologist*, 50, 965–974.

Shapiro, M.B. (1961) A method of measuring psychological changes specific to the individual psychiatric patient, *British Journal of Medical Psychology*, 34, 151–155.

Spitzer, R.L., Kroenke, K., Williams, J.B. and Löwe, B. (2006) A brief measure for assessing generalized anxiety disorder: the GAD-7. *Archives of Internal Medicine*, 166, 10, 1092–1097.

Tracey, J., Arrol, B., Richmond, D. and Barham, P. (1997) The validity of general practitioners' self-assessment of knowledge. *British Medical Journal*, 315, 1426–1428.

Whipple, J., Lambert, M., Vermeersch, D., *et al.* (2003) Improving the effects of psychotherapy: the use of early identification of treatment failure and problem-solving strategies in routine practice. *Journal of Counseling Psychology*, 58, 59–68.

Wilson, A. and Ross, M. (2000) From chump to champ: people's appraisal of their earlier and present selves. *Journal of Personality and Social Psychology*, 80, 572–584.

Wooliscroft, J., Tenhaken, J., Smith, J. and Calhoun, J. (1993) Medical students' self-assessments: Comparisons with external measures of performance and the students' self-assessments of overall performance and effort. *Academic Medicine*, 68, 285–294.

8

Ideas in Action

People load themselves with anxiety and grief because they will discuss their lives as if they were engineers on a job . . . Nice people talk like this and then worry themselves sick for here are the 'problems' but where are the neat solutions, settling them once and for all? They forget that human relationships don't belong to engineering, mathematics, chess which offer problems that can be perfectly solved. Human relationships grow, like trees; they cannot reach checkmate in four moves. (J.B. Priestley [1969] Journey Down a Rainbow)

Introduction

As alert readers will no doubt have gathered, promising though the notion of practice-based evidence appears, there are a number of substantial gaps in our understanding. A somewhat surprising lacuna in our existing knowledge base is that the various research groups who have demonstrated that providing sessional feedback to therapists on client progress improves outcomes in psychotherapy don't appear to know with any certainty how that information has been used. Another uncomfortable aspect of the research literature thus

Maximising the Benefits of Psychotherapy: A Practice-Based Evidence Approach, First Edition. David Green and Gary Latchford.
© 2012 John Wiley & Sons, Ltd. Published 2012 by John Wiley & Sons, Ltd.

far reviewed in this book is that it has been overwhelmingly presented at a group rather than individual level. This bias sits ill with
the convincing arguments already reviewed that there is great heterogeneity in the way that individual clients respond to ostensibly
similar therapeutic interventions. The myth of uniformity (Kiesler,
1966) has no place in our account of clients' experience of participating in the practice-based evidence experiment. There is also an
embarrassing dominance of stories told from the psychologist's
perspective (be they researcher or clinician) even when the model
being espoused titles itself as 'client directed' as well as 'outcome
informed'(CDOI). Haven't the consumers of these innovative services also got a tale to tell? Finally, while the PCOMS package includes
sessional measures for monitoring both outcomes (the ORS) and
alliance (the SRS), there have been remarkably few attempts to
describe, let alone evaluate, the particular contribution that SRS
scores have made to the course of treatment.

All this preamble is our attempt to justify the inclusion of a series
of frankly narrative case studies in this chapter to illustrate how we
as clinicians have made use of both the ORS and SRS questionnaires
in everyday therapeutic work. All the examples that follow concern
the experiences of clients who had been referred to a clinical health
psychology service based in a large general hospital in West Yorkshire
and were treated by DG. Although I have (occasionally) used a
number of other feedback systems in the past, such as repertory grids
(Green, 1997) and goal attainment scales (Green and Yeo, 1982), this
is the first time I have made a concerted effort to incorporate a single
system, the PCOMS package, in every consultation.

The chapter concludes with a few candid reflections from both
the therapist and client perspectives.

When it Went According to Plan . . .

Norma was a 45-year-old woman who had suffered from cancer
as a teenager and had a leg amputated at the age of 15. She subsequently married and had a son in her early 20s. However, Norma

found that her anxieties about both his and her own survival interfered with her ability to bond with her newborn baby. Norma's mother had stepped into a maternal role with the boy and this had become a continuing source of tension within the family. Although Norma had not experienced any recurrence of cancer, she dreaded the discovery of any secondary symptoms. As a consequence, she became increasingly anxious and panicky whenever she was due to attend her annual appointments at the long-term follow-up clinic designed to monitor the physical and psychological health of survivors of childhood cancer. One way she had developed to cope with these disabling fears was to engage in a number of medically related checking behaviours (such as scouring the environment for hypodermic needles), which she hoped would, in some way, protect her and her loved ones from harm. Her view of these beliefs was characteristic of many sufferers from obsessional compulsive symptoms in that she thought the ideas were fundamentally a bit crazy but nonetheless she could not resist the impulse to carry out her rituals 'just in case'.

Norma attended our first appointment with her husband Brian who had ostensibly come along as her chauffeur on a journey of more than 60 miles from their home. However, he was also immediately called upon to check that the consulting room and, in particular, the chair on which Norma was to sit were free of hypodermic needles. I noted Brian's unease at being asked to support his wife in this fashion and we rapidly got down to a serious three-way discussion about the possible origins of Norma's obsessive compulsive disorder (OCD) behaviour and how she might best be helped.

Although I have previously found behavioural techniques devised to treat obsessional compulsive problems very successful (Green, 1980), the approach that Norma and I developed together in this instance was more exploratory in style. Our discussions covered four major themes:

- The challenge of living with the threat of recurrent life-threatening disease – the so-called 'Damocles Syndrome' (Koocher and O'Malley, 1981).

- The impact of Norma's illness on her evolving relationships with her mother and her son. Norma's husband had observed at close hand how this family tale had unfolded and he contributed passionately and constructively to our conversations.
- The perverse way that so-called 'safety behaviours' (Thwaites and Freeston, 2005) that are intended to protect so often end up doing more harm than good.
- The role of consumer preference in deciding ideal follow-up care packages for survivors of childhood cancer.

Over a period of approximately six months, Norma felt increasingly able to confront her fears about a returning cancer. She had a consultation with the oncologist and specialist nurse from the long-term follow-up clinic she attended, and she was able to pose risk-related questions that she had not previously been able to even contemplate. As a result of this meeting, she took an independent initiative to visit a breast-screening unit near her work where radiography identified a number of pre-cancerous cells. She opted for further preventative surgery that she managed impressively. Furthermore, she also found the strength to resist responding to any of her checking compulsions. She reckoned that, because none of these elaborate precautions had prevented the development of the pre-cancerous cells, it was all 'stuff and nonsense' (though her own language was somewhat more colourful than that).

This was undoubtedly a successful and maybe life-saving intervention. How was the process of therapy tracked and influenced by the sessional measures that I collected during each of our meetings?

Figure 8.1 plots both the ORS and SRS scores recorded over the 6 consultations held over an eight-month period.

Norma's initial ORS score fell only just in the clinical range, indicating that despite her anxieties she continued to function surprisingly well at a social and personal level. Brief generic measures such as the ORS do not always pick up particular clusters of psychopathological symptoms and there is an argument for supplementing their use with more focused condition-specific questionnaires. Nonetheless, the changes in ORS scores from baseline to follow-up clearly

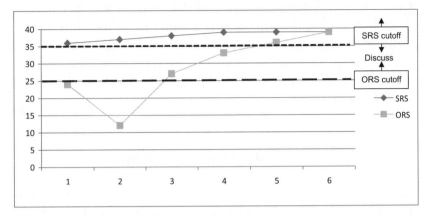

Figure 8.1: Norma – SRS and ORS scores

meet the criteria for both statistically and clinically significant change (Jacobsen and Truax, 1991). The low score recorded at the start of the second treatment session (after a strong sense of therapeutic engagement during the initial meeting) deserves comment. Norma attributed this deterioration in her mental state to an extra-therapeutic event – a very distressing visit to her dentist – and reassured me that she liked the tack we were taking. I have regularly found that it has not been the feedback scores themselves that I have valued most as a clinician but the conversations with clients that they have stimulated.

This principle also applied to the SRS scores that I collected throughout my work with Norma. The graph provides plenty of evidence of consistently positive feedback, which was in complete accord with my sense of the strong therapeutic alliance we were rapidly able to develop and maintain. However, the ritual of requesting a consumer's view near the end of each session had a number of other beneficial consequences. Norma felt able to ask if, in the light of the long distance that she had to travel, we could meet less frequently but for a longer period. It proved straightforward to respond positively to this request so we extended the length of our face-to-face sessions from 60 to 90 minutes and supplemented these meetings with brief telephone consultations. Since Norma's husband

Brian attended all our meetings, we decided that he too should complete SRS forms at the end of every session. Brian used this opportunity to offer his personal endorsement of the approach we were adopting and to explain how much he preferred being cast in a supportive therapeutic role as opposed to the thankless task of checking for dangerous needles.

When it Just Wasn't Working ...

Joanne was a woman who was also in her early 40s. She too had suffered from a childhood cancer that had been successfully treated albeit at a long-term cost to her fertility. When she was about 30 years old, she and her husband had been offered the opportunity to join an assisted fertility programme. After due consideration, the couple had decided not to accept this invitation. A decade or so later Joanne and her husband divorced. She subsequently found herself increasingly preoccupied with thoughts about the family she never had. She felt lonely and experienced overwhelming pangs of sadness whenever she dwelt on what might have been.

We contracted to meet monthly for a series of exploratory therapy sessions in which we would consider ways to help Joanne find a greater sense of purpose and direction in her life. First signs were encouraging. Joanne proved to be an open and thoughtful client who made good use of the space provided by this style of therapy to reflect on her feelings and her future options. Our conversation roamed widely but relevantly and I found myself drawing on a satisfying range of theoretical models in my attempts to make psychological sense of Joanne's experiences (such as solution-focused therapy, positive psychology and personal construct theory). She attended all sessions promptly and gave every indication that she was strongly engaged in treatment. The only problem was that she did not seem to be deriving any significant benefits from our conversations . . .

As Figure 8.2 illustrates, Joanne's ORS score at baseline fell securely in the clinical range and remained resolutely stuck in that position

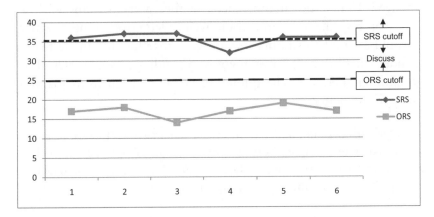

Figure 8.2: Joanne – SRS and ORS scores

throughout our work together. Her SRS scores were consistent with my impression that we had established a decent therapeutic alliance. However, at the end of one session, Joanne's SRS response broke what had become an established pattern. While she appeared to have appreciated the relationship and approach aspects of the interview, her ratings on the 'goals and topics' sub-scale were atypically low. The positive pole of this scale states that 'we worked on what I wanted to work on and talk about', while the negative pole states the reverse ('we did not . . .', etc.). I was somewhat surprised at this feedback because most of the session had centred on a fixed-role sketch that I had written for Joanne according to Kellian precepts (Winter, 1992). I was rather pleased with my efforts. When I asked Joanne to explain how come she had made this judgement, she let me down gently: 'You seemed to be more interested in this approach than I was.' The problem with being an enthusiastic therapist is that it is all too tempting to assume that your clients share your enthusiasms . . .

I tried hard to learn from this salutary lesson and determined to adhere more closely to my client-directed principles. Joanne's SRS responses suggested I had indeed taken note of her feedback but her ORS scores stubbornly refused to shift from the clinical range. We looked at the pattern of scores over a six-month period and both acknowledged that, despite our best efforts, nothing much had changed. Under the circumstances, neither party had any wish to 'carry on regardless'. I said I would write a letter to Joanne in which I would attempt to summarise our work together and invite her to ponder what her next move might be, including possible referral on to another therapist. The quotation below is taken from Joanne's reply to that letter:

> After consideration and reflections on our meetings I think I have moved on in the right direction, while I feel the job is not completed. I shall take on board some of the discussions we have shared and help myself with assistance from family and friends.

This is how Joanne and I concluded our work together. I cannot paint it as a stunning therapeutic success but neither of us judged it an abject failure. It could not, however, be classified as a treatment dropout. I suspect that when therapy is not producing the goods, the most likely outcome is that clients just quietly absent themselves. Joanne and I were able to openly acknowledge our disappointment that we had been unable to find an effective way of alleviating her suffering, and to choose to end our involvement in a dignified and constructive manner. I even managed to find a way of positively connoting the way Joanne had delivered her unambiguous feedback about my over-zealous advocacy of personal construct therapy. Consumer surveys in healthcare settings are notorious for their tendency to elicit an unconvincing 'we are all happy here' message. Joanne had not only been prepared to tell me where I had gone wrong but had done so at a time when I could try and do better next time. I take this as a compliment to the solidity of the working alliance that we had previously established. I also doubt that we could have held such a candid and constructive discussion without the prompt provided by the PCOMS feedback system.

Sticking With It

Despite the strong evidence supporting the effectiveness of psychotherapy, most clinicians are also keenly aware of the limitations of their trade. We are regularly confronted by clients who continue to suffer despite our (and their) best efforts. In the field of health psychology, individuals who have chronic medical conditions will also often find themselves obliged to cope with recurrent crises when their physical fitness is compromised. While there is no straightforward relationship between physical and psychological health, as illustrated by the intriguing phenomenon of post-traumatic growth after life-threatening illness (Baraket, Alderfer and Kazak, 2006), there are a significant number of patients with chronic health conditions who have a legitimate call on long-term psychological support services. It is, however, rarely obvious quite what form that support should take; who should provide it; and for how long.

When I first met Ruth, she was in her early 20s and suffering from an array of debilitating medical problems. She had been treated for Hodgkin's disease as an adolescent; had subsequently undergone a heart transplant; and was severely handicapped by chronic fatigue syndrome. Unfortunately, the immuno-suppressive medication that Ruth was obliged to take as part of her cardiac care meant she was at increased risk of developing another form of cancer. Another side-effect of the treatment Ruth had received was that her ovaries had ceased to function properly. In addition to this challenging set of medical symptoms, Ruth was also deeply frustrated by her home circumstances. She lived with her parents but felt she had a highly unsatisfactory relationship with her father. Under other circumstances she would have moved out but her health problems meant she could not realistically consider independent living. Ruth felt trapped, tired and forlorn.

I saw Ruth on about a monthly basis for over three years. Occasionally she missed appointments because of illness or exhaustion but otherwise she was very committed to our meetings, which she valued highly. Our conversation covered a range of salient topics such as her ambivalent attitude to the medical profession; how to make the most of her limited energy supplies; how she could construct a viable adult identity when predictions of her life expectancy seemed to vary; and whether there was any way to resolve her troubled relationship with her father. As Figure 8.3 indicates, Ruth was

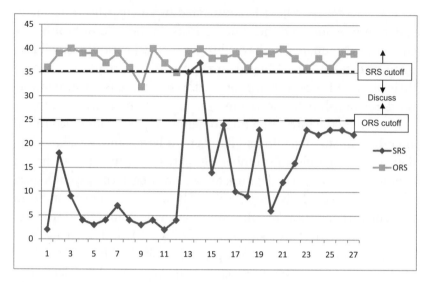

Figure 8.3:   Ruth – SRS and ORS scores

in a bad way throughout the first 12 months of our work together. She was frequently tearful during our sessions and had to endure recurrent bouts of exhaustion.

Although my involvement appeared to be having little impact in reducing Ruth's distress, which remained at a high and worrying level, her feedback on the SRS persistently indicated that she viewed our therapeutic alliance positively. However, Ruth consistently gave lower scores on the 'goals and topics' sub-scale ('we worked on and talked about what I wanted to work on and talk about') than on the other three sub-scales. The discerning reader may sense something of a pattern emerging here. She explained that there was some important material that she felt she ought to bring to our discussions but somehow she never seemed to get round to saying what she intended to say. We reckoned this was partly a function of her wariness about raising personally difficult matters and partly the result of my unhelpful preparedness to fill silences with wise therapeutic observations! I determined to listen more and say less while Ruth committed herself to trying to share her concerns more openly. Ruth subsequently elected to disclose that she had been hoarding some of her tablets for several months so that she had built up a cache of drugs so powerful that she could end her life if ever she felt there was no point in carrying on. We then held a very grown-up conversation about how I should best respond to this important information. Ruth did not want to have what little autonomy she felt she possessed further restricted by her parents monitoring her behaviour even more closely. I did not want to leave her at risk of killing herself. Ruth insisted that she did not consider herself a current suicide risk and that she now intended to destroy all the stored medication. We eventually agreed that I would not alert her family or GP about this disclosure but that we would return to the topic at some point in all our future consultations. While I remain uncertain about whether this was the best course of action to take under those circumstances, I am very clear in my view that Ruth would very probably not have decided to reveal her suicidal plans had the conversation prompted by the SRS feedback not have taken place.

As the pattern of ORS scores shows, this episode did not herald any dramatic improvement in Ruth's well-being. The positive spike in the record occurred some time afterwards and coincided with Ruth and her mother moving into accommodation away from her father. This was the only occasion during my three-year contact with Ruth that her ORS scores fell in the non-clinical range, albeit only briefly. However, the final five sessions suggest that she was coping more successfully with her difficult circumstances than when we had first met (i.e., there was evidence of statistically significant change). At this point I was due to leave the oncology service. Ruth and I reviewed the ORS data and she decided that she would not request transfer to another psychologist but would see how she fared without regular psychotherapeutic support.

I am not sure how and when our involvement would have ended if I had not changed my job. However I am convinced that the data provided by the PCOMS system will aid clinicians who are faced with difficult decisions concerning the discharge of clients who have enduring problems that do not appear to be alleviated by their existing psychotherapy provision.

A Psychotic Breakdown

Although the psychology department in which we both work serves patients with a wide range of medical complaints, some of those individuals can also suffer from major mental health difficulties. Gordon had been diagnosed with chronic myeloidleukaemia at age 14 and had subsequently received a bone marrow transplant. Some four years later he developed some very disturbing psychotic symptoms. He experienced troubling intrusive thoughts and voices (and some visual distortions as well), which directed him to harm himself and other members of his family. Gordon became increasingly self-absorbed and rarely left his family home. He reported having very disturbed sleep and feeling worn down by his constant battle with these pernicious voices. Gordon and his mother initially turned for advice to the oncology team who continued to monitor his medical fitness. They in turn referred the family to me as the psychologist attached to the long-term follow-up clinic.

At our first appointment Gordon was very reliant on his mother to give an account of his circumstances. He was frequently distracted by aspects of the consulting room environment, such as paintings on the walls, and was generally uncommunicative and very hard to engage. He seemed sad, solitary and scared.

Although Gordon would rarely make direct eye-contact with me and such conversation as we managed was often disjointed and peppered with non-sequiturs, he was perfectly prepared to complete both the ORS and SRS feedback forms. As Figure 8.4 illustrates, his ORS scores varied considerably from session to session, which fairly reflected the 'up and down' way Gordon's mood would swing not just from day to day but from hour to hour. On only one occasion did Gordon's total ORS score move into the non-clinical range and he attributed this to a change of medication that had enabled him to have a decent night's sleep for a change.

The SRS feedback also varied considerably from session to session. At our first meeting Gordon gave me the lowest possible rating on all four sub-scales. At the end of our second meeting he awarded me

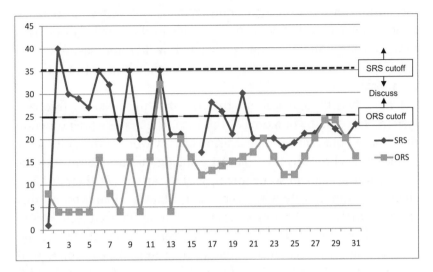

Figure 8.4: Gordon – SRS and ORS scores

maximum marks on all four sub-scales. Thereafter I received distinctly mixed feedback that never met the normative standard described in the SRS handbook (Duncan *et al.*, 2003). Sometimes Gordon would complete the form in a perfunctory fashion and just skim through mid-point ratings without much evident consideration. On other occasions he would use the sheets to make a pointed comment about some aspect of our discussion (e.g. to deter me from pursuing conversations about his future plans). However, Gordon only once opted out of completing the SRS ratings when invited. The voices, he explained, were instructing him not to cooperate with me.

My therapeutic strategy in Gordon's case could be fairly characterised as 'hang on in there until we find someone who really knows what they're doing.' I kept in close touch with the family's GP and referred Gordon to the local specialist service for young adults with severe and enduring mental health difficulties. Unfortunately he did not establish a viable alliance with staff from that team but continued to be prepared to attend appointments with me despite his less than enthusiastic feedback about what I had on offer. However, when the family moved house to another district, I was able to make another referral to the equivalent service in the new location. This time Gordon and his family connected swiftly and securely with team members and I was able to cease my involvement in a timely manner.

I have two thoughts about the role that the PCOMS feedback system played in the outcome of this case. The first is a phenomenon that I have noted on several occasions in my work with adolescents. While some clinicians fear that introducing questionnaires into the therapeutic arena will somehow upset the capacity of therapist and client to communicate with each other, I have regularly found that the opportune use of rating scales has helpfully allowed teenagers to express their views without having to say very much at all. My second observation is the recognition that, in situations like Gordon's, population norms have limited value in interpreting feedback. In this case Gordon functioned as his own control and both his ORS and SRS scores were best understood by being viewed in the unique context of his own previous responses. For example, when Gordon gave me an unremarkable SRS score of 21 and commented that he thought a session had been 'not too bad', I felt quietly elated.

Another Brick in the Wall?

Trevor was 12 years old when we first met. He lived with his single parent mother and had suffered from an unusual gut ailment since his birth. He regularly became so constipated that he needed to take time out of education to be treated with enemas. He had never settled in the secondary school to which he had moved at age 11. His attendance was patchy at best. He could not identify a single friend in his class. He described both the staff and students at the school in very disparaging terms. The teachers didn't know their subject material. The pupils were disruptive and gross. It also emerged from our initial consultation that Trevor had been subjected to hurtful teasing by other boys in his class and that both he and his mother felt criticised by the school over his poor attendance record. I suspected he was getting his retaliation in first. If they seemed to dislike him, he was going to dislike them even more. While this strategy allowed Trevor to keep up his morale and retain a positive view of himself in trying circumstances, it also had its downside. Tensions developed in his close relationship with his mother when she urged him to get ready for school in the morning but he maintained he was too sick to get out of bed. He was also falling behind in his studies, which would ultimately have a detrimental impact on his long-term aspirations to get to university and pursue a career in politics.

Like many adolescents who end up seeing psychologists, Trevor had been referred more because of the troubles he'd caused others than the troubles he himself had experienced. Although initially somewhat reticent and reliant on his mother's support in our sessions, he gradually found his voice. He also took to the ORS and SRS feedback forms with great enthusiasm. He took great care over his ratings and developed his own personal way of conveying his opinions. Rather than simply putting a slash mark across each of the four continuous lines on the two questionnaires, he chose to draw a neat continuous line of his own under each scale, the length of which precisely reflected his judgements. In this idiosyncratic manner he used the SRS to convey his contentment with the way we were going about our business, and expressed his satisfaction at having his preferences taken into account – for a change! He also used the ORS scales to communicate how his sense of well-being varied across contexts. In particular, I noticed a pattern whereby his ratings were consistently lowest on the sub-scale asking how he had been doing socially over the last week in terms of work, school or friendships. Since he did not have a job at this stage, his scores reflected his school-based experiences. Figure 8.5 illustrates how his ratings on this social scale closely tracked his overall ORS scores but invariably indicated a lower level of satisfaction with his lot.

As the data suggest, Trevor and his mother made good use of our sessions together. Over an 18-month period he grew in confidence; repaired his relationship with his Mum; made a number of new friends; and began to manage his health difficulties more

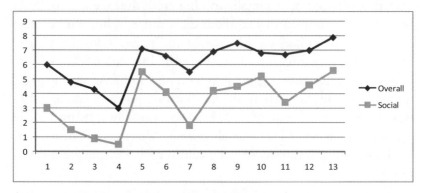

Figure 8.5: Trevor – ORS overall and social subscale scores

autonomously and more successfully. His school attendance record improved markedly but, as the ORS ratings indicate, he continued to feel uneasy in the school setting. However, he summed up his changed status in the classroom as 'I'm just a normal pupil now'. Nonetheless, he reckoned the education system had not seen the best of him yet. In the fullness of time he may well prove to be right . . .

Afterthoughts . . .

Having experimented with both the ORS and SRS for some three years now, I'm in a position to step back a little and review my experiences – and those of my clients.

I am aware through the responses to the various workshops we have run for fellow clinicians that there is a fear among colleagues, particularly those of a psychodynamic persuasion, that the introduction of questionnaires into day-to-day consultations will disrupt the natural flow of communication between therapist and client. The concern is basically that rather than contribute to improved outcomes the use of psychometric measures will ultimately prove antitherapeutic. Although I have more than once felt that the resistance to sessional feedback came primarily from the therapist side of the partnership, the hesitation has generally been expressed in terms of worries about how clients might respond to being asked to fill in forms as an integral part of their treatment. Our experience has been overwhelmingly that our patients have reacted positively to the invitation to complete the ORS and SRS feedback questionnaires. No one has opted out though they of course have the right to do so. Any sceptical readers who suspect that our enthusiasm for this approach may have coloured our clients' inclination to cooperate are probably on to something. Whatever the reason, not only has everyone acceded to our request but we have both had the experience of clients reminding us of the need to complete feedback forms when we have overlooked them. These instances have been oversights on our part that we have been happy to correct, but there have also been occasions when we have made a deliberate decision not to introduce either the ORS or SRS forms because we felt it would have jarred with the mood of the moment. These decisions have been made infrequently and, in our experience, have not hindered the regular flow of feedback between client and therapist.

It is odd, to say the least, that the evidence base supporting the collection of ongoing client feedback in psychotherapy does not yet appear to include investigations into clients' views on the role they are being asked to play. The following quote goes a tiny way to fill that embarrassing gap:

> The session feedback measure sheet was very helpful to me as it helped me to have a clearer insight of how much the issues and problems we talked about were affecting me and how correctly addressing them allowed me to feel much better equipped at approaching the issues and moving forward. It was also very helpful to understand how I progressed from the last and previous sessions and actually see improvement or deterioration and reflect upon why the pattern was so. When progress was noted it gave me a sense of satisfaction and positive gain.

These comments were made by a medical student whom I had supported during his return to studies following treatment for a recurring cancer. His attitude may well therefore be atypical. But then again it may not be.

One of the appeals of the PCOMS system is its flexibility. As the case studies have demonstrated, the ORS and SRS forms can be used by clients with a variety of presenting problems and a range of ages and capabilities. There is an even simpler variation that features a smiley (and not so smiley) faces format that was developed for use with younger children and colleagues from the learning difficulties field have also found helpful. Miller and Duncan (personal communication) also experimented with presenting the ORS and SRS questions verbally and requesting ratings on a 1–10 scale. They found this variant correlated highly with the traditional visual 'put a mark on this line please' format. My own experience of using this approach with a teenage girl whose eyesight had been compromised by treatment for a brain tumour proved very successful. It goes without saying that the spoken format is also well suited to telephone consultations. It is also important to remember that any generic assessment of well-being such as the ORS can be supplemented by the complementary use of symptom-specific measures such as the Beck Depression Inventory (BDI).

Unlike the relatively well-documented feedback system favoured by Lambert and his colleagues (2010), my interpretation of the information I have collected from clients has not been heavily reliant on normative data sets. Rather than wait for computer analysis of results, we have simply 'eye-balled' the ORS and SRS scores and made sense of any notable variation by referring to the individual's previous pattern of responses. Although these collaborative conversations have sometimes been informed by mathematical definitions of clinically and statistically significant change, it has more often been a case of using the client as their own control (i.e., using idiographic rather than normative research methods). In practice, clients tend to have a number of credible theories to explain why their ratings have moved in a positive or negative direction. In our work it has been these reflections, more than the scores themselves, that have tended to influence the future course of therapy. The approach pioneered by Duncan and Miller was never only intended to be outcome informed. It was also fundamentally client directed. When therapists request feedback from their clients, they do not only solicit information – they also convey an important attitude. As George Kelly asserted, 'The client, like the proverbial customer, is always right.'

There are many unanswered questions about the best way to use client feedback in psychotherapy. Which questionnaires to use? When and how to analyse responses? What are the most useful and efficient ways of interpreting ratings? What part can clients play in helping therapists make sense of their judgements? These issues will eventually be answered by well-controlled empirical research – we hope. In the meantime, I have tried to be transparent about my experiences (and those of some of my clients) of using the ORS and SRS measures in the hope that these informal reflections add 'a little something' to the evolving evidence base.

My final thought after more than 30 years of clinical practice is, 'Why on earth didn't I do this before?'

References

Barakat, L., Alderfer, M. and Kazak, A. (2006) Posttraumatic growth in adolescent survivors of cancer and their mothers and fathers. *Journal of Pediatric Psychology* 31, 4, 413–419.

Duncan, B., Miller, S., Sparks, J., *et al.* (2003) The Session Rating Scale: preliminary psychometric properties of a 'working' alliance measure. *Journal of Brief Therapy*, 3, 3–12

Green, D. (1980) A behavioural approach to the treatment of obsessional rituals: an adolescent case study. *Journal of Adolescence*, 3, 297–306.

Green, D. (1997) An experiment in fixed role therapy. *Clinical Child Psychology and Psychiatry*, 2, 553–564.

Green. D. and Yeo, P. (1982) Attitude change and social skills training: potential techniques. *Behavioural Psychotherapy*, 10, 79–86.

Jacobsen, N. and Truax, P. (1991) Clinical significance: a statistical approach to defining meaningful change in psychotherapy research. *Journal of Consulting and Clinical Psychology*, 59, 12–19.

Kiesler, D. (1966) Some myths of psychotherapy and the search for a paradigm. *Psychological Bulletin*, 65, 110–136.

Koocher, G. and O'Malley, J. (1981) *The Damocles' Syndrome: Psychological Consequences of Surviving Childhood Cancer*, McGraw Hill, New York.

Lambert, M. (2010) *Prevention of Treatment Failure. The Use of Measuring, Monitoring and Feedback in Clinical Practice*, American Psychological Association, Washington, DC.

Priestley, J.B. (1969) *Journey Down a Rainbow*, Penguin, Harmondsworth.

Thwaites, R. and Freeston, M. (2005) Safety-seeking behaviours: fact or function? How can we clinically differentiate between safety behaviours and adaptive coping strategies across anxiety disorders? *Behavioural and Cognitive Psychotherapy*, 33, 177–188.

Winter, D. (1992) *Personal Construct Psychology in Clinical Practice. Theory, Research and Applications*, Routledge, London.

9

Transforming Training and Supervision

I have never let my schooling interfere with my education. (Mark Twain)

Introduction

The practice-based evidence movement clearly has a raft of implications for how we conduct our clinical work but this chapter considers a number of ways its principles could both inform and transform our traditional approaches to training psychological therapists. Several commentators (Bickman, 1999; Binder, 1993; Green, 2004) have noted the marked contrast in the resources that have historically been invested in researching process and outcome research in psychotherapy as opposed to investigating the efficacy of our long-established procedures for helping trainee clinicians acquire their professional skills. It appears that the design of the educational curricula of even our most respected training programmes owes more to historical 'custom and practice' than to empirical evidence of proven efficacy. For instance, Bickman cited the belief that doctoral level professional qualifications will improve a therapist's treatment outcomes as one of six 'myths' prominent in the field of mental

Maximising the Benefits of Psychotherapy: A Practice-Based Evidence Approach,
First Edition. David Green and Gary Latchford.
© 2012 John Wiley & Sons, Ltd. Published 2012 by John Wiley & Sons, Ltd.

health (Bickman, 1999). He could find minimal evidence to support that contention. We too sometimes suspect that the widespread phenomenon of 'qualification drift' has been motivated more by aspirations towards exalted professional status than a commitment to improved patient care.

However, there is some undoubted sense in prioritising research into the efficacy of psychological treatments over investigation of the effectiveness of strategies for training psychotherapists. Let's do our damnedest to improve the quality of the product first and then pay close attention to our means of production. Or so the logic goes. Unfortunately, the relentless demands on community mental health services mean that fresh troops are continuously needed to be sent to the front line. Training providers will rarely have the luxury of being able to undertake a 'root and branch' reconstruction of their educational procedures. Running repairs will probably be the height of their ambitions. We think that the incorporation of client feedback into several strands of professional training might be just such a manageable venture.

Clinical Supervision

Ongoing clinical supervision is seen as the 'sine qua non' of both initial training as a psychological therapist and continuing professional practice in that role. The rationale for this resource-intensive commitment is simple. Much like the apprentice's relationship with his master in a medieval guild, novice psychotherapists are expected to provide their supervisors with a regular flow of feedback on their experiences with clients and colleagues. Supervision meetings provide a forum in which supervisors prompt supervisees to reflect on their work in a systematic manner. Where appropriate, supervisors are also empowered to make direct suggestions about shifts in therapeutic strategy. The dual aims of this approach are to provide a quality assurance mechanism that maintains high standards of client care, and to enhance the supervisees' professional and personal development (Hughes and Youngson, 2009). In many ways this is a highly defensible system. During initial training, the supervisor retains clinical responsibility for the treatment provided to clients and is therefore highly motivated to keep abreast of all relevant developments in their supervisee's practice. At post-qualification level, the discipline of regular supervision should ensure that no therapists find themselves ploughing a lone furrow deprived of informed collegiate feedback (Green, 2006). Furthermore, in theoretical terms we would expect supervision to be an effective educational intervention because, unlike say attending a one-off CPD event such as a day conference, all parties who have contracted to regular supervisory meetings have committed themselves to a continuous process of review and experiment (Cape and Barkham, 2002). It is the completion of these cycles of action and reflection that lies at the core of all successful experiential learning (Kolb, 1984).

So it all makes sense but does it work? If we focus on the role that clinical supervision is assumed to play in guaranteeing standards of care, it's easy to see why some have seen improvement in client outcomes as the 'acid test' by which our established supervisory procedures should be judged (Ellis and Ladany, 1997). In a meta-analytic review of the evidence purporting to demonstrate the impact of psychotherapy supervision on client outcomes Freitas (2002) echoed previous criticisms of research in the field (Ellis *et al.*, 1996). The measures employed tended to lack psychometric rigour. Experimental designs did not adequately account for the possibility of both Type 1 and Type 2 errors (missing a real difference between groups, or claiming a difference when there isn't one). The clients treated by supervisees in individual studies were so varied that it was hard to test whether disparities in outcome were primarily related to the nature of the supervision their therapists received. Finally, not all studies had involved a convincingly random system for allocating cases to the intervention or control condition. Freitas' sympathetic analysis acknowledged the challenges in designing and conducting research into the efficacy of supervision, particularly tracking the complex causal chain of events involved, and made a series of recommendations for future investigators to follow, but his conclusions were clear enough. The case that supervision improves client outcomes remains 'not proven' to use the verdict still employed in Scottish Courts of Law.

Supervisory Models

While novice supervisors who are looking for a solid empirical base on which to found their future practice might experience some frustrations at the dearth of convincing data published to date, they might find some solace in the richness of theoretical writing in the field. It is not appropriate at this stage to take the reader on an extensive tour of this ever-burgeoning literature (Watkins, 1997) but one recurrent focus of debate is worth reviewing in some depth. Should supervision be conducted on model-specific lines or are there canons of generic good practice that should be followed by all psychotherapy supervisors whatever their theoretical affiliations? Each of these positions has its own balance of strengths and weaknesses.

It's always refreshing when psychotherapists practise what they preach. If therapists believe that a particular brand of therapy is good for their clients, why wouldn't they be highly motivated to induct their trainees into that way of working? If the process of supervision can itself be informed by the principles of change defined by that theoretical model, then so much the better. Not only will supervisory conversations have an attractive intellectual coherence but the supervisees might also get a taste of what it's like to be on the receiving end of some of their planned therapeutic strategies before experimenting on their clients. So model-specific approaches to supervision are to be commended for their honest adoption of a reflexive psychology and the opportunities for safe practice of techniques that they frequently provide. The limitations of this approach lie primarily in the assumption (already challenged in earlier chapters of this book) that the policy of following prescribed therapeutic protocols will deliver the best results for clients (Pereplechicova and Kazdin, 2005). If supervision functions as a managerial check that the supervisee is adhering to explicit treatment guidelines (basically following the rules), there is a danger that the dominant response to an unresponsive client will be 'more of the same' – except done properly this time! We do not wish to set up a Straw Man argument here. It is of course quite possible to find creative solutions to a therapeutic impasse and still operate within the confines of your favoured therapeutic model. As the saying goes, 'There is nothing so practical as a good theory.' However, the very discipline of working within the constraints of a single theoretical framework that gives model-specific supervision its coherence and intellectual appeal inevitably limits the flexibility with which practitioners can respond to client feedback.

By contrast, those adopting a generic approach to the art of supervision can draw upon ideas from the full panoply of theoretical psychology to inform both their supervisory and therapeutic conversations. While it is possible to imagine a style of supervision that is simultaneously generic and model specific (which might have an exclusive focus on developing and maintaining the therapeutic alliance, for example) in practice, most generic supervision is a looser affair in which discussions roam freely with the broad intention of developing the supervisee's capacity to function as a 'reflective practitioner'. This stance emphasises the importance of supervisees' constructions of the therapeutic episodes that they choose to discuss in supervision (Feixas, 1992) and relies on their preparedness to provide their supervisors with full and honest accounts of their experiences at both a personal and professional level.

Unfortunately there are several convincing research papers that cast doubt on the assumption that supervisees, particularly those in training roles, are capable of providing such full and faithful reports of their practice (Farber, 2006; Hess *et al.*, 2008; Mehr, Ladany and Caskie, 2010) and even question whether they would choose to disclose these details in supervision even if they could!

Both the model-specific and generic traditions in psychotherapy supervision have a long history. However, it is only relatively recently that any systematic 'compare and contrast' research has been conducted to examine empirically whether one approach or the other is more likely to deliver patient benefits. An innovative

Australian study reported by Bambling *et al.* (2006) warrants careful consideration.

The paper reports an investigation of the impact of supervision with a skill (i.e. model specific) or process (i.e. generic) focus on the treatment of depressed adults using problem-solving therapy (PST). This is a structured and well-researched cognitive therapy popular in Australia. All therapists were trained to a demonstrated level of competence in PST and delivered a standardised eight-session intervention to their clients. Participating therapists were randomly allocated to one of three groups – no supervision; skill-focused supervision; and process-focused supervision. Consistent supervisory practice was ensured by manualised training and monitoring to check adherence. The first supervision session served as an introduction explaining to both groups of supervisees what they should expect of their supervisors; then weekly supervision sessions continued as per the two supervision manuals.

The measures taken in this carefully designed study were as follows:

- The Working Alliance Inventory (WAI) measuring the client/ therapist alliance was completed by clients at the end of sessions 1, 3 and 8.
- The BDI was completed at sessions 1 and 8.
- An assessment of client satisfaction was made at the end of therapy.
- Dropout rates were recorded for each condition.

The results of this study proved both encouraging and somewhat confusing for clinicians interested in gaining a better understanding of the mechanisms of supervision, and are worth reviewing in detail:

- At end of treatment, both BDI and WAI scores were significantly better for clients who had been treated by therapists in the supervised than in the unsupervised groups, but there was no difference in outcome between the two supervised groups. Precisely the same pattern held for measures of client satisfaction and dropout rates. Supervised therapists got significantly better results than unsupervised therapists but there was no difference between the two supervision groups.

- Adherence to the problem-solving therapy manual was similar across all three groups and, interestingly, proved unrelated to the final outcome of treatment. However, WAI and BDI scores were strongly correlated as predicted by the therapeutic alliance literature.
- The difference between the alliance scores reported by clients seen by supervised as opposed to unsupervised therapists was firmly established at the end of the first therapy session and stayed relatively constant thereafter. The only supervision discussion to precede this opening therapy session was the initial contracting conversation in which the two parties agreed how they would operate once the official supervision started.

The results of this experiment are reasonably clear-cut. It seems supervision worked in that clients appear to have gained more benefit from seeing a supervised as opposed to an unsupervised therapist, even though all therapists were following a treatment protocol in which they had received recent and thorough training. The specific style adopted by the supervisor conferred no advantage either way.

Quite how these results were achieved remains a complete mystery.

Improving Supervision Outcomes

A number of commentators have been critical of what might be described as standard supervisory practice in psychotherapy. One particular area of concern is the heavy reliance on supervisees' self-report as the evidential basis on which most supervisors operate. At best this is a poor proxy for direct feedback about client progress, which would better come from the proverbial 'horse's mouth'. At worse supervisors might find themselves working with deliberate disinformation: 'What you don't know won't hurt me' was one of the common games that people play in supervision identified by Kadushin in social work training (Kadushin, 1968). The net result has been described as akin to an archer trying to improve his accuracy without ever getting to discover where, or even if, his previous arrows have landed on their target (Bickman, 1999). It is hardly surprising that Lambert has posed the obvious question, 'Where is the client's voice in this process?' (Lambert and Hawkin, 2001). If clinical outcomes have been improved by the introduction of continuous feedback loops to help therapists stay in closer touch with their clients' experiences, would there not be potential benefits in making that information available to those charged with supervising the therapists as well?

The logic behind this argument is compelling. In addition to opening up a direct channel of communication between client and supervisor, this initiative would also help decide which issues should have priority in supervision sessions (where there is rarely enough time to consider all cases in depth) and provide a powerful and credible basis on which supervisors might base their judgments on trainees' competence. It should work splendidly but, as we have already seen, the 'Road to Hell' is littered with therapists who believe they know in advance how things are going to work out in psychotherapy research . . .

An Empirical Study

As noted earlier, tracing the impact of supervision initiatives on subsequent client outcomes is a complex and infrequently attempted task. It therefore makes sense to review in detail a recent study attempting to gauge the effect of providing regular feedback on the progress of supervisees' cases to their supervisors (Reese *et al.*, 2009b), referred to briefly in Chapter 6. This paper describes an exploratory study that allocated 28 Master's level students on two family/marital therapy and clinical/counselling psychology programmes in the United States to a 'feedback enhanced' versus supervision as normal condition. Over the course of a single academic year, these students worked under the supervision of nine different supervisors and saw 110 clients in total. Clinical outcomes were tracked using the ORS sessional measure (Miller *et al.*, 2006) described in previous chapters. For the supervision as usual group, this information was collected and analysed by independent research-ers. In contrast, the 'enhanced feedback' supervisees administered, scored and reviewed this data with their clients as an integral part of every session. Furthermore, they shared this information with their supervisors on a regular basis. In keeping with the PCOMS system recommendations, therapists in the feedback group also employed the SRS alliance measure in a similar fashion with both their clients and their supervisors. Members of both groups received both individual and group supervision every week. The effect of this admittedly imperfect manipulation of the independent variable of client feedback in supervision was evaluated using a series of depend-ent measures chosen to capture changes in the functioning of both the supervisees and their clients:

- ORS scores were completed by clients at the beginning of each therapy session for both groups of supervisees.
- Two measures, one of supervisee satisfaction, the Supervisory Outcome Survey (SOS) and the other of the perceived strength of the supervisory alliance, the Supervisory Working Alliance Trainee version (SWAI-T), were completed by all students in the study at the mid- and end-point of the two semesters during which the study was conducted.
- A measure of self-efficacy, the Counselling Self-Estimate Inven-tory (COSE) was completed by all students at the beginning and end of both semesters.

The results of this pragmatic investigation proved to be interesting, reassuring and surprising in equal measure.

Overall the clients seen by the students on both the college pro-grammes derived significant benefit from their consultations as indi-cated by the differences between pre- and post-treatment scores on the ORS. However, the clients seen by the enhanced feedback sub-group reported significantly greater mean changes (8.9 as opposed to 4.01 points) on this measure. As might have been expected, therapists in both supervisory groups differed markedly in their clinical effectiveness. Effect sizes calculated for those in the enhanced feedback condition ranged from 0.43 to 1.72 whereas effect sizes in the supervision as usual condition ranged from *minus* 0.22 to 1.0. That minus score is worth remembering because it is a rare reminder that not all therapists are consistently helpful to their clients. Pleasingly from the point of view of the supervisors and educators associated with the two training programmes, students in both groups seem to have become more effective over time in that the clients they saw in the second semester derived more benefit from therapy compared with those seen during the first semester. Again, however, greater improvements were recorded for the enhanced feedback (increased mean effect size from 0.70 to 0.97) as opposed to the supervision as normal condition (increased mean effect size from 0.30 to 0.37).

So far we suspect the reader might have construed these results as falling within the reassuring and interesting categories. The analysis of the questionnaires completed by the supervisees rather than their clients may prove more surprising.

Despite the reasonably compelling evidence that the enhanced feedback group achieved better results for their clients than the supervision as usual group, there were no significant differences recorded between the two conditions on the measures of satisfaction with supervision (SOS) or supervisory alliance (SWAI-T). Although trainees in both groups reported an increased sense of self-efficacy as they moved through their training, analysis revealed no differences between the enhanced feedback and supervision as usual groups on the COSE measure on any of the four occasions on which it was administered. Since the ORS data indicated that there were in fact significant differences between the two groups in terms of client-reported clinical outcome, it follows that someone, somewhere is a little out of touch with reality here. When correlations between self-efficacy and clinical outcome scores were calculated, the picture became clear. The average mean correlation in the feedback enhanced condition was .51 whereas in the supervision as usual condition the mean correlation was *minus* .38. Yes, *minus* .38. The higher the therapists' self-esteem, the lower the outcome. This at least goes to show that psychotherapists are not immune to the 'above average effect' so widely demonstrated in the self-appraisal literature (Williams, 2004).

Before considering some of the training implications of this intriguing study, it is important to acknowledge its limitations. There are some serious design flaws that the researchers themselves recognise. Numbers are small. Randomisation to intervention and control groups was partial at best. We don't know how the data on client progress were used by any of the supervisory pairings. Crucially we cannot determine whether making this information available to supervisors provided any 'added value' in terms of client outcome to that already achieved by the use made of those data by the therapists themselves. There is no way of differentiating between the effects of client feedback on outcome (ORS) and alliance (SRS). Finally, of course, we need to remember the allegiance effect (Luborsky *et al.*, 1999). Reese and his colleagues (2009a) have published research using the ORS and SRS in the and so can reasonably be assumed to have some sympathies with the practice-based evidence movement that may well have subtly influenced both the design of their study and the analysis of their results. Further research is undoubtedly needed.

Having determined that the findings of this work should be taken with at least a pinch of salt, it is nonetheless worth considering some of their implications for psychotherapy supervision. First, the students in this study were employing a range of different therapeutic models (both systemic and individual) but the benefits of enhancing supervision with direct client feedback appeared to be universal. So there is something here for those affiliated to both model-specific and generic approaches to supervision. Second, it behoves all those involved in the professional training of psychotherapists to recognise that our trainees will always be imperfect reporters and appraisers of their own work. They, and we, need our clients' help if we are to paint a more accurate picture of our therapeutic effectiveness both corporately and individually. Finally, it appears that supervisors who systematically use client feedback in supervision may well do their supervisees' clients a considerable good turn but their own reputations on the trainee grapevine will probably remain unaltered.

What's Sauce for the Goose . . .

Earlier in this chapter we indicated our respect for the way that supervisors who adopt a model-specific approach in their role transparently practise what they preach. If you believe, as a CBT specialist, that your clients have benefitted from keeping a thought diary to record and monitor their cognitions, why would you not recommend that the trainee psychotherapist whom you are supervising follow the same discipline? In similar vein, if you are a supervisor who has become convinced that therapy outcomes improve when clinicians seek regular feedback on their clients' experiences, will this not have implications for how you choose to manage your working relationships in supervision? Certainly you are likely to encourage your trainees to use some form of ongoing feedback measure in their therapeutic work (such as those described in previous chapters of this book) and to use this information in your supervisory discussions. However, to be fully true to the practice-based evidence code, supervisors would also need to consider how a parallel flow of regular feedback from supervisees regarding *their* experience of supervision might improve educational outcomes for trainee psychotherapists as well as clinical outcomes for their clients.

If trainee clinical psychologists (to use an example with which we are familiar) are on a supervised placement that is an integral component of a university-based training programme leading to the award of a professional qualification, it is highly likely that their educational progress over time will be systematically monitored. Formal documentation will be available to enable the supervisors to assess how successfully the individual trainees are meeting their stated learning objectives. There will even be a structured timetable for reviewing that process at various points during the placement, often assisted by a third party such as a tutor from the training course. While these review discussions may include some enquiry into the nature of the working relationship established between supervisor and supervisee, this is unlikely to be their primary focus. What options are available for supervisors who want to track the quality of their alliance with supervisees in a comparable manner to the way they might look to keep abreast of their clients' experiences of therapy?

There are a number of existing measures that have been designed specifically to measure aspects of the supervisory relationship, such as the SWAI-T mentioned in the Reese et al. (2009b) paper and the Supervisory Relationship Questionnaire (SRQ), a measure developed in the United Kingdom (Palomo, Beinart and Cooper, 2010). However, these are lengthy measures (the SRQ has 60 items) and were designed primarily for research use rather than as a vehicle for providing ongoing feedback in everyday professional practice. There is currently no brief but psychometrically sound instrument for gathering sessional feedback on the supervisory alliance comparable to the SRS developed for regular clinical use (Duncan *et al.*, 2003). A recent doctoral study by Nigel Wainwright in Leeds, UK, has sought to fill that gap (Wainwright, 2010).

The Leeds Alliance in Supervision Scale

Nigel Wainwright's research, which we supervised, aimed to use sound psychometric principles to develop a brief, user-friendly measure of the supervisory relationship that also demonstrated good reliability and validity. The starting point was to review the existing questionnaires and the aspects of supervision measured by them. Although too long to be a practical choice for use every session, several are well established and well regarded. It was important therefore to note the focus of the different items, and ensure that the constructs measured by them were reflected in the new measure. To this end Nigel read through each one and conducted a thematic analysis of the items, producing 12 themes. These were used to generate new items to represent each theme. A pilot measure was produced and tested, and data from this used to whittle down the number of items to three. These measure the approach of the supervisor (focused vs. not focused), the relationship with the supervisor (whether they understood each other) and whether the supervision met the supervisee's needs (whether it was helpful or not). It is not allied to any particular model of supervision but aims to reflect the aspects of supervision that most previous work would agree are important. It uses visual analogue scales (where a cross is placed on a line) and is quick and easy to complete.

Nigel tested the new measure for validity (whether it measures what it is supposed to measure), and reliability (whether it performs consistently and is also sensitive to change) with 137 trainee clinicians. The new measure performed very well. It is valid, correlating highly with existing measures, and reliable – it produces similar results when administered a week apart, but not so similar that there is a concern that it is incapable of detecting change. Crucially it is able to discriminate between satisfied and unsatisfied supervisees.

As it is such a new measure, there is no literature on whether it has an impact on the quality of supervision or outcomes for clients, but our initial work with it suggests that it is easy to incorporate into regular supervision and is at least a useful tool. The Leeds Alliance in Supervision Scale (LASS) is printed at the end of this chapter with Nigel's permission, and you are free to use it in your own practice.

Then Maybe . . .

If the principles of practice-based evidence become more widely accepted by the psychotherapy training community, there are two other developments that tickle our fancy. One has a warm visionary quality about it while the other will no doubt send a minor chill down the spine of some readers. In an inversion of the usual order of things, we shall start with what some might construe as the bad news.

We have both publicly expressed the opinion that it is currently possible for trainee clinical psychologists in the United Kingdom to gain their professional qualification without ever having demonstrated that any of their clients have significantly benefitted from the treatment they have provided. It is important to stress that this is a hypothetical point and we certainly wish to cast no aspersions on the quality of the many cohorts of splendid therapists who have emerged from the doctorate in clinical psychology programme at the University of Leeds on which we have been employed for many a long year! However, there are limitations to the manner in which therapeutic competence is assessed even on that august course . . .

Within the last decade, clinical psychology training in the United Kingdom has embraced a 'competency-based' educational model (Division of Clinical Psychology, 2010). The rationale behind this initiative has been both clear and defensible. First, a professional consensus has to be established as to what the core skills of a capable clinical psychologist (or family therapist or specialist nurse or whatever) should be. A number of novel consultation methods have been developed to help structure this diplomatically sensitive task such as Nominal Group Technique (Horton, 1980) and Delphi Panels (Green and Dye, 2002). Then broadly defined skills need to be operationalised explicitly enough for supervisors to be able to judge with confidence whether trainees have met the standard of performance expected at a defined point in their training. This stage is more easily achieved for some competences that for others. For example, while the correct way of administering and scoring a particular psychometric test will be unambiguously described in the test manual, it is much harder to pin down the ideal format for writing letters to referral agents. Nonetheless, the move to competency-based assessment has delivered a number of distinct benefits to clinical psychology training. Supervisors are much less likely to offer bland, global and generally unhelpful comments such as 'you're doing fine' to their trainees. The structure and rhetoric of competency-based evaluation procedures lend themselves to more specific and explicit feedback. As a result, the supervisees themselves are both more obliged and more inclined to take this feedback seriously. When the views of a credible supervisor are at odds with trainees' prevailing views of their own ability, a healthy cognitive dissonance should ensue (Festinger, 1957) that will hopefully be resolved by the trainee embarking on a fresh cycle of self-assessment.

However, there is a downside to the persuasive logic of competency-based training. It follows the same thread as the arguments concerning manualised training in psychotherapy. Here again we uncover two important implicit assumptions. First, that those people who determined what the competences of a particular professional group should be knew what they were talking about. In saying this, we do not wish to besmirch the reputations of 'the great and the good' in our own or any other trade. Rather, we are reminding readers of how complex research into the mechanisms of change in psychotherapy has proved to be even when the investigatory focus has been on very specific therapeutic hypotheses (Kazdin, 2008). Statements that presume to cover the full gamut of the essential competences of clinical psychologists are therefore acts of faith (or political expediency depending on your point of view). Second, in another repetition of the 'what works in psychotherapy?' debate, there are also reasons to doubt the reassuring assumption that if competent psychologists work competently then their clients will inevitably benefit – as night follows day. This clumsy tautology begs two questions: What is the relationship between therapists 'doing it right' and subsequent outcomes for their clients? How can it be possible to be defined as a competent therapist without having demonstrated that your clients have improved?

If research linking levels of technical adherence to clinical outcomes is anything to go by (Pereplechicova and Kazdin, 2005), there is no guarantee whatsoever that those trainees who receive highest marks on competency-based assessments will prove to be the most effective therapists. The only truly convincing way of deciding the relative competence of a cohort of trainee therapists is to track the results of their interventions over time. In our experience this occurs all too rarely on professional training courses (including our own). There are some good reasons for this troubling oversight. As Wampold's elegant meta-analyses have demonstrated (Wampold, 2001), the amount of variance in therapy outcome that can be

explained by factors related to the 'who' and 'how' of treatment variables is surprisingly, but consistently, small (a mere 8% in total, he
reckoned, of which <1% could be attributed to the use of specific
techniques). In contrast, client and extra-therapeutic factors such as
the resourcefulness of the individual or the chronicity of their problems exert a markedly more significant influence (estimated as
explaining 40% of total variance by Lambert [1992]). It therefore
follows that, if tutors were merely to compare their students' success
rates without recognising important differences between the clients
they had treated, the results would be both invalid and unfair. It
would be like producing a league table of school examination results
while paying no heed whatsoever to the social backgrounds of any
of the pupils. However, we might reasonably expect that most of
these inter-trainee differences in caseload would even out over the
course of an extended period of postgraduate training, though not
to the extent that might be achieved by deliberate randomisation.
Therapy dropout rates for individual trainees could also be compared with typical retention patterns within the services in which
they have completed clinical placements. Overall it should not be
beyond the ken of any psychotherapy training community to collect
more and better data on the therapeutic effectiveness of their trainees. Why do so few seem prepared to do so?

An obvious but perhaps unfair answer is that failure and re-sit
rates would be likely to increase substantially, which would make life
much more uncomfortable for both staff and students. Funding
agencies might start asking difficult questions too if they found
themselves being presented with bigger bills from training programmes whose levels of completion appeared to be decreasing. But
the ramifications of collecting reliable data on the clinical performance of student therapists could spread far and wide. It would be
hypocritical in the extreme to subject trainees to that form of
accountability and not ask their trainers to undergo a comparable
degree of scrutiny. Some fine reputations could then be at stake.
Clinical supervisors and the services within which they work would
also be drawn sooner or later into the practice-based evidence web.
As Shakespeare observed, comparisons can be odious.

This embarrassing scenario is not just malicious anticipation on our part. It is highly likely that whenever detailed information is gathered about the clinical effectiveness of a group of psychotherapists, their performance will be seen to be highly variable (Okiishi *et al.*, 2006; Wampold and Brown, 2005). In a now famous example of the implications of making outcome data public, when the survival rates of various cystic fibrosis treatment centres across the United States were systematically compared, patients attending the best clinics had a mean life expectancy of 46 years in contrast with an overall average of 30 years (Gawande, 2004). Furthermore, the centre in which two of the physicians who had produced the national evidence-based practice guidelines on good practice in cystic fibrosis care worked had only 'average to poor outcomes'. Gawande argues that making such information public is an excellent way of inducing change in poorer performing clinics, as long as the comparison data are a fair reflection of performance. A similarly dramatic spread of competence has also been reported when comparisons of doctors' abilities to diagnose pre-cancerous polyps have been made (Chen and Rex, 2008). So it would be pretty surprising if empirical evidence regarding the treatment outcomes of individual clinical psychologists supported the 'myth of uniformity' that still surrounds therapist efficacy (Kiesler, 1995). No doubt some treasured views of therapeutic self-efficacy (including our own) would need some painful revision. But this immediate 'bad news' for some individual practitioners could prove to be encouragingly 'good news' for the future direction of psychological therapy.

Brave New World?

While Aldous Huxley's version of the future was of an autocratic and over-controlled dystopia (Huxley, 1932), we have a gentler vision in mind for the psychotherapy training community. We imagine generations of novice psychotherapists being painlessly bitten by the practice-based evidence bug. They develop good habits during their training, such as continuously seeking feedback from their clients and honestly reviewing their own therapeutic effectiveness, that will stay with them throughout their careers. They see this form of personal experimentation as a way to integrate research skills and clinical expertise and function as genuine scientist practitioners (Barlow, Hayes and Nelson, 1984). They voluntarily coalesce into like-minded groupings peopled by both professionals and clients – let's call them 'practice networks' – within which everyone strives not just to maintain but constantly improve standards of psychological care: the embodiment of creative accountability, or perhaps accountable creativity.

Well, we're all allowed to dream . . .

References

Bambling, M., King, R., Raue, P., *et al.* (2006) Clinical supervision: its influence on client-rated working alliance and client symptom reduction in the brief treatment of major depression. *Psychotherapy Research*, 16, 317–331.

Barlow, D., Hayes, S. and Nelson, R. (1984) *The Scientist Practitioner: Research and Accountability in Clinical and Educational Settings*, Pergamon Press, New York.

Bickman, L. (1999) Practice makes perfect and other myths about mental health services. *American Psychologist*, 54, 965–978.

Binder, J. (1993) Is it time to improve psychotherapy training? *Clinical Psychology Review*, 13, 301–318.

Cape, J. and Barkham, M. (2002) Practice improvement methods: conceptual base, evidence-based research and practice-based recommendations. *British Journal of Clinical Psychology*, 41, 285–307.

Chen, S. and Rex, D. (2008) Variable detection of nonadenomatous polyps by individual endoscopists at colonoscopy and correlation with adenoma detection. *Journal of Clinical Gastroenterology*, 42, 704–707.

Division of Clinical Psychology (2010) *Clinical Psychology: The Core Purpose and Philosophy of the Profession*, The British Psychological Society, Leicester.

Duncan, B., Miller, S., Sparks, J., *et al.* (2003) The Session Rating Scale: preliminary psychometric properties of a 'working' alliance measure. *Journal of Brief Therapy*, 3, 3–12.

Ellis, M. and Ladany, N. (1997) Inferences concerning supervisees and clients in clinical supervision: an integrative review, in *Handbook of Psychotherapy Supervision* (ed. C. Watkins), John Wiley & Sons, Inc, New York.

Ellis, M., Ladany, N., Krengel, M. and Schult, D. (1996) Clinical supervision research from 1981 to 1993: a methodological critique. *Journal of Counseling Psychology*, 43, 35–50.

Farber, B. (2006) *Self-disclosure in Psychotherapy*, Guildford Press, New York.

Festinger, L. (1957) *A Theory of Cognitive Dissonance*, Stanford University Press, Stanford, CA.

Feixas, G. (1992) A constructivist approach to supervision: some preliminary thoughts. *Journal of Constructivist Psychology*, 5, 183–200.

Freitas, J. (2002) The impact of psychotherapy supervision on client outcome: a critical examination of 2 decades of research. *Psychotherapy: Theory, Research, Practice, Training*, 39, 354–367.

Gawande, A. (2004) The bell curve.What happens when patients find out how good their doctors really are? *The New Yorker*, 6 December, 82–91.

Green, D. (2004) Organizing and evaluating supervisor training, in *Supervision in Clinical Psychology. Theory, Practice and Perspectives* (eds I. Fleming and L. Steen), Brunner-Routledge, Hove.

Green, D. (2006) CPD –why bother? in *Continuing Professional Development for Clinical Psychologists. A Practical Handbook* (eds L. Golding and I. Gray I), BPS Blackwell, Oxford.

Green, D. and Dye, L. (2002) How should we best train clinical psychology supervisors? A Delphi survey. *Psychology Learning and Teaching*, 2, 108–115.

Hess, S., Knox, S., Schultz, J., *et al.* (2008) Predoctoral interns' nondisclosure in supervision. *Psychotherapy Research*, 18, 400–411.

Horton, J. (1980) Nominal group technique. A method of decision-making by committee. *Anaesthesia*, 35, 811–814.

Hughes, J. and Youngson, Y. (2009) *Personal Development and Clinical Psychology*, BPS Blackwell, Chichester.

Huxley, A. (1932) *Brave New World: A Novel*, Chatto and Windus, London.

Kadushin, A. (1968) Games people play in supervision. *Social Work*, 13, 23–32.

Kazdin, A. (2008) Evidence-based treatment and practice – new opportunities to bridge clinical research and practice, enhance the knowledge base, and improve patient care. *American Psychologist*, 63, 146–159.

Kiesler, D. (1995) Research classic: 'Some myths of psychotherapy research and the search for a paradigm': revisited. *Psychotherapy Research*, 5, 2, 91–101.

Kolb, D. (1984) *Experiential Learning: Experience as the Source of Learning and Development*, Prentice-Hall, Englewood Cliffs, NJ.

Lambert, M. (1992) Psychotherapy outcome research: implications for integrative and eclectic psychotherapists, in *Handbook of Psychotherapy Integration* (eds J. Norcross and M. Goldfield), Basic Books, New York.

Lambert, M. and Hawkins, E. (2001) Using information about patient progress in supervision: are outcomes enhanced? *Australian Psychologist*, 36, 131–138.

Luborsky, L., Diguer, L., Seligman, D., *et al.* (1999)The researcher's own therapy allegiances: a 'wild card' in comparisons of treatment efficacy. *Clinical Psychology: Science and Practice*, 6, 95–106.

Mehr, K., Ladany, N. and Caskie, G. (2010)Trainee nondisclosure in supervision: what are they not telling you? *Counselling and Psychotherapy Research: Linking Research with Practice*, 10, 103–113.

Miller, S., Duncan, B., Brown, J., *et al.* (2006) Using formal client feedback to improve retention and outcome: making ongoing, real-time assessment feasible. *Journal of Brief Therapy*, 5, 5–22.

Okiishi, J., Lambert, M., Eggett, D., *et al.* (2006) An analysis of therapist treatment effects: towards providing feedback to individual therapists on their patients' psychotherapy outcome. *Journal of Clinical Psychology*, 62, 1157–1172.

Palomo, M., Beinart, H. and Cooper, M. (2010) Development and validation of the Supervisory Relationship Questionnaire (SRQ) in UK trainee clinical psychologists. *British Journal of Clinical Psychology*, 49, 131–149.

Pereplechicova, F. and Kazdin, A. (2005) Treatment integrity and therapeutic change: issues and research recommendations. *Clinical Psychology: Science and Practice*, 12, 65–383.

Reese, R., Norsworthy, L., and Rowlands, S. (2009a) Does a continuous feedback system improve psychotherapy outcome? *Psychotherapy: Theory, Research, Practice, Training*, 46, 418–431.

Reese, R., Usher, E., Bowman, D., *et al.* (2009b)Using client feedback in psychotherapy training: an analysis of its influence on supervision and counselor self-efficacy. *Training and Education in Professional Psychology*, 3, 157–168.

Wainwright, N.A. (2010) The development of the Leeds Alliance in Supervision Scale (LASS): a brief sessional measure of the supervisory alliance. Doctoral thesis. University of Leeds.

Wampold, B. (2001) *The Great Psychotherapy Debate. Models, Methods and Findings*, Lawrence Erlbaum, Mahwah, NJ.

Wampold, B. and Brown, G. (2005) Estimating variability in outcomes attributable to therapists: a naturalistic study of outcomes in managed care. *Journal of Consulting and Clinical Psychology*, 73, 914–923.

Watkins, C. (1997) *Handbook of Psychotherapy Supervision*, John Wiley & Sons, Inc, New York.

Williams, W. (2004) Blissfully incompetent. *Psychological Science in the Public Interest*, 5, 1–2.

The Leeds Alliance in Supervision Scale

The Leeds Alliance in Supervision Scale (LASS) was developed as a sessional measure of the supervisory alliance.

The LASS is based upon a number of research measures designed to tap the supervisory alliance, and a number of alliance theories that underpin these measures.

The LASS should be completed *at the end* of each supervision session, in the last 10 minutes. Completion of the LASS provides an opportunity for the supervisee to provide feedback on how they felt about the supervisory working alliance in that session. This feedback can then be used as a discussion point, opening up a conversation about how the supervisee and supervisor feel about the supervisory alliance.

Completion of the LASS in each supervision session also allows for changes in the alliance to be monitored and discussed by both supervisee and supervisor.

The aim of the LASS is to promote open feedback and discussion about the supervisory alliance so that it can be fostered and used as an effective component of clinical supervision.

Please note: the length of the visual analogue scales is designed to be 10 cm; take care that they do not change when being photocopied.

The Leeds Alliance in Supervision Scale (LASS)

Instructions: Please place a mark on the lines to indicate how you feel about your supervision session

This supervision session was not focused	(Approach) I--------------------------------I	This supervision session was focused
My supervisor and I did not understand each other in this session	(Relationship) I--------------------------------I	My supervisor and I understood each other in this session
This supervision session was not helpful to me	(Meeting my needs) I--------------------------------I	This supervision session was helpful to me

Wainwright, N.A. (2010) The development of the Leeds Alliance in Supervision Scale (LASS): a brief sessional measure of the supervisory alliance. Doctoral thesis. University of Leeds.

10

Conclusions and Some Recommendations

'Your talk,' I said, 'is surely the handiwork of wisdom because not one word of it do I understand.' (Flann O'Brien [1967] *The Third Policeman*)

Introduction

In this chapter we try and tie up the different topics we have discussed, pull out the most useful ideas for practice and give some final guidance on how they might be used to make all of us better therapists. For those looking for a quick and handy guide, there's a (tentative) list of recommendations at the end of this chapter.

If you are still reading, we'll dip into the previous chapters to try to make sense of the confusing – but fascinating – current state of the literature on psychotherapy research.

Is it What You Do or the Way That You Do it?

There is no question that psychotherapy is an exceptionally effective intervention. It is different from having a friendly conversation with

Maximising the Benefits of Psychotherapy: A Practice-Based Evidence Approach, First Edition. David Green and Gary Latchford.
© 2012 John Wiley & Sons, Ltd. Published 2012 by John Wiley & Sons, Ltd.

someone. Though we don't know quite why it works, there is something about the interaction between a client and a trained therapist trying to understand the client's problems and using their knowledge and experience to guide the client to a solution that is very powerful. We know the confidence the client has in the therapist is important, and probably reflects the confidence the therapist has in what they do. We know that the alliance between the therapist and client is important, but so too are many other factors. The therapy, too, is important in that it needs to be a recognised therapy shown by research to be effective. On the question of whether some therapies are better than others, however, there is no clear evidence.

Given the amount of research demonstrating the influence of a number of factors on outcome, it is perhaps surprising that so much effort still goes into trying to show that one particular therapy is superior to another. As discussed in earlier chapters, though this has generated a great many articles and some very interesting data, no clear winner has emerged. CBT is probably the therapy that – at the moment – most feel is the leading contender, and most often at the centre of heated debate. It is an excellent therapy, accessible but capable of great complexity. We have no reservations in recommending it (among other therapies) and in doing so are unmoved by the debate about whether it is superior or not to others.

Why does this debate generate so much heat? We wonder whether the uncertainties about the mechanisms of change in psychotherapy have led to some insecurity among therapists who fear that this undermines the scientific basis of the approach. Perhaps it makes some feel uncomfortable arguing for therapy as a viable alternative to medication when they see drug trials as being 'more scientific' (though drug trials, of course, have their own problems; see, for example, Turner *et al.*, 2008). One response is to adopt the tools of medical research and apply them to psychotherapy, hoping for either a useful investigative approach or a reflected increase in credibility, depending on your point of view. CBT lends itself well to this approach. It may be broken down into component parts and relatively easily manualised, and the hypothesised mechanisms of action are easily understandable to therapist, medical professional and client. It all sounds very plausible. Our main point is that there is nothing at all wrong with this approach to psychotherapy research, but it only answers certain types of questions. The most important thing, it seems to us, is to avoid simplistic explanations. RCTs are useful but are limited in telling us what happens in therapy. CBT is a good therapy but not necessarily the best. The way CBT is suggested to work may not actually be that accurate.

There may well be a desire for certainty in some psychotherapy researchers with which to banish any doubts. Uncertainty is very hard for many to tolerate, yet in psychotherapy research a great deal remains uncertain and we will, for now, have to live with it. There are many proponents of therapies (not just CBT) who passionately believe that their approach to therapy is the most effective. Our response is to say that, though we can never rule out the possibility that this may one day turn out to be true, belief, no matter how strongly held, is not the same as evidence. Claims for primacy of one therapy over another should be subjected to very close scrutiny because 1) the proponents may really want to believe this is true and therefore not be as impartial as they might be (and there are also likely to be allegiance effects), and 2) if true, this would be extraordinarily important, so we would need to be convinced it was a reliable and durable finding.

At the moment, then, two camps can be identified amid the uncertainty and they are at the centre of what Bruce Wampold (2001) has called 'the great psychotherapy debate'. One believes that technique is the most important factor in therapeutic change and the other that it is but one of many factors, less important than the alliance or the 'common factors' of therapy. The debate has sparked some fascinating research, and a spread of thoughtful and provocative ideas (e.g. Hubble, Duncan and Miller, 1999). It's a very interesting time to be a therapist.

In our view, the work produced by both camps enlivens the debate and adds to the richness of the data that inform the ongoing discussion. We don't as yet see much convincing evidence that one therapy is more effective than another for particular problems, but we understand the reason for looking. It may be that all attempts to show, say, that CBT has an advantage for OCD are undermined by the sheer number of other factors affecting the outcome of therapy so that any advantage for type of therapy gets lost in the mix. On the other hand, a finding like this may yet emerge clearly from the literature and it may turn out to be robust enough to stay the test of time (or at least until usurped by an even better therapy). In that case we would be foolish not to take notice of the benefits for this therapy with a particular client group, until research proves otherwise, so therapists might be advised to adapt their approach when working with clients with particular problems. This is not without potential pitfalls, however. For example, is there a good fit with the client's wishes and the therapist's style and confidence? As we saw in Chapter 3, the requirements for training therapists to a level at which they can reliably deliver a new treatment is no easy undertaking.

Regardless of the messiness of the implications, research focused on technique is clearly potentially useful. On the other hand, it would also be foolish if such research were the only (or even the major) focus of work on psychotherapy. If our research is to be truly guided by evidence, we need complementary approaches to research using the RCT, research that opens the black box of therapy. We also need to acknowledge the many other ways of improving outcome that do not focus on technique, the evidence for which is often already available.

What's Happening?

As if all this uncertainty wasn't enough to unnerve even the most confident of therapists, we saw in Chapter 3 that there is very little evidence even for the most celebrated mechanisms of action proposed to be the key ingredients in our major therapies. To be fair, it's actually very hard to show a causal link between a therapeutic technique and client outcome, and just because we have little evidence now does not mean that the theories are wrong. We feel justified in pointing out, however, that proponents of all therapies tend to skip over this part of the evidence base in the very many papers and books they write about the theory and practice of their therapy. Just because experienced and wise researchers reach a consensus that, say, a formulation based on sound CBT principles is a key part of successful outcome in CBT does not in itself make this true. We'd point out too that the great effort that has gone into the training of practitioners to achieve an agreed standard of proficiency in particular therapies also – with a few honourable exceptions (e.g. Keen and Freeston, 2008) – tends not come clean about the variability in practice of therapists already meeting those standards. Mechanisms of change in psychotherapy are undoubtedly difficult to investigate. First, therapist and client may have different opinions about what works, and without a rigorous experimental design it's pretty much impossible to say who (if any) might be right. Client views are obviously the most valuable, but may not be accurate. It's perfectly possible, for example, for clients to feel that a therapy has been helpful when actually it has done them harm, as was found in research on de-briefing after trauma (Rose *et al.*, 2002).

Second, if therapists and/or clients are enthusiastic about a therapy and believe that a particular component is really important, a successful outcome may naturally be attributed to this component by them. In this way, characteristics that are distinctive of new therapies become accepted and talked about, and ways of training other therapists in the technique are developed. The accumulating evidence, however, tends to stay at the level of proving general effectiveness against no-treatment conditions. Therapies, as with so many other things in Western society, are subject to the vagaries of fashion. Old therapies tend not to become disproved, but instead get replaced by newer, more fashionable models. It's rare that a component of a therapy can be dissected and evaluated in such a way as to allow a comprehensive assessment of its contribution to outcome. Finger movement in EMDR, as described in Chapter 3, is an unusual example of a component that does lend itself to such an assessment. As you'll recall, alternative ways of occupying working memory were found to be equally effective (Gunter and Bodner, 2008). The years since the publication of this study have not seen a noticeable decline in the claims made for finger movements by advocates of EMDR, however. One of our colleagues even has a machine that flashes lights synthesising the sideways movement of fingers in EMDR (presumably to save them the effort of moving their own fingers). We suspect that this machine lends an air of scientific credibility to their EMDR sessions and the confidence it inspires in client and therapist may well make a difference to outcome, but we seriously doubt that any effect is actually due to the direction of movement of the lights.

Third, therapy is just so complicated. Demonstrating the effect of single variables against the background of so many others is daunting. Think of the number of different variables influencing outcome in a single case – the therapist (therapeutic orientation, confidence, experience, interpersonal style, training, etc.), the client (nature and severity of problem, interpersonal style, cultural background, readiness to change, preferences for therapy, social situation, etc.), the therapy (explanatory model of the client's problem, hypothesised mechanisms of action, particular techniques such as homework tasks), the setting (number of sessions, context, etc.). And this will be different between every combination of therapist and client, even between individual sessions. In addition, we know that the contribution of the client far outweighs that of the therapist in terms of influence on outcome. Against this background it is understandably difficult to demonstrate the unique contribution of one component of therapy. Further, it may well be that the contribution is not fixed – it may vary depending on interactions with other characteristics. Actually, a moment's thought about the complexities of human behaviour suggests that this is far more likely to be a true representation of reality in therapy.

Shadish and Sweeney (1991) have described this issue in terms of the need to identify therapeutic moderators (characteristics that affect the impact of a treatment on outcome) and mediators (variables that directly intercede between treatment and outcome). They make the point that these may differ between different therapies. For example, one therapy may work well for a particular problem when delivered by any therapist; another therapy may be equally effective for this particular problem but only when delivered by an experienced therapist (experience as moderator). Similarly, outcome in

couples' therapy may ultimately depend upon improved communication between the couple, but different therapies may influence this
in different ways (improved communication as mediator). Basically,
they argue that therapeutic orientation may well make a difference
to outcome, but by virtue of its moderating and mediational effects.
Generalisations therefore are problematic, and the ability to map
such relationships in most psychotherapy research is limited by the
design.

Does this matter? We think it's a good thing that we are becoming
more sophisticated in our appreciation of the complexities of therapy
and a focus on the dynamic undercurrents of therapy may well point
the way to improved interventions. We should be mindful, too,
however, of Rosenzweig's notion from 1936: maybe the important
variable is whether client and therapist believe a therapy to be effective. In this case, what is really required of the different explanations
of distress and proposed mechanisms of change of different therapies is that they are plausible to those using them[1].

If this is all getting a bit too much, we offer a little metaphor.

Evidence-based music

For several years now an influential body of music researchers have
claimed that rock is the best music. They have conducted several
RCTs looking at the musical appreciation of listeners, comparing a
rock CD with a treatment as usual condition in which they listen to
a blank CD. Most show more enjoyment listening to the rock CD.
Such research has led to claims that all musicians now need to move
with the times and play rock. More controversially, the researchers

---

[1] In Victorian times, this would probably have involved allusions to magnetism;
when Rosenszweig wrote this paper, theories of personality. More recently, hypothesised links to neuroscience have been used in an attempt to give credence to a
number of therapies, from neurolinguistic programming to EMDR. Currently, with
the growth of interest in third-wave cognitive therapies such as mindfulness, there
seems particular interest in citing spirituality as an inspiration.

have carried out some trials comparing rock with other forms of music such as jazz, and claimed superiority. This has led to a backlash among jazz lovers who argue that research on jazz also gets good results, though it's not as popular a topic. The big issue in the literature, though, is what are the factors that effect the enjoyment of listeners? Advocates of rock music argue that it is the guitar solo, but so far no association has been found to link this with overall enjoyment. Some rock musicians don't even do solos and people still like them. Others have questioned whether it is the type of music or something else such as the skills of the performer that makes the difference, leading to the ill-fated trial comparing Miles Davis on banjo with Elvis Presley on jazz trombone. A new notion is that it is, perhaps, a mixture. Perhaps it also depends on the context: rock might have the advantage at parties because it leads to dancing, though many people might also end up dancing to jazz when moderated by beer. Perhaps, too, it all depends on the preferences of the listener . . .

What's Next?

We'll be quite happy if this book has contributed in a small way to making you a more sceptical consumer of psychotherapy research, but we also hope that as well as the limitations of research we have communicated some of the benefits. We've also focused on practice-based evidence, with an emphasis on providing a hands-on guide as well as an overview of the potential contribution of this approach to our understanding of psychotherapy. Our approach is to encourage the adoption of both evidence-based practice and practice-based evidence in planning research and guiding our clinical practice. It is not either/or: both are valid and important for our understanding about how and why therapy works, and for developing better interventions in the future.

In reality, it's hard to see how any other way is fit for tackling the big questions facing psychotherapy in the twenty-first century.

Therapy works but we are relatively ignorant of how it works, and why some therapists seem to consistently get better results than others. The relatively recent appearance of the feedback literature is a reminder that there are still many important things to discover, and they may well lead to significant improvements in outcome. The big issues are still out there.

On the ground, there is still a considerable gulf between psycho-therapy research and clinical practice, and we feel that closing that gap has the potential for enormous benefit for both camps. We are not alone in adopting that position (Beutler, 2009). Clinicians need to become more involved, perhaps through scientifically exploring their own clinical work, perhaps through linking with other clini-cians in a practice research network, perhaps through becoming better informed about psychotherapy research and asking awkward questions next time a set of guidelines is foisted upon them by someone or some group in authority.

Above all, we need some appreciation for the fact that, as impres-sive and informative as the literature on psychotherapy is, the com-plexities and limitations of the evidence base means that on the ground, when working as a therapist with a particular client, nothing will guarantee to tell you exactly what will happen next or what you should do!

Improving Practice

How does all this help us become better therapists?

Nothing in the literature has ever suggested that anything other than a bona fide psychotherapy gets results, and when therapy works it works very well. That's the first reassuring note to sound and the implication is that we should have faith in our therapeutic interventions. The literature also suggests that the biggest reason for poor outcomes is that clients drop out and this is a sensible target for improving practice. Apart from that, the literature also points to a large number of variables that influence outcome.

We don't yet know why some therapists consistently do better than others, but perhaps they are attentive to signs of dropout and the needs of their individual clients, and modify their approach accordingly.

So, the first and easiest decision is to incorporate regular feedback from the client in therapeutic work. Our preference is to routinely include an alliance measure as well as a symptom-focused measure. We've given you a few options, but our preference is for the SRS and ORS. Whatever you use, it is important that you make time to check the feedback you are getting and respond appropriately. Again, our preference by far is to follow the method suggested by Miller and Duncan (2004):

- At the beginning of each session, hand out the ORS to the client to complete.
- Score it up straightaway, and have previous forms to hand.
- Discuss that day's scores with the client, with reference to previous scores, how they are feeling today, and what they think it would be useful to focus on in today's session.
- Five minutes before the end of the session, hand out the SRS to the client to complete.
- Score it up straightaway, and have previous forms to hand.
- Discuss that day's scores with the client, with reference to previous scores, how they felt the session went today and how helpful you were, and what they think would be useful to focus on in the next session.

As you can see, the therapist reflects on the meaning of the scores *with the client*. This can lead to some very interesting conversations.

This approach to feedback also accords with our view of the importance of involving the client in the direction of therapy. As research is starting to suggest, this should be pitched at several levels, from respecting a client's cultural or spiritual beliefs, or adapting the style of therapy to match a client's level of resistance, to adapting the therapy provided to match the preferences of the client. As can be seen, the therapist responds to the unique characteristics of the client in various ways. This includes the therapist's empathic reaction to the presentation of the client. It should also include the explicit invitation to the client to express their beliefs about their problem and preferences for treatment, and to jointly plot the direction therapy should take.

Historically, most research into psychotherapy has focused on therapists and what they do. We have always known that the client is important too, of course, and more recent years have seen a growing acknowledgement of this contribution. We know that the client is best placed to give feedback on the therapeutic alliance and progress of therapy, for example. The client also has a role to play in feeding back on services as a whole, contributing to their evaluation and development, and adding a personal voice to the more general discussion of what constitutes a good outcome. Slowly the client's perspective is beginning to become influential in determining the priorities and methodologies of mental health research.

In clinical situations we have evidence that the preferences of the client can influence outcome, and there is encouragement – at least in the United States – for clinicians to implement evidence-based practice thoughtfully, with due respect to 'client characteristics, culture, and preferences'. Tailoring treatment to individual clients, then, seems a legitimate approach to therapy. What might this mean in practice? It is, in our view, essential to recognise that the client is an active participant in deciding both the form and direction of therapy. This should be done not just at the start of therapy, but as a conversation that continues in every session, informed by the process of 'checking in' with the client using the feedback tools described earlier. The literature on feedback in therapy suggests that this is a powerful way to reduce dropout and rescue clients from treatment failure. We suspect it also helps treatment that is already progressing satisfactorily. We further suspect that it not only benefits the individual client, but also has the potential to provide the feedback on performance necessary for the therapist to develop.

In all walks of life, exceptional performance – whether in music or sport – tends to be associated with effortful practice. Often talent is cited as the most important factor, something that gets those of us who do not feel particularly talented off the hook from practising. Research is suggesting otherwise, however, showing that exceptional performance is achieved by essentially the same means as normal performance, just much more of it. Professional musicians, for example, will have put in around 10,000 hours of practice to achieve the appropriate standards (Ericsson, Krampe and Tesch-Römer, 1993). Even Mozart, a figure often cited as a perfect example of a genius born and not made, had studied for around 3500 hours by his sixth birthday, and did not produce a piece of work recognised as a masterwork until he had been composing for 10 years (Howe, 1999). A key notion here, though, is *effortful* practice. This does not mean randomly trying to pick up a tune on the piano while watching TV. It means practising piano, preferably with a tutor providing feedback. If you want to be an elite performer, you have to be dedicated, willing to commit to 'a decade or more of maximal efforts to improve performance in a domain through an optimal distribution of deliberate practice' (Ericsson *et al.*, 1993, p. 400). What does this mean for psychotherapy? Well, most therapists will already be at a professional standard. We suggest, though, that to get even better may require more than continuing to do the same thing. Getting regular feedback from clients, thinking about it, discussing it with clients, and above all being prepared to reflect on what you do and change if need be, seems to us to be an obvious way of achieving *effortful* practice as a psychotherapist.

And Finally . . .

Finally, we offer 10 recommendations for practice based on our understanding of the literature. This list is tentative and may change later if and when we change our minds! We offer this merely as a guide to things that may be worth trying . . .

Box 1: Ten tentative recommendations for practice (or things that may be worth trying)

1. Find a valid therapy that you feel comfortable with and enthusiastic about, and get good at it.
2. Use this therapy, but do not develop notions that because you like it (or perhaps because there is some research on it) it is necessarily better than other therapies.
3. Keep informed about the debate about differences between therapies. At the moment, we don't think there is convincing evidence for any significant differences in effectiveness. Keep checking in though, because the debate is fascinating.
4. Be prepared to change your mind if convincing evidence showing some advantage for one therapy over another for certain types of presenting problem emerges. Be mindful that, if this does happen, you should consider changing what you do and using this therapeutic approach with this particular problem, providing a) you know what you are doing, and b) that other factors such as client preferences do not outweigh the advantages of the new approach.
5. Whatever your therapeutic orientation, consider adapting your approach when necessary in ways that we know can affect outcome. This means taking into account characteristics of clients where evidence shows that these are relevant to how well they do, especially treatment preferences. Discuss this with your clients. Seek and be guided by their opinions. Other important aspects are clients' culture, readiness to change and their spirituality. Keep an eye on the literature for more information on these and other relevant factors.
6. Mechanisms of change in psychotherapy are extremely complex and not at all well understood. Anyone who offers an account reducing this to one theory (perhaps related to the therapy they are promoting) should be reminded of this at every available opportunity.

7.　You are really poor at telling how well your clients are doing. Don't feel bad, because other therapists are no better at it. Do something about it and you can make a real difference to your outcomes, so incorporate routine feedback into your practice. Do this every session, using whatever system feels right or is available. Remember, some people get worse in psychotherapy and we need to be alert to this. Some people drop out and receive no benefit. Using feedback is an excellent way to spot the likelihood of this before it happens. Detailed information on client progress is also likely to prove a very useful addition to supervision.

8.　Think about how you measure what you do and adopt a curious stance towards finding out more. Consider spending time exploring the process of change with your clients using whatever approach suits you best. Consider linking with other like-minded practitioners to measure outcomes and processes using the same measures, sharing your findings and thoughts about what they mean. Join or set up a practice research network in your geographical or theoretical area. And don't forget to include your clients as genuine partners in the enterprise. You could be instrumental in shedding light on some of the important things we don't yet know about, like how therapists actually use the feedback they receive and what sense clients make of the practice-based evidence approach.

9.　Psychotherapy research is extremely good at showing what therapies don't work and should be avoided, and it is getting better and more sophisticated in mapping out the many factors that contribute to outcome. Papers can be difficult to obtain, and sometimes even more difficult to understand. It's worth it.

10.　And lastly . . . remember, we don't know how exactly, and we know it's not for everyone, but psychotherapy really works.

Sorry we took so long to get round to these few basic proposals but we feared you would not have taken us seriously without the lengthy preamble . . .

References

Beutler, L. (2009) Making science matter in clinical practice: redefining psychotherapy. *Clinical Psychology Science and Practice*, 16, 301–317.

Ericsson, K.A., Krampe, R.T. and Tesch-Römer, C. (1993) The role of deliberate practice in the acquisition of expert performance. *Psychological Review*, 100, 363–406.

Gunter, R.W. and Bodner, G.E. (2008) How eye movements affect unpleasant memories: support for a working-memory account. *Behaviour Research and Therapy*, 46, 913–931.

Howe, M.J.A. (1999) *Genius Explained*, Cambridge University Press, Cambridge.

Hubble, M.A., Duncan, B.L. and Miller, S.D. (1999) *The Heart and Soul of Change: What Works in Therapy*, American Psychological Association, Washington, DC.

Keen, A.J.A. and Freeston, M.H. (2008) Assessing competence in cognitive-behavioural therapy. *British Journal of Psychiatry*, 193, 60–64.

Miller, S.D. and Duncan, B.L. (2004) *The Outcome and Session Rating Scales Administration and Scoring Manuals*. The Institute for the Study of Therapeutic Change, Chicago, IL.

Rose S.C., Bisson J., Churchill, R. and Wessely, S. (2002) Psychological debriefing for preventing post traumatic stress disorder (PTSD). *Cochrane Database Systematic Reviews*, Issue 2. Art. No.: CD000560. DOI: 10.1002/14651858.CD000560.

Rosenzweig, S. (1936) Some implicit common factors in diverse methods of psychotherapy. *American Journal of Orthopsychiatry*, 6, 422–425.

Shadish, W. and Sweeney, R. (1991) Mediators and moderators in meta-analysis. *Journal of Counselling and Clinical Psychology*, 59, 883–893.

Turner, E.H., Matthews, A.M., Linardatos, E., *et al.* (2008) Selective publication of antidepressant trials and its influence on apparent efficacy. *New England Journal of Medicine*, 358, 252–260.

Wampold, B.E (2001) *The Great Psychotherapy Debate: Models, Methods and Findings*, Lawrence Erlbaum Associates, Mahwah: NJ.

Subject Index

Notes: Page numbers in *italics* refer to Figures

A-B designs, 90
'above average effect', 181
academia, practice *vs.*, 35–7
adherence, 55–7
  outcomes, 56–7
The Affluent Society, 45
Agnew Relationship Measure
  (ARM), 100
alcohol abstention, 117
alcohol abuse trials, 17
allegiance effect
  client feedback, 124–5
  supervision, 181
American Psychological
  Association
  Division 12 (Clinical
  Psychology), 4
  effective practice guidelines,
  37
  therapy adaptation, 80

anti-social behaviour problems,
  71–2
anxiety disorders
  cancer patients, 153
  exposure therapies, 54
  IAPT project, 142
'at risk' clients, 72
auditory tracking tasks, 50

barriers to treatment, 71–2
Barriers to Treatment Participation
  Scale (BTPS), 72
Beck Depression Inventory (BDI),
  168, 175–6
Begley, Sharon, 1
belief in progress, 2
bell and pad treatment, 48–9
  classical conditioning, 48–9
  operant conditioning paradigm,
  49

Maximising the Benefits of Psychotherapy: A Practice-Based Evidence Approach,
First Edition. David Green and Gary Latchford.
© 2012 John Wiley & Sons, Ltd. Published 2012 by John Wiley & Sons, Ltd.

benchmarking, 94
Beutler, Larry, 37–8
'big picture' analysis, 143
bone marrow transplant, 162
bulimia nervosa, 117

California Psychotherapy Alliance
    Scales (CALPAS), 100
cancer, 153, 156, 159, 162
case studies, 151–70
    Gordon, 162–4, *163*
    Joanne, 156–8, *157*
    Norma, 152–6, *155*
    psychotic breakdown, 162–4,
        163
    Ruth, 158–61, *160*
    therapy not working, 156–8, *157*
    Trevor, 164–6, *166*
    young people, 162–6
catharsis, 6
CBT *see* cognitive behavioural
    therapy (CBT)
change interview, 101
checking behaviours, medically
    related, 153
'checking in' process, 205
chronic fatigue syndrome, 159
chronic myeloid leukaemia, 162
'chronic' self-appraisals, 132
classical conditioning, 48–9
client(s), 67–86
    accounts of session, 134–5
    attachment style, 81
    barriers to treatment, 71–2
    coping style, 81
    culture, 81
    deterioration *see* client
        deterioration
    dropout *see* client dropout

evaluation measures, 100–101
expectation, 81
feedback *see* client feedback
outcome, contribution to, 200
outcome predictors, 68–9
preferences, 75–7, 82–3, 205
rapid improvements, 53
religious beliefs, 82
resistance/reactance level, 83
self-awareness, 104
spiritual beliefs, 82
stages of change, 81
treatment customization, 79–83,
    205
treatment failure, 110
treatment progress information,
    113, 119–20
client deterioration
    detection by therapist, 110–111,
        134–5
    estimates, 35
    'head to head comparison',
        110–111
client directed as well as outcome
    informed (CDOI), 152
client dropout, 69–73
    average rate, 69–70
    preferences in, 76
    reduction strategies, 72–3
client feedback
    allegiance effect, 124–5
    bigger picture, 122–4
    clinical model, 124
    clinical support tools, 113
    condition-specific measures,
        141–2
    consensus, 118–19
    current *vs.* previous scores, 122
    effectiveness variables, 123

idiographic approaches, 137–40
immediate, 113–14
incorporation, 204, 208
Lambert's work, 111–14
measures, 120–122
meta-analysis, 118–19
motivational interviewing, 117
need for, 110–111
normative approaches, 140–141
performance and, 123
in practice, 129–50
research, 109–27
research needs, 123
scores *vs.* wider population,
    121–2
self-esteem effects, 123
in supervision, 178, 181–2
symptom change measures, 121
therapist's use of, 122–3
timing, 113–14
traffic light system, 112, 144–5
unknowns, 119–24
clinically significant change
criteria, 91, *92*
definition, 91
Clinical Outcomes in Routine
    Evaluation (CORE), 143–4
five item version (CORE-5),
    98–9, 144
ten-item version (CORE-5), 144
Clinical Outcomes in Routine
    Evaluation – Outcome
    Measure (CORE-OM), 98,
    143–4
initial intention, 143
clinical support tools (CSTs), 113
Cochrane Collaboration, 3
cognitive behavioural therapy
    (CBT)

insight-oriented therapy, 38
mechanisms of change,
    196–7
mediators of change, 52
other therapies *vs.*, 196
relational therapies *vs.*, 38
simplification, 29
therapist competence, 61–2
Cohen's *d*, 12
common factors, 4–7, 197
definition, 4–7
community partnership model,
    eating disorders, 62
competency-based educational
    model, 185–7
downside to, 186
therapist effectiveness, 186–7
component analysis study, 52
conclusions, 195–209
conscious competence, 132
conscious incompetence, 132
Consumer Reports, 130
unconscious competence, 133
continued professional
    development (CPD)
commitment reluctance, 59
impact of, 61
conventional wisdom, 45–66
definition, 45
Counselling Self-Estimate
    Inventory (COSE), 179
Counselor Rating Form (CRF),
    100
Counselor Rating Form shortened
    version (CRF-S), 100
couples therapy, 115–16
Creating a Patient-Led NHS, 74
criminology, 47–8
critical summaries, 3

Damocles syndrome, 153
databases, 95
debriefing interventions, 30
Delphi Panels, 185
depression
    client resistance/reactance level,
        83
    IAPT project, 142
    treatment meta-analysis,
        15–16
*Developing and Delivering Practice-
    based Evidence*, 88
Diagnostic and Statistical Manual
    of Mental Disorders (DSM),
    26
dismantling strategy design, 82
dodo bird hypothesis, 5
dodos, 4–7
drug abuse problems, 83
drug trials, 26

eating disorders, community
    partnership model, 62
effect sizes, 11–12
    partially randomised preference
        trial, 76
effortful practice, 206
empirically supported Treatments
    (ESTs), 4
    effectiveness, 38
evidence-based music, 201–2
evidence-based practice, 3–4
    aims, 3
    client-directed treatment *vs.*,
        78–9
    inconvenient questions, 46
    other sources, 18
    service-user movement, 75
    traditional model, 79–80

evidence-based practice in
    psychology (EBPP), 79
exceptional performance, 206
exposure therapies, 54
extinction model, 54
eye movement desensitization and
    reprocessing therapy (EMDR),
    49–50
    alternative explanations, 49–50
    finger movement, 49, 199–200
    mechanism of change, 50
    principles, 49
    relaxed state, 50
Eysenck, Hans, 8
    methodology, 11

family therapy, multidimensional,
    56
fear conditioning, 36

Galbraith, J.K., 45
Generalised Anxiety Disorder
    Assessment (GAD-7), 142
Glass, Gene, 8, 11–13
goal attainment scaling (GAS),
    138–9
    principle, 138
    scaling question *vs.*, 139
'the great psychotherapy debate',
    197
growth potential, 74
guidelines, 3–4
    meta-analysis, 15

heart transplant, 159
Helpful Aspects of Therapy form
    (HAT), 101
Helping Alliance Questionnaire
    (HAq-II), 100

hermeneutic single case efficacy
   design, 92–4
 benefits, 93–4
 effectiveness evidence, 93
hierarchical linear modelling, 33–5
 therapist *vs.* therapy, 33–5
 underpowered studies, 34
high-fidelity feedback, 133
high internal validity, 27
Hodgkin's disease, 159

IAPT project, 141–2
imiprimine, 33
implicit knowledge, 132–4
insight-oriented therapy, 38
intention to treat sample, 71
inter-hemispheric communication
   hypothesis, 50
internet
 clinically significance change, 91
 practice research networks, 101
 reliable change, 91

Kelly, George, 135–6
 personal construct therapy, 67
 therapeutic relationship, 68
Kelly's First Principle, 135–6

Lambert, Michael, 111–14
latent growth curve analysis, 54
Leeds Alliance in Supervision Scale
   (LASS), 183–4, 192–3
 reliability, 184
 validity, 184
low external validity, 27

'the magical number', 12
manuals *see* therapy manuals
mechanisms of change, 46–52

challenges, 52–3
client views, 199
common factors, 5
meta-analysis, 53–5
recommendations, 207
uncertainties, 196–7
medicine, belief in progress, 2
memory conditioning, 36
mental disease
 classification, 25–6
 comorbidity, 27
mental distress quantification, 25
mental health, generic measures,
   142–3
meta-analysis, 11–13
 average client dropout rate,
   69–70
 client feedback, 118–19
 cultural adaptations, 81
 mechanisms of change, 53–5
 particular conditions, 15–16
 psychotherapy effectiveness, 12
mini-RCTs, 17
miracle question, 51
mixed effect modelling *see*
   hierarchical linear modelling
motivational interviewing (MI)
 bulimia nervosa, 117
 client feedback, 117
 'one-shot' workshop, 60–61
 training follow-up, 61
Multicenter Collaborative Study
   for Treatment of Panic
   Disorders, 32
multidimensional family therapy,
   56
multilevel modelling *see*
   hierarchical linear modelling
multi-site trials, 17, 32

narrative reviews, 10
National Institute for Health and
    Clinical Excellence (NICE)
    depression guidelines, 3–4
National Institute for Mental
    Health (NIMH) Treatment of
    Depression Collaborative
    Research Project, 17, 33–5
naturalistic evidence gathering, 18,
    103
nocturnal enuresis, 48
Nominal Group Technique, 185

obsessive compulsive disorder
    (OCD)
  case study, 153
  treatment meta-analysis, 15
occupational psychology, 59
omnibus instruments, 143
operant conditioning paradigm,
    49
OQ-30, 145
ORS *see* Outcome Rating Scale
    (ORS)
outcome data, in public domain,
    188
Outcome Questionnaire (OQ-45),
    121, 144–5
  revision, 145
  scoring, 144
Outcome Rating Scale (ORS), 99,
    114, 145–6, 204
  Gordon case study, 162, *163*
  Joanne case study, 156–7, *157*,
    157–8
  Norma case study, 154–5,
    155
  patient reaction to, 167
  Ruth case study, *160*, 161

Session Rating Scale and, 146
Trevor case study, 165, *166*
verbal presentation, 168

parents, 72
partially randomised preference
    trial (PRPT), 76
Partners for Change Outcome
    Monitoring System (PCOMS),
    114–16, 146
  automated feedback, 115
  couples therapy, 115–16
  flexibility, 168
  Gordon case study, 164
  symptom change measure, 121
  teenagers, 164
  telephone-based intervention,
    115
Patient Health Questionnaire
    (PHQ-9), 142
patients *see* client(s)
patient-therapist relationship *see*
    therapeutic relationship
personality, 6
personal questionnaire, 93, 122,
    139–40
person involvement, 74
person orientation, 74
Peterson, Donald, 39
phobias, 15
Pilgrim, David, 25
post-traumatic stress disorder
    (PTSD), 16
practice, academia *vs.*, 35–7
practice-based evidence, 87–108
  change in a number of cases, 94
  definition, 88
  implications, 94–6
  outcome monitoring, 95

single cases, change in *see* single
    case studies
therapist *vs.* therapy, 95
practice research networks,
    96–105, 189, 208
    administrators, 101
    aims, 97
    client evaluation measures,
        100–101
    client/therapist characteristics,
        100
    criticisms, 103
    data, 102–3
    data, research use, 103–4
    measurement objectives, 97–101
    measurement timing, 101, *102*
    online support, 101
    paperwork, 101–2
    practice improvement, 104–5
    routine measurement, 96
    setting up, 97–103
    therapy outcome (problem
        severity) measures, 98, 101
    therapy process (therapeutic
        alliance) measures, 99–100,
        101
    therapy progress measures,
        98–9
Prime-MD, 142
problem-solving therapy (PST),
    175–6
    manual adherence, 177
process research, 109–10
Procrustes, 79–80
Project MATCH, 17
    hypotheses failure, 31
    therapist differences, 32
psychotherapeutic competence,
    58–9

psychotherapy
    action, 35–6
    effectiveness, 6, 7–8
    equivalence of, 1–22
    harmful effects, 35
    ideas in action, 151–70
    key components, 26
    mechanisms of change *see*
        mechanisms of change
    outcome influencing variables,
        200
    outcome predictors, 68–9
    practice improvement, 203–6
    quantification, 25
    research into *see* psychotherapy
        research
    success, 2, 7
    technique-outcome link,
        198–9
    training recommendations, 36
    trials, 23–7
psychotherapy research, 23–43
    big trials, 16–17
    clinicians' awareness of, 38, 203
    dropout rate, 69–71
    future directions, 202–3
    myths, 38

qualification drift, 172
questionnaires, 166–7

Radio Luxembourg, 130–131
randomised controlled trials
    (RCTs), 8–11, 29–31
    allocation, 9
    client feedback, 116
    client preferences, 76
    cognitive behavioural therapy,
        197

randomised controlled trials
    (RCTs)(*cont'd*)
  little black box, 29–31
  motivational interviewing and
    client feedback, 117–18
  non-specific factors, 29–30
  problems with, 10
  psychotherapy effectiveness, 24
  randomisation, 9
  sample size, 10
  theory, 9
  treatment comparisons, 30–31
  value, 30
rational-emotive therapy (RET),
    47
RCTs *see* randomised controlled
    trials (RCTs)
real experimenter *see* client(s)
real-world practice, 103, 130
recommendations, 195–209
recovery, 74
recovery movement, 74
reflective practitioner, 175
regression analysis, 54
relational therapies, 38
Reliable Change Index (RCI),
    90–91
repertory grids, 137–8
  constructs, 137–8
  elements, 137–8
research allegiance, trial outcome
    and, 30–31
resistance, 83
Rosenzweig, Saul, 4–7
  non-specific factors, 7
  psychological problem
    complexity, 6–7
routine outcome assessment, 18
running race format, 82

safety behaviours, 154
sample size, 10
scaling questions, 137
  goal attainment scaling *vs.*,
    139
self-appraisal bias, 131–2
self-determination, 74
self-monitoring, systematic, 133
service-user movement, 73–5
  definition, 73
  economic reasons, 74
  evidence-base practice
    recommendations, 75
  moral reasons, 73
service users, 73
Session Rating Scale (SRS), 100,
    114, 204
  Gordon case study, 162–3,
    163
  Joanne case study, *157*, 157–8
  Norma case study, *155*, 155–6
  Outcome Rating Scale and,
    146
  patient reaction to, 167
  Ruth case study, 160, *160*
  Trevor case study, 165, *166*
  verbal presentation, 168
Shapiro, David, 13–14
Shapiro, Diana, 13–14
shared decision making (SDM),
    77–8
  advocates, 77
single case studies, 88–94
  analysis depth, 89
  clinically significant change,
    90–91
  hypothesis testing *vs.*, 89
  quantitative measures, 89–90
  reliable change, 90–91